Ferries
OF
The British Isles
and Northern Europe

Compiled by
Nick Widdows

Published by

FERRY
Publications

ISBN 1 871947 57 X

Ferry Publications, PO Box 9, Narberth
Pembrokeshire SA68 0YT
Tel: +44 (0) 1834 891460   Fax: +44 (0) 1834 891463

CONTENTS

Introduction   3

Foreword   4

A guide to using this book   6

New Ferries for the New Millennium   12

Round Britain Review   21

Scandinavian and Northern Europe Review   42

GB & Ireland international passenger operations   60

GB & Ireland domestic services   98

GB & Ireland freight-only ferries   124

Chain, cable etc ferries   160

Major passenger-only ferries   162

Northern Europe   166

Other vessels and recent changes   208

Late News   219

Index   220

© Ferry Publications 2000

Caedmon (Andrew Cooke)

INTRODUCTION

THIS is the thirteenth edition of this book, which first appeared in 1983 as the 24 page 'home published' *Car Ferries from Great Britain and Ireland*. This year we run to 224 pages and for the first time the book in is hard covers. We are pleased to be sponsored by *P&O Ferries*, whose wide-ranging operations are undertaken though subsidiaries *P&O Irish Sea*, *P&O Portsmouth*, *P&O North Sea Ferries*, *P&O Scottish Ferries*, *P&O Ferrymasters* and the partly owned *P&O Stena Line*. The book aims to list every passenger/vehicle ferry in Great Britain and Ireland, ro-ro freight vessels which operate regular services between Great Britain and Ireland and to nearby continental destinations and major passenger/vehicle ferries in other parts of Northern Europe. The coverage of Northern Europe is not fully comprehensive (to make it so would probably triple the size of the book) and does not include freight-only operations and vessels. Also, ro-ro vessels engaged in 'deep sea' and Mediterranean trade and those operated solely for the carriage of trade cars are not included in the book.

Each operator is listed alphabetically within sections – international and Northern Ireland routes, domestic services, freight-only operations, chain, cable and float ferries, passenger only ferries, other North European passenger operators and vehicle/passenger vessels owned by companies not currently engaged in operating services. After details relating to each company's management, address, telephone numbers, email, web site and services, there is a fleet list with technical data and then a potted history of each vessel with previous names and dates.

The year 1999 was the year when duty-free between EU countries ended and the implications are still being felt. It was a mixed year for fast-ferries with some new ones introduced but others withdrawn. But perhaps the most exciting development has been the growth of convention ferries – both freight and passenger – which are several knots faster than what has been the norm in the past. Passengers undoubtedly like speed – but they also like comfort and reliability, something that fast-ferries of the type that have been introduced over the past decade cannot always provide. On the freight side, faster ships not only speed transit times but can often lead to economies in terms of number of vessels needed to run the service. With many new faster ships being introduced over the next couple of years – including the promise or threat (according to your point of view) of Greek Superfast vessels on the Baltic – the ferry scene will undoubtedly continue to fascinate.

Whitstable, Kent
March 2000

Nick Widdows

FOREWORD

Graeme Dunlop

It is now some six years since I was last invited to write the introduction for this publication. As predicted then, the intervening years have certainly proved exciting and challenging for those of us with a vested interest in the ferry industry.

Last year's abolition of tax and duty free sales within the EU has arguably played the major role in determining the future of the ferry industry.

We have seen the demise of a number of ferry operators, the closure of several routes and consolidation amongst those players left. There are some who believe there are still a few companies operating who will lose the battle for profitability.

As predicted, the loss of tax and duty free sales has led to an increase in ticket prices, although it should be noted that today's prices are only now coming into line with those charged in the early nineties. The dilemma is to what extent an increase in ferry fares will cut demand.

Ferry companies have not been idle whilst these changes have been taking place. Onboard retailers now offer as diverse a choice of goods as any high street department store in an effort to mitigate the losses from the traditional range of best sellers.

As we enter a new century, operators are planning for a very different type of future. With the addition of the Channel Tunnel the days of high demand and low capacity have gone. In addition the European ferry industry faces the challenge of modifying its fleet to comply with the new SOLAS regulations.

On one issue I would suggest all operators are agreed, the very real need to increase yield. Capital expenditure to meet the SOLAS requirements will be substantial - whether in updating existing vessels or in newbuilds. The past 12 months have seen a number of operators placing orders for new ships, predominantly multi-purpose vessels offering plenty of space for freight (a business with continued strong growth) together with enhanced passenger facilities.

The number of high speed craft in operation is likely to continue to increase. They offer the chance to grow the market by creating day-trip and short break travel and enhancing a crossing that is seen by some potential travellers as too long on a conventional ferry. They are of course susceptible to inclement weather and therefore the solution for many routes may well be high speed craft running in parallel with conventional ferries.

As I mentioned at the outset, I believe we are likely to see further consolidation before the industry finally overcomes the dramatic changes it has undergone in the last few years. However, the fittest will survive as ferry travel will remain an integral part of our transport infrastructure.

Graeme Dunlop,
Chairman, P&O Ferries.

European Envoy (P&O)

A GUIDE TO USING THIS BOOK

Sections Listing is in seven sections: *Section 1* – Services from Great Britain and Ireland to the continent and between Great Britain and Ireland (including services to/from the Isle of Man and Channel Islands), *Section 2* – Domestic services within Great Britain and Ireland, *Section 3* – Freight only services from Great Britain and Ireland and domestic routes, *Section 4* – Minor vehicle ferries in Great Britain and Ireland (chain and cable ferries etc), *Section 5* – Major passenger only operators, *Section 6* – Major car ferry operators in Northern Europe, *Section 7* – Companies not operating regular services possessing vehicle ferries which may be chartered or sold to other operators.

Order The company order within each section is alphabetical. Note that the definite article and words meaning 'company' or 'shipping company' (eg 'AG', 'Reederei') do not count. Sorting is by normal English convention eg 'Å' comes at the start, not at the end of the alphabet as is the Scandinavian convention. Where ships are numbered, order is by number whether number is expressed in Arabic or Latin digits or words (eg SUPERSEACAT THREE comes before SUPERSEACAT FOUR).

Company information This section gives general information regarding to status of the company ie nationality, whether it is public or private sector and whether it is part of a larger group.

Management The managing director and marketing director or manager of each company are listed. Where these posts do not exist, other equivalent people are listed. Where only initials are given, that person is, as far as is known, male.

Address This is the address of the company's administrative headquarters. In the case of some international companies, a British and overseas address is given.

Telephone and Fax Numbers are expressed as follows: +[*number*] (this is the international dialling code which is dialled in combination with the number dialled for international calls (00 in the UK, Ireland and most other European countries); it is not used for calling within the country), ([*number*]) (this is the number which precedes area codes when making long distance domestic calls – it is not dialled when calling from another country or making local calls (not all countries have this)), [*number*] (this is the rest of the number including, where appropriate, the area dialling code). In a few cases free or local call rate numbers are used for reservations; note that these are not available from overseas. Telex numbers are also included where applicable; it should be noted that many operators no longer use this service, its role having largely been taken over by fax and Email.

Internet Email addresses and Website URLs are given where these are available; the language(s) used is shown. Note that use of the Internet is increasing quickly and new sites may come into use during the currency of this book. If a web site is not shown for a particular operator, it may be worth trying one or more search engines to see if a new site has opened. In a few cases Email facility is only available through the Website. To avoid confusion, there is no other punctuation on the Internet line. All these addresses can be accessed from: http://homepages.enterprise.net/nickw00000 and this will be updated at regular intervals as new web sites come on line. It should be noted that some sites are not always up to date and it is disappointing that few operators use this facility for 'real time' data showing day by day service changes.

Routes operated After each route there are, in brackets, details of *1:* normal journey time, *2:* regular vessel(s) used on the route (number as in list of vessels) and *3:* frequencies (where a number per day is given, this relates to return sailings). In the case of freight-only sailings which operate to a regular schedule, departure times are given where they have been supplied. Please note that frequencies can vary over the year and freight operations are often restricted at weekends.

Winter and Summer In this book, **winter** generally means the period between October and Easter while **summer** means, Easter to October. The **peak summer period** is generally June, July and August. In Scandinavia, the summer peak ends in mid-August whilst in the UK it starts rather later and generally stretches into the first or second week of September. Dates vary according to operator.

Spelling The 'Cook's European Timetable' convention is used in respect of town and country names

– local names for towns (eg Göteborg rather than Gothenburg) and English names for countries (eg Germany rather than Deutschland). Many towns in Finland have both Finnish and Swedish names; we have used the Finnish name except in the case of Åland. In the case of Danish towns, the alternative spelling of 'å' or 'aa' follows local convention. The following towns, islands and territories have alternative English names: Antwerpen = Antwerp, Dunkerque – Dunkirk*, Fyn – Funen, Genova – Genoa, Gent – Ghent, Göteborg – Gothenburg, Helsingør – Elsinore*, Jylland – Jutland, København – Copenhagen, Oostende – Ostend, Sevilla = Seville, Sjælland – Sealand, Venezia – Venice, Vlissingen – Flushing*. (* local name now in common usage in UK).

Terms The following words mean *'shipping company'* in various languages: Redereja (Latvian), Rederi (Danish, Norwegian, Swedish), Rederij (Dutch), Reederei (German), Zegluga (Polish). The following words mean *'limited company'*: AB – Aktiebolag (Swedish) (Finnish companies who use both the Finnish and Swedish terms sometimes express it as Ab), AG – Aktiengesellschaft (German), AS – Aksjeselskap (Norwegian), A/S – Aktie Selskabet (Danish), BV – besioten vennootschap (Dutch), GmbH – Gesellschaft mit beschränkter Haftung (German), NV – naamloze vennootschap (Dutch), Oy – (Finnish), Oyj – (Finnish (plc)), SA – Société Anonyme (French).

Types of Ferry

Car Ferry Up until about 1970, most vehicle ferries were primarily designed for the conveyance of cars and their passengers and foot passengers. Little regard was paid to the conveyance of lorries and trailers, since this sort of traffic had not began to develop. Few vessels of this type are still in service.

Multi-purpose Ferry From about 1970 onwards vehicle ferries began to make more provision for freight traffic, sharing the same ship with passengers and cars. Features usually include higher vehicle decks, often with retractable ramps enabling two levels of cars or one level of freight and coaches, and separate facilities (including cabins on quite short crossings) for freight drivers.

Cruise Ferry In the 1980s the idea of travelling on a ferry, not just to get from A to B, but for the pleasure of the travel experience became more and more popular and ferries were built with increasingly luxurious and varied passenger accommodation. Such vessels also convey cars and freight but the emphasis is on passenger accommodation with a high level of berths (sometimes providing berths for all passengers).

Ro-pax Ferry A vessel designed primarily for the carriage of freight traffic but also carry a limited number of ordinary passengers. Features generally include a moderate passenger capacity – up to about 500 passengers – and a partly open vehicle deck. Modern ro-pax vessels are becoming increasingly luxurious with facilities approaching those of a cruise ferry.

Ro-ro Ferry A vessel designed for the conveyance of road freight, unaccompanied trailers and containers on low 'Mafi' trailers. Some such vessels have no passenger accommodation but the majority can take up to 12 passengers. On routes where there is a low level of driver accompanied traffic, ordinary passengers, with or without cars, can sometimes be conveyed. On routes with a high level of driver accompanied traffic, passenger capacity will sometimes be higher but facilities tend to be geared to the needs of freight drivers eg lounge with video, high level of cabins on routes of 3 hours or more. Technically such vessels are passenger ferries but are included in the freight section when exclusively or largely conveying freight drivers.

Fast Ferry Streamlined vessel of catamaran or monohull construction, speed in excess of 30 knots, water jet propulsion, generally aluminium built but some have steel hulls, little or no freight capacity, no cabins.

List of vessels

NO		YEAR BUILT	NUMBER OF PASSENGERS		VEHICLE DECK ACCESS (C)		FLAG (D)
1 NAME	26433t	87	22k	290P	650C	100L BA2 Town, GY	GB

NAME	GROSS TONNAGE (A)	SERVICE SPEED (KNOTS)	VEHICLE (B) DECK CAPACITY	WHERE BUILT (D)

(A) ‡ = not measured in accordance with the 1969 Tonnage Convention; c = approximate.

(B) C = Cars, L = Lorries (15m), T = Trailers (12m), R = Rail wagons, – = No figure quoted, p = passenger only vessel, • = laid up vessel.

(C) B = Bow, A = Aft, S = Side, Q = Quarterdeck, R = Slewing ramp, 2 = Two decks can be loaded at the same time, C = Cars must be crane loaded aboard, t = turntable ferry.

(D) The following abbreviations are used. Note that where the code relates to place of construction, it relates to the country that the shipyard was in at the time the vessel was built. Thus vessels built in Split (and other Croatian yards) when it was part of Yugoslavia are shown as 'YU' whilst those built since 1991 are shown as 'CR' for Croatia. All references to Germany refer to the Federal Republic except where indicated by '(DDR)' meaning the former Democratic Republic ('East Germany')

AL = Australia	FA = Faroes	JA = Japan	PO = Poland
AU = Austria	FI = Finland	KE = Kerguelen	RO = Romania
BA = Bahamas	FR = France	Islands (FR)	RU = Russia
BB = Barbados	GB = Great Britain	LB = Liberia	SI = Singapore
BD = Bermuda	GE = Germany (DDR)	LT = Lithuania	SK = South Korea
BE = Belgium	GI = Gibraltar	LX = Luxembourg	SP = Spain
CA = Canada	GR = Greece	MA = Malta	SV = St Vincent &
CH = China	GY = Germany	NA = Netherlands	Grenadines
CI = Cayman Islands	(Fed Rep)	Antilles	SW = Sweden
CR = Croatia	IM = Isle of Man	NL = Netherlands	TV = Tuvalu
CY = Cyprus	IN = Indonesia	NO = Norway	UY = Uruguay
DK = Denmark	IT = Italy	PA = Panama	YU = Yugoslavia
ES = Estonia	IR = Irish Republic	PL = Portugal	

In the notes ships are in CAPITAL LETTERS, shipping lines and other institutions are in *italics*.

Capacity In this book, capacities shown are the maxima. Sometimes vessels operate at less than their maximum passenger capacity due to reduced crewing or to operating on a route on which they are not permitted to operate above a certain level. Car and lorry/trailer capacities are the maximum for either type. The two figures are not directly comparable; some parts of a vessel may allow cars on two levels to occupy the space that a trailer or lorry occupies on one level, some may not. Also some parts of a vessel with low headroom many only be accessible to cars. All figures have to be fairly approximate.

Ownership The ownership of many vessels is very complicated. Some are actually owned by finance companies and banks, some by subsidiary companies of the shipping lines, some by subsidiary companies of a holding company of which the shipping company is also a subsidiary and some by companies which are jointly owned by the shipping company and other interests like a bank, set up specifically to own one ship or a group of ships. In all these cases the vessel is technically chartered to the shipping company. However, in this book, only those vessels chartered from one shipping

Red Jet 3 (John Hendy)

Commodore Clipper (Miles Cowsill)

company to another or from a ship owning company unconnected with the shipping line, are recorded as being on charter. Vessels are listed under the current operator rather than the owner. Charter is 'bareboat' (ie without crew) unless otherwise stated. If chartered with crew, vessels are 'time chartered'.

Gross Tonnage This is a measure of enclosed capacity rather than weight, based on a formula of one gross ton = 100 cubic feet. Even small alterations can alter the gross tonnage. Under old measurement systems, the capacity of enclosed car decks was not included but, under a 1969 convention, all vessels laid down after 1982 have been measured by a new system which includes enclosed vehicle decks as enclosed space, thereby considerably increasing the tonnage of car ferries. Under this convention, from 1st January 1995, all vessels were due to be re-measured under this system; in a few cases, details were not available at the time of going to press. All vessels measured by the old system are indicated with a double dagger '‡'. Note that this generally only applies to larger vessels with enclosed vehicle decks; many open decked vessels have not been re-measured as the changes that the new formula would make are fairly marginal. Tonnages quoted here are, where possible, those given by the shipping companies themselves.

The following people are gratefully thanked for their assistance with this publication: Graeme Dunlop, Chairman of P&O Ferries and many others in ferry companies in the UK and abroad, Anders Ahlerup, Gary Andrews, Cees de Bijl, Dick Clague, Geoffrey Hamer, Erik B Jonsen, Barry Mitchell, The Ostend Ferry Crew, Jack Phelan, Pekka Ruponen, Michael Speckenbach (Speckus Ferry Information), Andrew Cooke, Mike Louagie, Philippe Holthof, William Mayes, Colin Smith, Gordon Hislip, Jenny Williamson, Henk van der Lugt, Ian Smith (Bézier Design), Foto Flite, Haven Colourprint and Pat Somner (Ferry Publications).

Whilst every effort has been made to ensure that the facts contained here are correct, neither the publishers nor the writer can accept any responsibility for errors contained herein. We would, however, appreciate comments from readers, which we will endeavour to incorporate in the next edition which we plan to publish in spring 2001.

Caledonian Isles (Colin Smith)

NEW FERRIES FOR THE NEW MILLENNIUM

P&O has currently on order four new ferries for its subsidiaries P&O North Sea Ferries and P&O European Ferries (Irish Sea) Ltd (trading as P&O Irish Sea). They are designed to considerably upgrade the service and represent a new confidence for the new millennium.

New Hull – Rotterdam ships

P&O have been operating on the popular Hull – Rotterdam route since 1965, both as part owners of North Sea Ferries and, since 1996, as sole owner of the route. Original vessels were the tiny, by modern standards, 4,000t *Norwind* and *Norwave* but nine years later they were replaced by the *Norland* and *Norstar*, at the time true giants and representing a major step forward. These were in turn in 1987 superseded by the *Norsea* and *Norsun*, again a major increase in size, although perhaps more typical of the sort of cruise ferries being built at the time for Baltic and Mediterranean service. In 1994 they were complemented by the *Norbank* and *Norbay*, two fast ro-ros which enabled the freight service to be greatly enhanced. Through the use of a riverside berth at Hull (as opposed to an enclosed dock) and their greater speed they are able to leave three hours later than the passenger ships yet arrive slightly before them – a major attraction for freight operators who take a vehicle over one night, have a full day to make deliveries and return the next night.

The purpose of the new ships, which are to be called the *Pride of Hull* and the *Pride of Rotterdam*, is to replace four ships – the two cruise ferries and the two freighters – with two ships. They will not only combine the features of both types of ship but offer enhanced facilities for all types of customer. The ships are currently under construction at the Marghera Yard in Venice of Italian builder Fincantieri and are due for delivery in April 2001 and December 2001. With a gross tonnage of 60,600 tonnes, they will be bigger than any ferry currently afloat. They will carry 1360 passengers and 136 crew, 250 cars and 3,400 running metres of freight. In addition 1,500 metres of freight space will be specifically designed for the carriage of double stacked containers on low 'Mafi' trailers.

Although the large freight capacity would qualify the vessels for the category of ro-pax, the notion of such vessels as having rather basic passenger accommodation will be confounded by the lavish provision on these vessels. As well as the usual buffet and à la carte restaurants there will be a Continental Café, Irish Bar, Skylounge and Bar and Wine Bar. A double deck show lounge will boast a bar, disco, live entertainment, a casino and slot machines. But for those looking for a more tranquil time there will be a quiet lounge and a business lounge for those who have to work. Indeed, for business people, the 21.00 departure and 08.00 arrival should prove an attractive alternative to the inconvenience of an early morning flight or the cost of a night in a hotel. An internet/cyber zone will make use of the latest technology – quite what it will have in it is probably not yet known by anyone, so rapid is the pace of development in this sphere! More conventional entertainment will be provided in the two cinemas.

The ships will leave from a berth in the River Humber, thus obviating the need for the entertaining but time consuming practice of locking in and out of the King George V Dock at Hull. Indeed, the existing ships are of the maximum size that can go through the lock.

The new riverside berth and terminal, currently under construction by Associated British Ports, owners of Hull Docks, will completely segregate cars from trucks and coaches. Despite the later departure times, passengers, both on foot and in cars and coaches, will still be able to join the ship in the early evening and enjoy the facilities for several hours in port. The opportunity to enjoy an evening meal when stationary could be an advantage on windy days, although the size of the vessels and their modern stabilisation system should make for a comfortable crossing on all but the most extreme occasions.

P&O North Sea Ferries have enjoyed a monopoly of passenger traffic from Northern England to the Netherlands and Belgium for many years but face a new challenge from DFDS Seaways Newcastle IJmuiden service, now daily for a large part of the year. The new ships should ensure that P&O North Sea Ferries continues as a major player in this field and that the North continues to enjoy excellent surface links with the heart of the European Union

New Cairnryan – Larne ship

Ever since the Cairnryan – Larne service started in 1973, it has always relied on vessels built for other routes. The first ship, the *Ionic Ferry* of 1958, was switched from the Preston – Larne route and this trend has continued to this date with such ships as the *Free Enterprise III* and *Free Enterprise IV* from Dover and the second *Ionic Ferry* (formerly the *Dragon*) from Southampton. The current ships, *Pride of Rathlin* (last of the successful 'Free Enterprise' class), *European Trader* and *European Endeavour*, were all built for the English Channel and long since replaced by bigger and better ships. Now at last the route is to have its own brand new custom built ship.

The *European Causeway* as she is to be called will be bigger and faster than any conventional ship previously used on the North Channel by any operator. Incidentally, *European Causeway* was the name to be carried by what is now the *P&OSL Burgundy* before it was decided to complete her as a passenger rather than a freight vessel. It is probably a rather more appropriate name than previously since Larne is only about 40 miles from the famous Giant's Causeway, which lies between Ballycastle and Portrush.

The *European Causeway* was ordered in February 1999 from Mitsubishi Heavy Industries in Japan and delivery is now expected in August 2000. She will share a common design with the second, slightly larger vessel being built for the Liverpool – Dublin route (see below). Her 23 knot service speed will cut the journey time from 135 to 105 minutes – it is perhaps no coincidence that P&O are seeking to match the time of Stena Line's fast ferry *Stena Voyager*, although this vessel does, of course, go all the way to Belfast! Should it be desired, there should be no problem in running four round trips per day on the route although operating such a schedule with the slower freight ships would lead to some difficulties.

There will be a wide range of passenger facilities including bars, restaurants, shops, video lounge, games room and children's play room. Freight divers will have their own restaurant, lounge and showers.

She will have two vehicle decks and drive through loading with double deck link spans at both terminals. Cairnryan terminal has just completed a £4.5 development scheme with a new terminal, vehicle check-in and marshalling area. Landscaping and environmental improvements will further enhance the travel experience. In April the

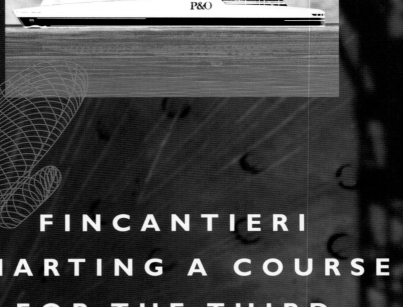

First keel section of the ***Pride of Hull***. (P&O)

complementary fast ferry service has been enhanced by the replacement of the *Jetliner* by the *Superstar Express*, which successfully ran at Portsmouth during the previous two summers, not only giving an increase in capacity and comfort but replacing what has proved to be a rather unsuccessful fast ferry design with an Austal Ships 82 craft, one of the most successful. However, due to the enhanced speed and capacity that the *European Causeway* will bring, it has been decided that the fast ferry will operate March to early November only rather than nearly all year as before.

New Liverpool – Dublin ship

P&O Irish Sea and, their predecessor Pandoro, have built up a successful network of freight routes between North West ports and Ireland, both to Northern Ireland and the Republic. As well as conveying a large number of unaccompanied trailers, the routes have always been popular with drivers travelling all the way with their loads, although the night sailings have been more heavily booked with this class of traffic than those during the day. This imbalance has in the past meant that facilities have been underused for half the day, and whilst it has for several years been possible for car passengers to book a passage for themselves and their vehicles on the Larne – Fleetwood day services, this has not been greatly promoted and knowledge of it has relied more on 'word of mouth'. In 1999 is was decided to allow cars and passengers on not only on that service but on the Liverpool – Dublin route and the recently introduced Rosslare – Cherbourg sailings in a more structured way under the 'Value Routes' branding. Prices charged offer savings when compared with other operators, although it has to be borne in mind that they are primarily freight ships and do not have all the facilities offered on modern passenger ships. There are however many people who welcome the quietness of such a crossing and the less formal atmosphere. There is also growing demand from passengers for a night service which allows them a full night's sleep, rather that a departure in the middle of the night with only 3 or 4 hours to get their heads down – something that the current vessels are unable to meet due to the need to provide for freight drivers (apart from Sunday nights when driver demand is low).

The vessels operating these services all date from the 1970s and although several have had their capacity enlarged through lengthening and provision of an additional vehicle deck, there is a limit to what can be done with such old vessels. A further factor has been the introduction of two new ro-pax vessels on Liverpool – Dublin by Merchant Ferries and their take over of Belfast Freight Ferries and Norse Irish Ferries

It is against the background of the growth in passenger traffic, the need to provide for night travel, the emergence of Merchant Ferries as a major player on the Irish Sea and the need to re-equip the current fleet and increase capacity, that P&O have ordered a new ro-pax vessels for the Liverpool – Dublin route. She is due for delivery in December 2000, replacing the *European Leader* which will transfer to the Fleetwood – Larne service. Similar in many ways to the new *European Causeway*, and from the same yard, the *European Ambassador* will be slightly longer and wider, thus offering greater freight capacity than her sister. The increase in power will be disproportionate to the larger size, thus giving even more speed – a very fast 25 knots. This will enable the journey time to be reduced to six hours – even shorter if and when a new riverside berth at Liverpool is completed, although this still remains at the planning stage at present. Such a timing will be highly competitive with the services offered at Holyhead, bearing in mind driving time to reach the port and especially the frequent delays experienced on A5 on Anglesey.

Passenger capacity will be similar but the new ship will be more geared to the needs of the longer distance passenger ie every passenger will be expected to have at least one full meal on board, whereas on the shorter journey many make do with a snack. Passengers and freight drivers will have their own restaurants along with the usual lounges and bars. She will have 53 two berth cabins and 29 with four berths, including two club cabins, thereby allowing over half her passengers to have a bed at night (although in practice full occupancy of cabins is rarely achieved). She will also have a club class lounge with overnight reclining seats.

For the first time on the North West England to Ireland routes, the ship will have both bow and stern loading and will be capable of loading on both levels given the provision of suitable berths.

The Future

When the new ships enter service and the consequential moves have taken place, P&O North Sea Ferries will have modern tonnage on most their routes. The Teesport – Zeebrugge route has recently been re-equipped with the new 20,000t *Norsky* and *Norstream*, and the Teesport – Rotterdam route is now in the hands of the *Norking* and *Norqueen*, which, although nearly 20 years old, have recently been lengthened and re-engined and so are good for many more years' more service. The Hull – Zeebrugge passenger service will be in the hands of the *Norsea* and *Norsun*, the previous generation on the Hull – Rotterdam route and the additional freight capacity that they will provide over the *Norland* and *Norstar* may well render the three times a week freight only service offered by the 1979 *Norcape* unnecessary. What happens to the *Norland* and *Norstar* remains uncertain. They need major work to bring them up to SOLAS standards under their present passenger capacity but could work with a low passenger certificate without modification. They could be sold or possibly re-deployed on a new route.

The Felixstowe – Rotterdam service will be greatly boosted by the arrival of the modern freighters *Norbay* and *Norbank* from Hull and these will serve along-side the lengthened 'Searunner' class vessels *European Freeway* and *European Tideway*, enabling the unstretched *Pride of Flanders* and *Pride of Suffolk* to be re-deployed. The recent agreement between P&O and the Shell Oil Company to redevelop the site of Shell Haven Oil Terminal as a major container port also raises the interesting possibilities of P&O moving into the Thames, as ro-ro berths will form part of the development.

The situation on the Irish Sea is rather more complex and the provision of these first two vessels must surely be just the start of a major re-equipment exercise.

A second ro-pax on Cairnryan – Larne would enable both the current freighters to be replaced and yet still result in increased capacity, even without an increase in frequency. If the ships operated four return trips per day, this would produce a further increase of 33% and lead to an almost doubling from the present situation. Eight fast ro-pax departures per day would offer an unparalleled service, although the increase in passenger provision would call into doubt the continued need for a fast ferry, even in the busier summer months.

On Liverpool – Dublin, running the new ship with the older, smaller and slower *European Envoy* (which cannot offer tourist accommodation on her night crossings) cannot be but an interim solution. Two such ships could possibly complete three round trips every 48 hours (such as happens at Portsmouth) giving three departures a day and thus allowing one or more of the chartered vessels on the route (the *Celtic Star and Celtic Sun*) to be disposed of. Much will depend on whether and when the new riverside berth is completed. The Fleetwood – Larne route is also in need of an upgrade and it may be that, to show equal commitment to the Northern Ireland route, the third or fourth new vessel, when ordered, will go there. Even if new vessels for that route are of the same speed, tidal restrictions at Fleetwood make it difficult to envisage vessels being able to make more than one return trip per day.

P&O have options on a further two vessels from Mitsubishi, unexercised at the time of going to print. Further orders could of course be made. It seems clear that there will further interesting developments in this area.

Whilst this article has been produced with the assistance of P&O Irish Sea and P&O North Sea Ferries, all comments and speculations are entirely my own.

Nick Widdows

TECHNICAL SPECIFICATION

NEWBUILDINGS FOR P&O NORTH SEA FERRIES – *PRIDE OF HULL* & *PRIDE OF ROTTERDAM*

Builders	Fincantieri, Venice, Italy
Delivery	*Pride of Hull* – April 2001 and
	Pride of Rotterdam – December 2001
Gross Tonnage	60,600 GRT
Deadweight	8,850 T
Length	215m
Breadth	31.5m
Draught	6m
Passengers	1,360
Cabins	546
Cargo	250 cars and
	400 Freight Units
Engine Power	37,800Kw
Service Speed	22 Knots
Stabilizers	2
Ship's Crew	136
Flag	*Pride of Hull* – Great Britain
	Pride of Rotterdam – Netherlands
Technical Consultants	Three Quays Marine
	Services, London.
Interior Design	Tillberg Design, London

TECHNICAL SPECIFICATION

NEWBUILDING FOR P&O IRISH SEA – CAIRNRYAN – LARNE – *EUROPEAN CAUSEWAY*

Builders	Mitsubishi, Shimonoseki, Japan
Delivery	August 2000
Gross Tonnage	20,800 GRT
Deadweight	4,335 T
Length	156 m
Breadth	23.4 m
Draught	5.5 m
Passengers	410
Cabins	82
Cargo	375 cars or 107 x 13.5m freight units
Engine Power	31,680 Kw
Service Speed	23 Knots
Stabilizers	2
Ship's Crew	55
Flag	To be decided
Technical Consultants	Three Quays Marine Services, London.
Interior Design	Dougdale Management and Design, Suffolk

TECHNICAL SPECIFICATION

NEWBUILDING FOR P&O IRISH SEA – LIVERPOOL – DUBLIN - *EUROPEAN AMBASSADOR*

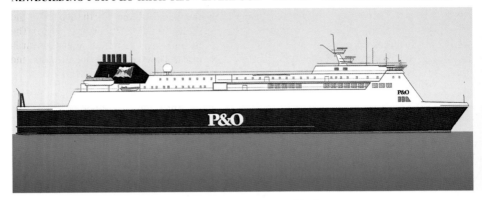

Builders	Mitsubishi, Shimonoseki, Japan
Delivery	January 2001
Gross Tonnage	24,500 GRT
Deadweight	5,000 T
Length	170 m
Breadth	24 m
Draught	6.0 m
Passengers	405
Cabins	82
Cargo	375 cars or 123 x 13.5m freight units
Engine Power	39,600 Kw
Service Speed	25.1 Knots
Stabilizers	2
Ship's Crew	45
Flag	Bahamas
Technical Consultants	Three Quays Marine Services, London.
Interior Design	Dougdale Management and Design, Suffolk

ROUND BRITAIN REVIEW

North Sea

P&O North Sea Ferries have continued to set the pace on the North Sea with the introduction of twin ro-ro vessels for their Middlesbrough - Zeebrugge route. The *Norsky* and *Norstream* entered service during July and November from Aker Finnyards at Rauma and, unusually, display this fact on their hulls. They replaced the *Norking* and *Norqueen* which were duly switched to the company's Tees- Europoort service.

The new £90 million cruiseferries for the Hull - Europoort service will be named *Pride of Hull* and *Pride of Rotterdam* and when they enter service in April and December next year the renamed *Norsun* and *Norsea* will be switched to operate the Zeebrugge service in place of the *Norland* and *Norstar*. Super-freighters *Norbank* and *Norbay* will switch to the Felixstowe - Europoort operation with the former Stena pair *European Freeway* and *European Tideway* while it is expected that the smaller *Pride of Suffolk* and *Pride of Flanders* will move to the company's Irish Sea operations.

The first of the new trio of DFDS Tor Line freighters, built at the Fincantieri yard in Ancona, finally made her way into service during 1999. Built for the AngloBridge service linking Immingham and Gothenburg, the *Tor Selandia* (24,196 gross tons) entered service in March. She was followed by the *Tor Suecia* while the *Tor Britannia* will be the final vessel.

The passenger/ vehicle ferry *Princess of Scandinavia* (Newcastle-Kristiansand-Gothenburg) was unexpectedly withdrawn from service in late September after major problems with her Pielstick machinery. All four main units were returned to St. Nazaire for repair while the ship was laid-up in Frederikshavn.

Norfolkline have greatly expanded their service between Scheveningen and Felixstowe and the final two of the Chinese series of freighters offer a further 30% increase in capacity. The *Maersk Flanders* took up service in January 2000 while the last of the series, the *Maersk Suffolk*, is due in May.

The well-known German -owned vessels *Thomas Wehr* and *Gabrielle Wehr* completed their charters in October on the P&O North Sea Ferries' Felixstowe - Zeebrugge route. They were replaced by the larger and faster Swedish twins *Sapphire* and *Rodona* (6,568 gross tons/ built 1980) which also offer internal ramps rather than lifts and therefore allow faster turnround times. The earlier pair were quickly taken on a further charter for Ferryways to operate a new service in February 2000 linking Ipswich with Ostend.

The Argomann Ferry Service weekly link between Turku, Bremerhaven, Harwich, Cuxhaven and Tallinn introduced the new 18,395 gross ton ro-ro vessel *Estraden* (later renamed *Amazon*) on 9th February. The Aker Finnyards vessel offers more than 50% freight capacity than the *Garden* which she replaced in service.

The historic link between Harwich and the Hook of Holland received a much needed boost during June when Stena Line BV announced that twin ro-pax 'Seapacer' vessels of 30,500 gross tons had been ordered from AESA in Cadiz. The 22 knot vessels will reduce conventional crossing times from 8 to 6 hours and will carry 452 passengers and 2,500 lane metres of freight. They are expected to be called *Stena Hollandica* and *Stena Britannica* and will replace the present ro-ro vessels *Stena Searider* and *Stena Seatrader* which date from 1969 and 1973.

P&OSL Provence and European Highway (FotoFlite)

Eastern Channel

The new *Dart 8* and *Dart 9* entered service on the Thames Europort - Zeebrugge service in August and September. The former Chinese (COSCO) deep-sea roll on - roll off vessels provide excellent driver accommodation in addition to freight space for 190 trailers. The Jacobs fleet have lost the familiar 'J' on their funnels in favour of the chequers of associated company Ropner Ship Management. The 'Bazias' connection has certainly been weakened with only the *Dart 4* (ex *Bazias 4*) and *Dart 5* (ex *Bazias 5*) now on the Vlissingen service and the *Dart 2* (ex *Bazias 2*) the third ship on Zeebrugge.

The Ramsgate - Ostend service continued to be operated by TransEuropa Shipping Line's former Belgian pair *Eurovoyager* (ex *Prins Albert*) and the *Primrose* (ex *Princesse Marie-Christine*). There has been much speculation relating to the recommencement of a passenger service both during November 1999 and at Easter 2000 but an announcement is still awaited.

Hoverspeed operated the summer 1999 season with the 74 metre *SeaCat Atlantic II* running in tandem with the twin hovercraft on the Dover - Calais link. The craft was originally the SeaCat Tasmania and had recently completed a five year charter across the River Plate. At the conclusion of the season she was sent to lay-up at Newhaven.

Both hovercraft and the Ostend 81 metre SeaCats have had First Class areas fitted and a further modification to the livery duly appeared with the addition of the strapline 'Fast Car Ferries.' The Sea Containers board are presently contemplating a new name for their ferries division. The 50% share of the Ostend operation which was previously held by Australian company Holyman was sold to Sea Containers during the year.

P&O Stena Line's freighter *European Pathway* rejoined the Dover - Zeebrugge service in April after which the chartered *Stena Royal* (ex *Prins Filip*) was taken on a seven year charter and renamed *P&OSL Aquitaine*. Such was the freight on offer that the 'Highway' was moved onto the Calais route for the summer before the 'Aquitaine' was sent for a major refit at Falmouth. The ship took up service to Calais in November and effectively saw off the *P&OSL Picardy* (ex *Pride of Bruges*) which retired for lay-up at Dunkerque in February 2000.

SeaFrance (the nationalised French ferry company) carried 20% of all Dover - Calais passenger traffic and 34% of the freight during 1999. At 32,000 gross tons, the largest and fastest conventional ferry ever built for Dover - Calais has been ordered from Aker Finnyards and should replace the *SeaFrance Manet* (ex *Champs Elysees*, ex *Stena Parisien*) on the link in September 2001. The reserve vessel *SeaFrance Monet* (ex *Stena Londoner*) appeared in service during the winter overhaul periods in both 1999 and 2000.

SeaFrance acquired the 49% share which Stena Line had held in the ship owning subsidiary SPN when the Calais - Dover service had been a joint service using the *Fiesta* (now *SeaFrance Cezanne*) and *Cote d'Azur* (now *SeaFrance Renoir*).

Norfolkline surprisingly entered the hectic Dover market in March when the new Merchant Ferries ro-pax *Northern Merchant* took up service to Dunkerque. If the route proves a success then sister *Midnight Merchant* could well join her.

At Folkestone Falcon Seafreight continued to operate the Boulogne freight service with the *Purbeck* alone following the departure of the Sea Containers ro-ro vessel *Picasso* in

From the M20 motorway, the dual carriageway leads directly into the Port of Dover where streamlined check-in systems make boarding quick and easy.

Ferries depart up to four times an hour around the clock on the short sea crossing to Calais - plus there are freight services to Zeebrugge and Dunkirk and a fast ferry service to Ostend.

PLAIN SAILING

PORT OF
DOVER

A brief but welcome break from driving, the ferry crossing provides the perfect opportunity to take in some sea air, to stretch your legs, to enjoy a meal, do some shopping, or simply relax whilst, at the same time, keeping on the move towards your continental destination.

It's the high road to Europe and a rewarding experience - from every point of view!

Port of Dover, Harbour House, Dover, Kent CT17 9BU
Website: www.doverport.co.uk E-mail: pr@doverport.co.uk

Norstream (FotoFlite)

Primrose (Mike Louagie)

March. However in February 2000 the Estonian-owned Neptunia (formerly Sealink's Darnia) came on the route and with the Purbeck returning to Truckline in May for the Portsmouth - Caen route, the larger Bonavista was earmarked to replace her. In April 2000, the French shipping firm Compagnie Maritime Marfret (CMM) acquired 51% of the company which in future is to be known as Falcon Marfreight.

Hoverspeed introduced the SuperSeaCat Two onto their Newhaven - Dieppe service as from 23rd April but their hopes of acquiring the four coach carrying 'SSC4' for the 2000 season were dashed when it was announced that she would run the Helsinki - Tallinn service instead. The SuperSeaCat One (from Gothenburg - Frederikshavn) has been transferred to the route while the 'Two' moves to Heysham - Belfast.

SeaTruck had hoped to introduce the Landi (ex Argo, ex Euroway) on the Dieppe freight service but problems with the French unions saw a lost window of opportunity.

Consolidation of operations was very much the theme at Portsmouth for both Brittany Ferries and P&O Portsmouth. Services were operated on a similar style and timetable to that of the previous year with both operators. P&O Portsmouth had another successful season with their fast-craft operation between Portsmouth and Cherbourg with the *Superstar Express*. The former Olau twins, the *Pride of Portsmouth* and *Pride of Le Havre*, continued their operation to the Normandy port of Le Havre, but with lower than expected traffic than the previous year.

P&O Portsmouth will be faced with having to replace the former 'Super Vikings' (*Pride of Cherbourg* and *Pride of Hampshire*) during the next 18 months or operating them on a reduced passenger certificate. At the time of writing no replacement vessels appear to have been found or ordered by the company.

Brittany Ferries, likewise, find themselves in the same position as P&O Portsmouth with two vessels required to replace their ageing *Quiberon* and *Duc de Normandie*. The company had hoped prior to Christmas to make an announcement of two replacement vessels but due to enquiries from the EU Commissioners into their previous operations the announcement was delayed.

With the strong pound, Brittany Ferries had a good trading year, despite the demise of duty-free. Meanwhile, Brittany Ferries launched one of possibly the most revolutionary aspects of their marketing to date when they produced their timetable for the year 2000 without a tariff for passengers and cars being quoted within their brochure. Potential customers are invited to telephone the company to obtain the rates of travel, on similar lines to that of cheap airlines, like EasyJet. Brittany Ferries had been talking about this strategy for some time and the move was made in the light of more passengers using the Western Channel operations, especially on their St. Malo route. P&O Portsmouth carried out a similar campaign with their brochure for 2000 but the price range was shown for their customers.

Both Brittany Ferries and P&O Portsmouth with their separate operations to Spain had mixed blessings during 1999. Both companies cut back on their winter schedule during 1999/2000 with less demand and interest being shown on the Spanish services during the winter period. Possibly two factors have reduced the interest in the sailings from the United Kingdom to the Iberian Peninsular - the advent of cheaper air fares and improved road connections through France and Spain.

P&OSL Provence (John Hendy)

Despite these problems for both P&O and Brittany Ferries, a new freight service between Southampton and Bayonne started during the year, initially with two vessels and later using one ship, only operating one round sailing per week. Eventually this service was suspended with lack of traffic.

Commodore Ferries and Condor took delivery of their new ro-pax *Commodore Clipper* in October from Van der Giessen. This extremely well appointed ship entered commerical service on 18th October with a weekly schedule of six round sailings a week from Portsmouth at 09.30, sailing first to Guernsey and then on to Jersey. The evening departure from both Guernsey and Jersey returns each day at 06.30. The new vessel, built on a similar line to the *Ben-my-Chree* for the Isle of Man Steam Packet Company, offers extremely well-appointed accommodation with a large club-class lounge, attractive bar, restaurant/cafeteria and well-appointed cabins. The ship is manned by British officers and Polish crew, while catering facilities are operated by Condor staff.

Condor Ferries, who operate the fast ferry operations from Poole and Weymouth, had a much more successful year during 1999, following the re-organisation of their operations. Their new Poole-Channel Islands-St. Malo fast-ferry opeation attracted good loadings, so much so that the operation has been expanded for the year 2000.

Emeraude, who maintain the fast-ferry operations from France to the Channel Islands, eventually concluded negotiations with both the Jersey and Guernsey States for a user agreement, on a similar line to that Condor/Commodore have for their operations between the UK and the Channel Islands. Both agreements should now offer a long-term transport strategy for the Islands; possibly the only vulnerable aspect of the agreement is that there is too much reliability upon fast-craft with Emeraude's operations from France.

On the Irish Sea there continues to be fierce competition between all operators. The demise of duty-free has not helped profitability of companies as the tax regimes between the UK and Irish Republic are so similar. There is very little initiative for bargain-hunters to travel across the Irish Sea, compared to France and Spain, as far as British citizens are concerned.

Swansea Cork Ferries continue to operate their seasonal service between Swansea and Cork with the Cypriot-registered *Superferry*. The company sought a replacement for the Japanese-built ship last year but with no success. It is understood that they expressed interest in chartering the former *St. Patrick II* but at the last minute the deal fell through. The former Irish Ferries' vessel would have offered improved facilities on the nine-hour service, however possibly there was some hesitation within the company following the ship's earlier career on the Irish Sea. The company are confident that they will be able to replace the *Superferry* as from the year 2001.

Irish Ferries' fortunes continue to expand once again during 1999, despite the problems in getting their new fast-ferry operation started due to union disputes in the summer. The *Jonathan Swift*, built in Australia, arrived with its new owners during late May. The company were unable to commence their new service between Holyhead and Dublin until 3rd July. The new operation proved extremely successful and reliable for them.

The entry into service of the *Jonathan Swift* was followed by a major announcement and

Dawn Merchant (Gordon Hislip)

Val de Loire (Miles Cowsill)

investment from Irish Ferries. On 8th July the company announced that they would build the world's largest car ferry for their Holyhead-Dublin route. The new EUR100 million vessel will be built at Finnyards and will be capable of carrying over 1,300 cars and 260 trucks, plus 2,000 passengers. The new vessel is due for lauch this autumn, will enter service by spring 2001 and will replace the *Isle of Inishmore*. It is envisaged, but not yet confirmed, that the *Isle of Inishmore* will replace the *Isle of Innisfree* on the Rosslare-Pembroke Dock route.

Irish Ferries were to see continued growth on their Irish/French services during 1999 with their chartered *Normandy*. The vessel was later purchased by the Irish Continental Group in the latter half of 1999 for use on their Rosslare-Cherbourg/Roscoff service. The former Sealink vessel is due to undergo a major overhaul during the winter of 2000/2001.

Stena Line's fortunes saw another downturn for them during 1999 on the Irish Sea, apart from their Fishguard-Rosslare route. Increased competition from Irish Ferries with their new fast-craft *Jonathan Swift* saw a downturn for them on their Holyhead route with the *Stena Explorer*. Fierce competition from Merchant Ferries, P&O Irish Sea, Sea Containers and Irish Ferries also saw a decline in freight traffic for Stena Line on their Central Corridor. Fortunes on the North Channel were not good for the Swedish company either during 1999 and continued rumours over the company's operations at Stranraer have not helped. There is continued speculation that the company might abandon Stranraer and concentrate their fast-ferry service between Holyhead and Belfast, leaving only their freight operations at Stranraer. At Fishguard the *Stena Lynx III* replaced the *Stena Lynx*, offering increased capacity on the Southern Corridor with the *Koningin*

Beatrix. If Stena Line are to compete against their aggressive rivals, Irish Ferries, a restructuring and reorganisation of tonnage will have to take place in the very near future, especially on the Central Corridor with the arrival of Irish Ferries' new conventional ferry. There is speculation that the *Koningin Beatrix* may be moved on to the Holyhead-Dublin route and that one vessel from the Baltic may be moved to replace her at the Pembrokeshire port.

Merchant Ferries introduced their new ferry service between Liverpool and Dublin with their two new purpose-built vessels *Brave Merchant* and *Dawn Merchant.* Both ships were to prove an overnight success. Cenargo, who own Merchant Ferries, acquired Norse Irish Ferries' operations (Liverpool-Belfast) in 1999. It is possible that the Italian-built vessels *Lagan Viking* and *Mersey Viking* will be replaced by the two new sister vessels of similar design to that of the Liverpool ships during 2001. Merchant Ferries also were able to consolidate their operations at Heysham, following their earlier acquisition of Belfast Freight Ferries.

Sea Containers' fortunes on the Irish Sea with their fast ferry operations were to see some fairly radical changes during 1999. The company introduced a new fast-ferry service between Heysham and Belfast, which was to prove an overnight success for them. Likewise, Sea Containers decided to split their Belfast services to Scotland, between Stranraer and the new port of Troon. The new Troon operation again was to prove successful for them, so much so that during March 2000 the company have decided to move all their operations in favour of Troon, instead of Stranraer. The fortunes of the Liverpool-Dublin fast-ferry service were not to be so positive, following the demise of

Superferry (Miles Cowsill)

duty-free between the UK and Ireland.

The Isle of Man Steam Packet Company also was to see growth once again during 1999. Their new ferry, *Ben-my-Chree*, maintained the passenger and freight operations between Heysham and Belfast, while the fast-ferry services once again were operated from Liverpool, Dublin and Belfast to the Island. Conventional back-up of their fast-ferry services was maintained once again by the *Lady of Mann*.

P&O Irish Sea ordered from Mitsubishi in Japan a replacement vessel for the *Pride of Rathlin*. The new 21,000 ton passenger and freight vessel is due to enter service between Larne and Cairnryan during this summer. The ship will maintain a service speed of 23 knots and will have a capacity for 375 cars or 107 commercial vehicles. Later in the year the company ordered a new ro-pax vessel for their Liverpool-Dublin route. It is envisaged that a second sister ship will be ordered for this operation in the not-too-distant future in the light of increased competition from Merchant Ferries on the route.

P&O Irish Sea's fast-ferry service between Larne and Cairnryan with the *Jetliner* continued to attract good loadings. The vessel will be replaced this summer by the *Superstar Express* from Portsmouth on the arrival of the *Catalonia* on charter to the company for their Portsmouth-Cherbourg route.

Both Irish Ferries and Brittany Ferries continue to attract good loadings on their services between France and Ireland. A new operator came on the scene during last year under the guise of Cork St. Malo Ferries. The new company, set up by Swansea Cork Ferries, chartered the *Venus* (ex. *Dana Gloria*) from Vetouris Ferries of Greece. The operation had mixed

Stena Lynx III (Miles Cowsill)

Rosslare Europort
Gateway to Europe

Jonathan Swift Gordon Hislip)

Clansman (Colin Smith)

fortunes but due to operational problems with the French Authorities the service temporarily was closed in October. At the time of writing the operation has not re-opened.

Scotland

During February an order was made at Ailsa's Troon yard for a replacement for the *Lochmor* on the Small Isles route. The £5.5 million *Lochnevis* will be a stern loading car ferry with a capacity for 200 passengers and 14 cars. She is due in April 2000 and will also be used for off-season work on the Mallaig- Armadale (Skye) route.

A further order was made in the same month for a £15.5 million replacement for the *Hebridean Isles* for delivery in November 2000. The *Hebrides* is being built at Ferguson Shipbuilders at Port Glasgow.

The contract to serve the Northern Isles from Aberdeen and Scrabster from 2002 has been narrowed down to four bidders - P&O Scottish Ferries, CalMac & Wightlink, Sea Containers and Serco-Denholm - with the decision likely to be made in spring 2000. The successful bidder will be left a tight timescale for the construction of new ships.

Miles Cowsill & John Hendy

DECK EQUIPMENT

DURASTIC
Decks for all Reasons

Durastic Ltd is one of the world's leading suppliers and installers of marine deck covering systems offering a wide range of specifications. From primary underlays; including Durastic's lightweight underlay, to weatherdecks, sound reduction and A60 Solas rated materials; all with associated finishes such as carpets, vinyls and epoxy resins.

A full specification service and experienced, supervised contract teams ensure the best deck coverings are installed to the highest standards. Durastic's products are covered by International Certifications and produced at its ISO 9002 Quality Assured manufacturing facility.

The company's 76 years of technical expertise is reflected in the fact that Durastic is frequently nominated as a supplier and sub-contractor by leading ship owners and is regularly called upon to supervise contracts overseas. For further information on products, specifications or contract services, contact:

Mr J Gallagher
Durastic Ltd
Howdon Yard
Willington Quay
Wallsend
Tyne & Wear NE28 6UL
United Kingdom..

Tel: +44 (0) 191 295 3333
Fax: +44 (0) 191 263 2173

Branch offices: Glasgow, Liverpool, Southampton, Jarrow and representation in 20 countries worldwide.

As one of the world's leading suppliers of marine deck covering systems...

we can provide a complete service package. From design and specification support through materials supply to installation.

From decorative deck finishes to functional underlays all manufactured to ISO9002

DURASTIC LTD
FLOORING AND DECKING

Howdon Yard, Willington Quay, Wallsend, Tyne & Wear NE28 6UL, United Kingdom..
Tel: +44 (0) 191 295 3333   Fax: +44 (0) 191 2173

A Member of the Rigblast Group

SCANDINAVIAN AND NORTHERN EUROPE REVIEW

The final year of the century in Scandinavia was marked by a number of major events. Firstly it saw the end of duty-free between EU countries, something which had a major impact on all international services, both in terms of changes made to preserve the opportunity to offer such goods for sale, and cut backs where the withdrawal made services uneconomical. It also saw the announcement of two important acquisitions. Sea Containers acquired 51% of Neptun Maritime, the parent company of Silja Line. They immediately disposed of 1%, leaving them with a half share in the company. Sea Containers' involvement in Scandinavian shipping had previously been restricted to the SeaCat fast ferry in the Kattegat and Silja Line, operating luxury cruise ferries, was a very different proposition. However, ownership by shipping people rather than bankers was generally welcomed. The second acquisition, that of Scandlines AB, previously a subsidiary of SJ, Swedish State Railways, by Stena Line AB was certainly not welcomed by Scandlines AG, the joint Danish/German company who had hoped to purchase the company themselves. Claiming that a previous agreement made between SJ and DSB (Danish State Railways) gave them first refusal to purchase the company should it be for sale, litigation was immediately launched in the courts to block the sale. The purchase is thus 'on hold' pending the arbitration in Olso which is to take place in the spring.

Another significant happening was a marked reduction in the once large Scandlines withdrawn fleet. Vessels had a variety of fates, such as scrapping *(Danmark)*, conversion to cable laying ship *(Kraka* and *Lodbrog)*, conversion to hospital ship *(Dronning Ingrid)*, service in the Mediterranean *(Prins Henrik* and *Tranekæer)* and service in Indonesia *(Romsø)*. Other vessels such as the *Holger Danske* and *Dronning Margrethe II* found new roles within the Scandlines network.

The following detailed review again takes the form of a voyage along the coast of The Netherlands and Germany, round the tip of Norway, down the Kattegat, through the Great Belt and into the Baltic (with a side journey to the Oresund) then up to the Gulf of Finland and Gulf of Bothnia.

The new ferry service between Cuxhaven and Brunsbüttel, across the mouth of the Elbe, finally got going in August. Problems in agreeing a site and then building a terminal at Brunsbüttel had frustrated the plans of formally freight only Harms Group to re-open the route but the three former Scandlines ferries *Hinrich-Wilhelm Kopf* (ex *Prinsesse Elisabeth)*, *Jochen Steffen* (ex *Prinsesse Anne-Marie)* and *Wilhelm Kaisen* (ex *Najaden)*, are now operating, providing a two hourly service.

Tragedy returned to the ferry world on Friday, 27th November, when the almost brand new Austal Ships built fast passenger ferry *Sleipner* of Hardanger Sunnhordlandske Dampskipsselskap sank in the entrance Bømlafjorden, between Haugesund and Bergen, with the loss of 16 lives. Sister vessel *Draupner* was taken out of service pending the outcome of the enquiry.

Both the former Moss – Horten ferries – the 1979 built *Østfold* and the 1991 built *Vestfold* – were sold to Italian operator Meridiano, who operate between Italy and Sicily, over the Straits of Messina. They had been withdrawn from the route when new operator, Bastø

Princess of Scandinavia (William Mayes)

Max Mols (William Mayes)

Fosen, took over the service in 1996 and had spent most of the intervening period laid-up.

On the Skagerak, Color Line's services were due to continue much as before except that the Skagan – Larvik fast ferry service, operated by the *Pegasus Two*, which proved unreliable in 1998, was not scheduled for summer 1999. However, the summer proved even more newsworthy when, in the early hours of 8th July the *Prinsesse Ragnhild* caught fire near Göteborg. About 1300 passengers and crew members were rescued by 20 other ships and, apart from one elderly lady who developed heart problems and subsequently died in hospital, there were no casualties. However a few days later the running mate *Kronprins Harald* was also out of action, having grounded near the mouth of Oslofjord. She was only away for a few days but the *Prinsesse Ragnhild* did not re-enter service until 3rd September.

Scandi Line was integrated into parent company Color Line during the year. Operating between Sandefjord (Norway) and Strömstad (Sweden), an increase in capacity was required to supplement the veteran *Bohus* and *Sandefjord* and in the autumn it was announced that in spring 2000 they would be joined by the former Dover – Calais vessel *Stena Invicta*, renamed the *Color Viking*.

In January Stena Line closed the Halmstad – Grenaa service and transferred the vessel used, the *Stena Nautica*, to the other former Lion Ferry route, between Varberg and Grenaa. This was in anticipation of the ending of duty-free in July and was the first of several moves by Scandinavian ferry companies to cope with the new threat to profitability. The previous Varberg vessel, the elderly *Stena Prince*, was withdrawn and subsequently sold.

The busy Göteborg – Frederikshavn route was little changed, except that in the autumn the

Skagen (William Mayes)

Povl Anker (John Hendy)

Sea Containers *SuperSeaCat One* began operating to Langesund in Norway at the expense of some of her Frederikshavn runs. With Norway being outside the EU, duty-free sales could continue. Another new Sweden – Norway service was provided by DFDS Seaways' Göteborg – Kristiansand – Newcastle route operated by the *Princess of Scandinavia*; the twice weekly through service was complemented by a weekly Göteborg – Kristiansand round trip aimed very much at the mini-cruise market.

When the Great Belt fixed link opened in 1998 it was planned that there would continue to be one ferry route between Jylland and Sjælland (and their associated islands) to the north and one to the south, if necessary subsidised by the tolls from the link. At the time of opening however, there were two competing companies – Scandlines and Mols-Linien both operating fast ferries and ro-pax type conventional ferries. The rationalisation was announced in December 1998 – Scandlines would acquire a 40% share in Mols-Linien and close their own Cat-Link Kalundborg – Århus operation and the parallel ferry service. The two Cat-Link Incats would switch to Mols-Linien and, whilst continuing to serve Århus, would serve Odden instead of Kalundborg. This duly happened in the spring, with the *Cat Link IV* becoming the *Max Mols* and the *Cat Link V* becoming the *Mads Mols*. The older *Cat-Link III* was withdrawn and sold to Tallink. The *Ask* was removed from the Kalundborg route, leaving sister vessel the *Urd* to continue alone until replaced by the *Rostock Link*, operating in freight only mode. These arrangements did not find total favour with truckers and in the autumn a new freight service using the *Dana Hafnia* of DFDS Tor Line, chartered for three years and renamed the *Kattegat Syd*, started. The new company, Århus-Kalundborg Linien, started operation in October but their efforts were frustrated by Mols-Linien's announcement that, from January, it was to transfer both its ro-pax vessels, the *Maren Mols* and *Mette Mols*, to the Århus – Kalundborg route and provide nine sailings a day. In the light of this prospect, the new service foundered after 29 days and the vessel was returned to DFDS Tor Line. At the same time, the Århus – Kalundborg fast ferry route was to become a single vessel operation and the chartered *Mads Mols* withdrawn.

The other Jutland – Sjælland route, that between Spodsbjerg (Langeland) – Tårs (Lolland), operated by Scandlines subsidiary SDFS continued on the reduced scale introduced after the link opened. The operation was put out to tender in the autumn but SFDS were the only bidder.

Routes between Denmark and Germany were particularly hit by the ending of duty free. In anticipation, Langeland – Kiel Linjen, sold their vessel, the *Langeland III* to Jadrolinija of Croatia in 1998, with delivery taken at the end of the year; they renamed her the *Petar Hektorovich*. The service duly ceased at the end of 1998 but, in the early months of the year there was considerable pressure within the EU to further defer the ending of duty-free, with all the larger countries in favour. Accordingly, the *Apollo* was chartered from Eckerö Linjen and the service reopened in March. Come the end of June, the needed unanimity to effect the deferment was not forthcoming and, when duty-free ended, so did the service. Ironically in was Denmark alone who stood out in favour of abolition. The service of sister company Faaborg-Gelting Linien also ceased at the end of June and their vessel, the *Gelting Syd*, was sold to *IMTC* of Spain and renamed the *Atlas*.

The intensive Scandlines service between Puttgarden and Rødby continued much as before, the only change being the replacement of the *Dronning Margrethe II* as the 'dangerous loads' vessel by the *Holger Danske*. The former vessel was transferred full time to the Gedser –

Dronning Margrethe II (William Mayes)

Delphin (William Mayes)

Rostock route, replacing the fast ferry *Berlin Express* which was initially sub-chartered out and then returned to her Norwegian owners. This was a reaction to a greater emphasis on freight on this route and increased competition from Easy Line, who introduced a second Superflex craft, the *Gitte 3*. Attempts by Easy Line and others to establish rival services on the shorter Puttgarden – Rødby route again failed.

In anticipation of the opening of the Oresund fixed link in July 2000, Scandlines withdrew their Limhamn – Dragør service in November. Although their was much public objection to the premature ending of the service, Scandlines saw little reason to operate during the loss making winter period when it was inevitable that the route would have to close at the end of June. The elderly *Scania* was snapped up by Saaremaa Lævakompanii of Estonia and the fast ferry *Felix* laid up for sale or charter. Helsingør – Helsingborg services continued as before, with Scandlines and HH-Ferries competing vigorously and the route looks likely to continue when the new link opens. The København – Helsingborg rail freight service will, however, end, with all rail freight using the link.

After 1998's problems with the manoeuvrability of the *Mecklenburg-Vorpommern* and the very late delivery of the *Skåne*, Scandlines Sweden – Germany routes enjoyed a quieter year. Rival operator TT-Line also continued much as before but announced the replacement of their two 'flagship' ferries *Nils Holgersson* and *Peter Pan* with new vessels carrying less passengers but enhanced freight capacity. BornholmsTrafikken had their last year of wholly conventional operation whilst their new fast ferry *Villum Clausen* was being built in Australia. The veteran *Peder Olsen*, used mainly on the Rønne – Ystad route during recent summers, was returned to her owners in the autumn and subsequently sold to Moby Lines

Bastø II (William Mayes)

Skåne (William Mayes)

of Italy.

Polferries withdrew their fast ferry, the *Boomerang*, from the Swinoujscie – Malmö service in the autumn. Although continuing to operate a conventional ferry on that route, they also re-introduced a service to Ystad, competing with Unity Line's *Polonia*, and reducing their service to Nynäshamn in Sweden to a single ship operation.

Euroseabridge, a Scandlines subsidiary operating from Germany to Latvia and Lithuania, chartered the *Ask* from Scandlines in the spring and placed her on their Travemünde – Klaìpeda (Lithuania) service. This enabled the chartered *Kalhlberg* to be transferred to the Rostock (Germany) – Liepaja (Latvia) route and establish a service with space for 70 passengers. In the autumn a deal was done with Lisco of Lithuania and a joint service established on Lisco's Kiel – Klaìpeda route. Only one Euroseabridge vessel was required and the *Ask* was withdrawn. In January 2000 she was switched to the Latvian link and the *Kalhlberg* to Scandlines' Amber Line Karlshamn (Sweden) – Liepaja route.

Destination Gotland's new fast ferry the *Gotland* entered service in the spring. Built in France, she has a steel (rather than aluminium) hull and has been designed to cope with the level of winter ice generally found in that area of the Baltic. However, the level of subsidy did not, during winter 1999/2000, make it economic to continue through the winter months, so the service was suspended in the autumn and will resume again in the spring. Meanwhile, parent company Rederi AB Gotland have ordered two new ro-pax vessels, at least one of which seems destined to replace one or both of the current fleet on the services to the island of Gotland.

SHIPS NEWS

World Breaking News Today

Publication date: annual

Hot News ■ AST and BSkyB together extending the boundaries of entertainment

Entire Premier League seen on North Sea Ferry

Marine Stabilised Antenna from Europe's Largest Manufacturer - AST

For nearly ten years AST has been manufacturing and supplying ferry companies all over the world.

With the widespread availability of low cost computer power their new designs are all microprocessor based. In other words based on data received from the ships on board GPS and compass, their software will predict the position of any satellite commercially available after which, the antenna will lock on with their patented and renowned conical scanning system.

Once the system has been commissioned it will never need to be touched as it is entirely automatic. Should one require to c h a n g e satellite to view alternative channels or obtain a one way high speed internet connection, this is very straightforward.

Designed to be user friendly their systems can be explained in just a

few minutes, allowing the complete novice or a non-technical operator to be fully conversant very quickly

Bearing in mind their massive experience in the North Sea, AST's enormous commitment to research and development and their determination to simply out perform the competition, an investment in AST antennas makes sense.

Evolution not revolution, that has to be AST.

Report by:
Kevin Franklin - AST

BSkyB & AST -
APPLIED SATELLITE TECHNOLOGY *Extending the Boundaries*

Interested???
Contact us Today!

European Office:
Tel: +44 (0)1493 440011
Fax: +44 (0)1493 441023
E-mail: kevin.franklin@ast-uk.com
Website: www.satcomms.com

Small Dish Big Performance

Unbelievable results have been found with recent tests carried out around the coast of the UK on Sky Digital. Irrespective of weather conditions or vessel size their little dish simply out performs anything of a similar size, refusing to be knocked off the satellite. With its super l i g h t w e i g h t construction we were able to test in a number of different locations, including high on a mast, and nothing we did to it could faze this little beauty.

Maritime BSkyB Now Available

Entertainment on board ferries will never be the same with the amazing new channel line up from BSkyB, everything from premier league to MTV and the movies.

With the inclusion of BBC1, BBC2 and Channel 4, terrestrial TV can be viewed as well with stunning picture quality.

AST / Toshiba Launch 61″ TV

To take full advantage of BSkyB, Toshiba via AST, has launched a whole range of TVs suitable for ferries - from their diminutive 14″ set, right up to their new monster 61″ cinema.

★ ★ ★ ★ **AST add BBC World to their programme portfolio** ★ ★ ★ ★

FCG

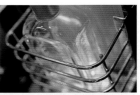

SPECIALISTS IN

MARINE INTERIOR DESIGN

PROJECT MANAGEMENT

AND BRANDING

34 West Street

Brighton East Sussex

BN1 2RE

Tel: 01273 220 992

Fax: 01273 220 993

email: fcg-design@finnegan.co.uk

Silja Europa (Philippe Holthof)

Finnlines' *Finnclipper* finally arrived in May, over a year late. First of four ro-pax vessels ordered by Stena Ro-Ro, she was one of two purchased by Finnlines before completion. She was placed on the Helsinki – Travemünde route, replacing the *Translubeca*. Sister vessel *Finneagle* was delivered in the autumn but did not, as anticipated, join her on the cross-Baltic service. Instead she was placed on the freight only FinnLink Kapellskär – Naantali route. Helsinki – Travemünde frequency was, however, doubled as announced as the smaller ro-pax *Finnsailor* was transferred from the FinnLink service to this route.

Early in the new year Silja Line's *Finnjet* switched her 22 hour cruises from the industrial port of Muuga to the main harbour in Tallinn. She resumed her sailings to Germany in the spring but her destination was changed from Travemünde to Rostock. The shorter sailing time enabled calls in both directions to be made at Tallinn. Being outside the EU, the Estonian calls enabled duty-free facilities to be maintained for the whole route. In the autumn, she resumed her cruises, but this winter was the sole Silja Line representative on this booming route, as the *Wasa Queen* was transferred to the Vaasa – Umeå route, replacing the much loved *Fennia*. This route, the only one operated by Silja Line no longer able to offer duty-free, is operated by subsidiary Vaasanlaivat. In need of subsidy in a post duty-free situation, the route was put out to tender. Vaasanlaivat was successful and part of their application involved the replacement of the *Fennia*.

The Ferry Serviss route between Stockholm and Riga (Latvia) was without a ship for a time during the early autumn due to the arrest of their vessel, the Russian owned *Russ*, for non-payment of port dues and staff wages. The Latvian operation was taken over by Russian interests and, after debts had been settled, the service was able to resume. This operator also re-started the Stockholm – St Petersburg service, using the *Mikhail Sholokov*, a sister vessel of the *Russ*.

1999 saw a 200% increase in fast vehicle ferries on the Helsinki – Tallinn route with Nordic Jet Line introducing a second craft – the *Baltic Jet* – and Tallink acquiring the *Cat-Link III* from Scandlines and renaming her the *Tallink Autoexpress*. The route continued to boom, although no new conventional tonnage was introduced.

Both Silja Line and Viking Line reacted to the ending of duty-free by diverting their services via the special tax status Åland Islands. Stockholm – Helsinki services now call at Mariehamn, but, for time reasons, it would not have been possible to divert both night and day Stockholm – Turku services to this port. Accordingly a new port was built at Långnäs, which is nearer to the direct route, and vessels on night crossings call there.

Silja subsidiary SeaWind Line finally acquired a second vessel of their own in the spring with the purchase of the train ferry *Rostock* from Scandlines. She was renamed the *Star Wind*. Although a passenger vessel, her accommodation was not deemed suitable for Baltic service, especially overnight, and she has operated on a freight only basis. In the longer term, it is planned to both lengthen her and upgrade the passenger facilities to enable a twice daily passenger service to be offered.

Nick Widdows

Crown of Scandinavia (Philippe Holthof)

**Low Weight Safety Barriers
ALUBAR, Norway**

ALUBAR

SeaFrance Cezanne (John Hendy)

Section 1 – GB & IRELAND PASSENGER
OPERATIONS
BRITTANY FERRIES

THE COMPANY *Brittany Ferries* is the trading name of *BAI SA*, a French private sector company and the operating arm of the *Brittany Ferries Group*. The UK operations are run by *BAI (UK) Ltd*, a UK private sector company, wholly owned by the *Brittany Ferries Group*.

MANAGEMENT Group Managing Director: Jean-Michel Masson, **Managing Director UK & Ireland:** Ian Carruthers, **Marketing Director:** David Longden.

ADDRESS Millbay Docks, PLYMOUTH, Devon PL1 3EW.

TELEPHONE Administration: +44 (0)1752 227941, **Reservations:** *All Services:* 0990 360360 (UK only), *Portsmouth:* +44 (0)23 9289 2200, *Plymouth:* +44 (0)1752 252200, **Fax:** +44 (0)1752 600698, **Telex:** 86878.

INTERNET Website: http://www.brittany-ferries.com *(English, French)*

ROUTES OPERATED *All year:* Roscoff – Plymouth (6 hrs (day), 6 hrs – 7 hrs 30 mins (night); *(5,6)*; up to 3 per day (summer), 1 per week (winter)), St Malo – Portsmouth (8 hrs 45 mins (day), 10 hrs 30 mins – 11 hrs 30 mins (night); *(2 (summer), 2,4 (winter))*; 1 per day), Caen (Ouistreham) – Portsmouth (6 hrs (day), 6 hrs 15 mins – 8 hrs (night); *(3,4)*; 3 per day), Plymouth – Santander (Spain) (24 hrs; *(6)*; 2 per week (March – November)), Cherbourg – Poole (4 hrs 15 mins; *(1)*; up to 2 per day), *Summer only:* Roscoff – Cork (14 hrs; *(6)*; 1 per week), *Winter only:* St Malo – Plymouth (8 hrs; *(4,5)*; 1 per week.

CONVENTIONAL FERRIES

1	BARFLEUR	20133t	92	19k	1173P	550C	125T	BA	Helsinki, FI	FR
2	BRETAGNE	24534t	89	21k	2030P	580C	40L	BA	St Nazaire, FR	FR
3	DUC DE NORMANDIE	13505t	78	21k	1500P	350C	44T	BA	Heusden, NL	FR
4	NORMANDIE	27541t	92	20k	2263P	630C	66T	BA	Turku, FI	FR
5	QUIBERON	11813t	75	20k	1302P	300C	35L	BA2	Rendsburg, GY	FR
6	VAL DE LOIRE	31395t	87	21k	1800P	550C	114T	BA	Bremerhaven, GY	FR

BARFLEUR Built for the *Truckline* Cherbourg – Poole service to replace two passenger vessels and to inaugurate a year round passenger service. In 1999 the *Truckline* passenger service was marketed as *Brittany Ferries* and she was repainted into full *Brittany Ferries* livery.

BRETAGNE Built for the Santander – Plymouth and Roscoff – Cork services (with two trips per week between Roscoff and Plymouth). In 1993 she was transferred to the St Malo – Portsmouth service.

DUC DE NORMANDIE Built as the PRINSES BEATRIX for *Stoomvaart Maatschappij Zeeland (Zeeland Steamship Company)* of The Netherlands for their Hoek van Holland – Harwich service. In September 1985 sold to *Brittany Ferries* and chartered back to *SMZ*, continuing to operate for them until the introduction of the KONINGIN BEATRIX in May 1986. In June 1986 delivered to *Brittany Ferries* and inaugurated the Caen – Portsmouth service.

NORMANDIE Built for the Caen – Portsmouth route.

QUIBERON Ordered by *Lion Ferry AB* of Sweden. The contract was sold to *Svenska Lastbils AB (Svelast)* of Sweden (a subsidiary of *Statens Järnvägar (SJ), Swedish State Railways*) before delivery and she was delivered to them as the NILS DACKE. She was initially chartered to *Svenska Rederi AB Öresund* (another SJ subsidiary) for their service between Malmö (Sweden) and Travemünde (Germany). Sister vessel the GUSTAV VASA (now NORRÖNA of *Smyril Line*) was owned by *Lion Ferry AB* of Sweden and was also chartered to *SRÖ*. In 1976, *Svelast* took over the marketing of the service and it was operated under the name *Malmö-Travemünde Linjen*, with *Lion Ferry AB* operating it as agents. Later in 1976, *Svelast* and *Linjebuss International* (a subsidiary of *Stockholms Rederi AB Svea*) formed a jointly owned subsidiary called *Saga-Linjen* and *Lion Ferry AB* continued as

Shouldn't getting there be as relaxing as being there?

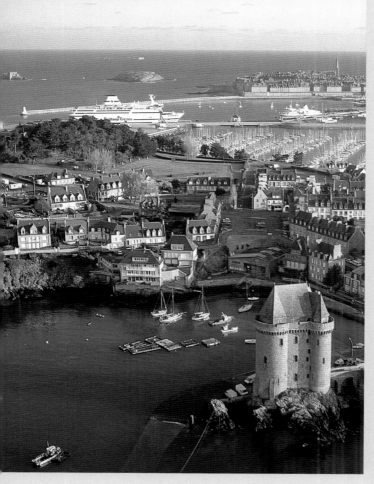

It's been our philosophy since
our maiden voyage in 1973.
It's one shared by our passengers.
Which is why that single route
has grown to six today.
And three of our passenger ships
have been awarded
the AA's coveted 5-star award for
on-board facilities and services.
Nor do things stop when we dock.
For more and more of our
passengers, sailing is just the first
part of a complete Brittany
Ferries' holiday. So if you haven't
yet, it's time to come aboard
and enjoy the philosophy.

www.brittanyferries.com 08705 360 360

administrative operator. In 1981 a joint marketing agreement was reached with the rival German owned *TT-Linie*, (running between Travemünde and Trelleborg (Sweden)) and the two services were marketed as *TT-Saga-Line*. In April 1982 the NILS DACKE was chartered to *Brittany Ferries* with an option to purchase. She was renamed the QUIBERON and placed on the Santander – Plymouth and Roscoff – Cork services; she also operated between Roscoff and Plymouth. The GUSTAV VASA continued as sole vessel on the Malmö – Travemünde route for a further year until the service was withdrawn. The QUIBERON was purchased by *Brittany Ferries* in 1984 and re-registered in France. Following the delivery of the BRETAGNE in July 1989, she was transferred to the Roscoff – Plymouth service.

VAL DE LOIRE Built as the NILS HOLGERSSON for *TT-Line* of Sweden and Germany for their service between Travemünde and Trelleborg. In 1991 purchased by *Brittany Ferries* for entry into service in spring 1993. After a major rebuild, she was renamed the VAL DE LOIRE and introduced onto the Plymouth – Santander and Roscoff – Plymouth/Cork service.

COMMODORE FERRIES

THE COMPANY *Commodore Ferries (CI) Ltd* is a Guernsey private sector company.

MANAGEMENT Managing Director: Jeff Vidamour.

ADDRESS PO Box 10, New Jetty Offices, White Rock, St Peter Port, GUERNSEY GY1 3AF.

TELEPHONE Administration: +44 (0)1481 728620, **Fax:** +44 (0)1481 728521, **Reservations (Passenger):** See *Condor Ferries*.

INTERNET Email: JVidamour@CommodoreFerries.com

ROUTE OPERATED Portsmouth – St Peter Port (Guernsey) (6 hrs 30 mins) – St Helier (Jersey) (10 hrs 30 mins) – Portsmouth (8 hrs 30 mins) (return Guernsey via Jersey, 12 hrs 30 mins); *(1)*; 1 per day.

RO-PAX FERRY

1	COMMODORE CLIPPER	14000t	99	18.25k	500P	100C	94T	A	Rotterdam, NL	BA

COMMODORE CLIPPER Ro-pax vessel built to operate between Portsmouth and The Channel Islands. She replaced the ISLAND COMMODORE, a freight only vessel. Her passenger services are operated as part of the *Condor Ferries* network and she carries the logos of both companies. Her passenger capacity is normally restricted to 300 but is increased to 500 when the *Condor* fast ferries are unable to operate.

CONDOR FERRIES

THE COMPANY *Condor Ferries Ltd* is a Channel Islands private sector company owned by *Commodore Shipping*, Guernsey.

MANAGEMENT Managing Director: Robert Provan, **General Manager, Sales & Marketing:** Nicholas Dobbs.

ADDRESS Condor House, New Harbour Road South, Hamworthy, POOLE, Dorset BH15 4AJ.

TELEPHONE Administration: +44 (0)1202 207207, **Reservations:** +44 (0)1305 761551, **Fax: Admin:** +44 (0)1202 685184, **Reservations:** +44 (0)1305 760776.

INTERNET Email: sales@condorferries.co.uk **Website:** http://www.condorferries.co.uk *(English)*

ROUTES OPERATED Fast Car Ferries: Winter Only: Weymouth – St Peter Port (Guernsey) (2 hrs 15 mins) – St Helier (Jersey via Guernsey) (3 hrs 35 mins) (Mon, Fri,); *(1)*; 2 per week). **Spring, Summer and Autumn:** Weymouth – St Peter Port (Guernsey) (2 hrs) – St Helier (Jersey via Guernsey) (3 hrs 25 mins) – St Malo (via Guernsey and Jersey) (5 hrs); *(1,2)*; 1 per day, Poole – St Peter Port (Guernsey) (2 hrs 30 mins) – St Helier (Jersey via Guernsey) (3 hrs 50 mins) – St Malo (via Guernsey and Jersey) (5 hrs 25 mins); *(1,2)*; up to 2 per day to Jersey, 1 per day to St Malo.

Barfleur (Andrew Cooke)

Condor Express (Miles Cowsill)

Fast Passenger Ferry: *Spring and Autumn:* St Malo – St Helier (Jersey) (1 hr 10 mins); *(4),* 2 per day (1 per day Mon & Fri), St Helier – St Peter Port (1 hr) (Mon & Fri); *(3);* 1 per day. **Summer only:** St Malo – St Helier (Jersey) (1 hr 10 mins); *(3);* 2 per day).

Ro-pax Ferry: The car and passenger facilities on the ro-pax service between Portsmouth and The Channel Islands operated by *Commodore Ferries* (see above) are marketed by *Condor Ferries.*

FAST CAR FERRIES

| 1 | CONDOR EXPRESS | 5005t | 96 | 39k | 774P | 185C | - | A2 | Hobart, AL | SI |
| 2 | CONDOR VITESSE | 5005t | 97 | 39k | 774P | 185C | - | A2 | Hobart, AL | BA |

CONDOR EXPRESS InCat 86m catamaran. She was delivered December 1996 and entered service in 1997.

CONDOR VITESSE InCat 86m catamaran. Built speculatively and launched as the INCAT 044. Moved to Europe in summer 1997 and spent time in the both the UK and Denmark but was not used. In 1998, she was chartered to *Condor Ferries* and renamed the CONDOR VITESSE. During winter 1999/2000 she was chartered to *TranzRail* of New Zealand. Returned to UK in spring 2000.

FAST PASSENGER FERRY

| 3p | CONDOR 9 | 752t | 90 | 30k | 450P | 0C | 0L | - | Fareham, GB | GB |

CONDOR 9 FBM Marinteknik catamaran built for *Condor Ferries* and initially mainly used between the Channel Islands and Weymouth. In spring 1994, she was chartered to *Viking Line* and operated between Helsinki and Tallinn as the 'VIKING EXPRESS' (although not officially renamed). During winter 1994/95 she went on charter to the Caribbean. On return in mid 1995 she was laid up for a period before starting a new service between the Channel Islands and Torquay. She operated on this route during summer 1996. In 1997 she operated between Jersey and Poole and Jersey and St Malo. Since 1998 she has operated between St Malo, Jersey and Guernsey.

LAID UP VESSEL

| 4• | HAVELET | 6918t | 77 | 19k | 500P | 200C | 37L | BA2 | Bergen, NO | BA |

HAVELET Built as the CORNOUAILLES for *Brittany Ferries* and used mainly on their Roscoff – Plymouth service. In 1984 she was chartered to *SNCF* for use on their Dieppe – Newhaven service. This charter terminated at the end of 1985 and she was transferred to *Truckline Ferries*. From January 1986 she operated on their Cherbourg – Poole freight-only service and then, in April, she inaugurated the Caen – Portsmouth service for *Brittany Ferries* on a freight-only basis. In June she returned to *Truckline Ferries* and inaugurated a car and passenger service between Cherbourg and Poole. Until 1989 she operated between Cherbourg and Poole all year round, conveying passengers between April and October only. In 1989 she was renamed the HAVELET and sold to *Channel Island Ferries,* holding company of *British Channel Island Ferries,* operating between Poole and the Channel Islands. It was intended that, in 1993, she would be used in a freight-only role; however, due to the level of demand it was decided to allow her to carry passengers and she was crewed accordingly. In 1994, *British Channel Island Ferries* ceased operations and she was chartered to *Condor Ferries* to operate between Weymouth and the Channel Islands. She was withdrawn in autumn 1996 and laid up. In 1998 purchased by *Condor Ferries* for use as a back-up vessel in time of bad weather for the fast ferries between the Channel Islands and the UK. She was withdrawn in November 1999 when the new COOMODORE CLIPPER was delivered. Currently laid up at Weymouth for sale.

Solidor 4 (Dave Hocquard)

Commodore Clipper (Commodore)

DFDS SEAWAYS

THE COMPANY *DFDS Seaways Group A/S* is the passenger division of the *DFDS Group*, a Danish private sector company. *DFDS Seaways Ltd* is a British subsidiary.

MANAGEMENT Managing Director *(DFDS Seaways Ltd):* John Crummie.

ADDRESS Scandinavia House, Parkeston, HARWICH, Essex CO12 4QG.

TELEPHONE Administration: +44 (0)1255 243456, **Reservations:** *National:* 08705 333000 (from UK only), *Harwich:* +44 (0)1255 240240, *Newcastle:* +44 (0)191-293 6262, **Fax:** *Harwich:* +44 (0)1255 244370, **Fax:** *Newcastle:* +44 (0)191-293 6222.

INTERNET Email: john.crummie@dfds.co.uk **Website:** http://www.dfdsseaways.co.uk *(English)* http://www.dfdsseaways.com *(Danish, Dutch, German, Norwegian, Swedish)*

ROUTES OPERATED *All year:* Harwich – IJmuiden – Esbjerg (call at IJmuiden northbound only) (23 hrs northbound, 19 hrs southbound; *(2)*; 3 per week or alternate days) (call at IJmuiden is for freight only), Newcastle – Kristiansand – Göteborg (25 hrs; *(5)*; 2 per week), Kristiansand – Göteborg (7 hrs (day), 13 hrs 30 min (night); *(5)* 1 per week), Harwich – Hamburg (20 hrs 30 mins; *(4)*; 3 per week (winter), every 2/4 days (summer), Newcastle (North Shields) – IJmuiden (near Amsterdam) (15 hrs; *(1,3)*; daily).

CONVENTIONAL FERRIES

1	ADMIRAL OF SCANDINAVIA	19292t	76	21k	1132P	400C	45L	BA	Rendsburg, GY	BA
2	DANA ANGLIA	19321t	78	21k	1372P	470C	45L	BA	Aalborg, DK	DK
3	KING OF SCANDINAVIA	13336t	74	22.5k	1100P	300C	38L	BA	Turku, FI	DK
4	PRINCE OF SCANDINAVIA	22528t	75	23k	1692P	385C	70T	AS	Lübeck, GY	DK
5	PRINCESS OF SCANDINAVIA	22528t	76	23k	1704P	385C	70T	AS	Lübeck, GY	DK

ADMIRAL OF SCANDINAVIA Built as the KRONPRINS HARALD for *Jahre Line* of Norway and used on their service between Oslo and Kiel (Germany). Acquired by *DFDS* in 1987, renamed the HAMBURG, re-registered in the Bahamas and replaced the PRINS HAMLET (see the NIEBOROW, *Polferries*) on the Harwich – Hamburg service. In March 1997 she was transferred to the Newcastle – IJmuiden and Newcastle – Hamburg services and renamed the ADMIRAL OF SCANDINAVIA. During winter 1997/98 she was temporarily transferred back to the Harwich – Hamburg service; this also happened during winter 1999/2000. For most of 2000 she will operate between Newcastle and IJmuiden, the Hamburg service having ceased.

DANA ANGLIA Built for the Harwich – Esbjerg service and has seldom operated elsewhere.

KING OF SCANDINAVIA Built as the PRINSESSAN BIRGITTA for *Göteborg-Frederikshavn-Linjen* (trading as *Sessan Line*) and *Ragne Rederi AB* of Sweden for their alternate day Göteborg – Travemünde service. The company was taken over by rival *Stena Line AB* in 1981 and later that year she was transferred to their Göteborg – Kiel route, the Travemünde route becoming freight-only. In 1982 a new PRINSESSAN BIRGITTA was delivered and she was renamed the STENA SCANDINAVICA. She remained on the Göteborg – Kiel route until 1987 when she was replaced by the new STENA GERMANICA. During summer 1987 she was chartered to *CoTuNav*, the Tunisian state shipping concern, and used on their service between Tunis and Marseilles (France) and Genova (Italy). In early 1988 a new STENA SCANDINAVICA was delivered and she was further renamed the SCANDINAVICA. In June 1988 she was taken on four months charter by *Sealink British Ferries* and used on additional sailings between Dover (Eastern Docks) and Calais (passenger and freight services) and Zeebrugge (freight-only services). In 1989, after further charter to *CoTuNav*, being renamed the TARAK L, she was sold to *Norway Line*. In 1990 she was renamed the VENUS, re-registered in Norway and took over the Bergen/Stavanger – Newcastle service from the JUPITER (9499t, 1966). In 1994 she was sold to *DFDS*, renamed the KING OF SCANDINAVIA and, in 1995, replaced the WINSTON CHURCHILL (8658t, 1967) on the Newcastle – Esbjerg/Hamburg services. In 1996 she operated alternate sailings from Newcastle to Hamburg and IJmuiden. In March 1997 she was replaced by the ADMIRAL OF SCANDINAVIA. During winter 1997/98 she returned to service, operating on the Newcastle – IJmuiden service. During summer 1998 she was again chartered to

Going to Europe?

Go from Newcastle or Harwich.

Go for the convenience.

Go for the price.

Go~easy
Go DFDS Seaways.

Cruise across to northern Europe with DFDS Seaways from £44 per person. Sail overnight with your car from Newcastle to Holland, Norway or Sweden. From Harwich to Germany or Denmark. Enjoy a good meal. Live entertainment. The shops, bars and cinema. Comfortable accommodation. Go on. For a brochure call **08705 333 666** quoting ref. 9B278. Or visit **www.dfdsseaways.co.uk**

DFDS SEAWAYS

AMSTERDAM – HAMBURG – ESBJERG – KRISTIANSAND – GOTHENBURG

CoTuNav of Tunisia. During summer 1999 she sailed between Newcastle and IJmuiden and she will sail on this route for most of 2000.

PRINCE OF SCANDINAVIA Built as the TOR BRITANNIA for *Tor Line* of Sweden for their Amsterdam – Göteborg and Felixstowe – Göteborg services. She was acquired by *DFDS* in 1981 and subsequently re-registered in Denmark. Since winter 1983/4 she also operated on the Harwich – Esbjerg service with the DANA ANGLIA. She has also operated Newcastle – Esbjerg and Amsterdam – Göteborg. During winter 1989/90 she was used as an accommodation ship for refugees in Malmö. In 1991 renamed the PRINCE OF SCANDINAVIA following a major refurbishment. In summer 1994 and 1995 she operated on the IJmuiden (Netherlands) – Göteborg (Sweden) and IJmuiden – Kristiansand (Norway) service and did not serve the UK. In 1996 she was chartered to *CoTuNav* of Tunisia for service between Tunisia and Italy. In March 1997 she was transferred to the Harwich – Hamburg route. During winter 1997/98 she covered for other ferries which were being refitted, including the København – Oslo vessels, and had major modifications made at Gdansk. In summer 1998 she operated every third trip from Hamburg to Newcastle instead of Harwich; this was repeated in 1999 but in summer 2000 she will operate solely between Harwich and Hamburg.

PRINCESS OF SCANDINAVIA Built as the TOR SCANDINAVIA for *Tor Line* of Sweden for their Amsterdam – Göteborg and Felixstowe – Göteborg services. In 1979 she was used on a world trade cruise and was temporarily renamed the HOLLAND EXPO. Similar exercises were undertaken in 1980, 1982 and 1984, but on these occasions her temporary name was the WORLD WIDE EXPO. She was acquired by *DFDS* in 1981 and subsequently re-registered in Denmark. She has also operated on the Harwich – Esbjerg service. Between 1989 and 1993 she also operated Newcastle – Esbjerg and Amsterdam – Göteborg services. In 1991, following a major refurbishment, she was renamed the PRINCESS OF SCANDINAVIA. Since 1994, she generally operated on the Harwich – Göteborg and Newcastle – Göteborg routes. During winter 1998/1999 she had major modifications made at Gdansk and during winter 1999/2000 she has a major engine rebuild. She now operates between Newcastle and Göteborg via Kristiansand.

EMERAUDE LINES

THE COMPANY *Emeraude Lines* is a French private sector company.

MANAGEMENT Commercial Manager (St Malo): Jean-Luc Griffon, **Managing Director (Jersey):** Gordon Forrest.

ADDRESS Terminal Ferry du Naye, PO Box 16, 35401, ST MALO Cedex, France.

TELEPHONE Administration & Reservations: *St Malo:* +33 (0)2 23 180 180, *Jersey:* +44 (0)1534 766566, **Fax:** *St Malo:* +33 (0)2 23 181 500, *Jersey:* +44 (0)1534 768741.

INTERNET Email: sales@emeraude.co.uk **Website:** http://www.emeraudelines.com *(English)*

ROUTES OPERATED Fast Car Ferries: St Malo (France) – St Helier (Jersey) (1 hr 10 mins; *(1,2)*; up to 4 per day), St Malo – St Peter Port (Guernsey) (1 hr 50 mins; *(1,2)*; up to 3 per day), St Helier – St Peter Port (1 hr; *(2)*; 1 per day), **Fast Passenger Ferry:** St Helier – Sark (45 mins; *(4)*; 1 per day), Granville (France) – St Helier (1 hr; *(4)*; 1 per day), **Fast Passenger Ferry operated by Alizés in joint venture with Emeraude Lines:** Carteret (France) – Gorey (50 mins; *(3)*; see note), Diélette – St Peter Port (1 hr 30 mins; *(3)*; see note). Note: on most days through the summer there is either a Carteret – Jersey or Diélette – Guernsey service. Timetable varies according to the tidal conditions at the French ports and Gorey.

FAST CAR FERRIES

1	SOLIDOR 3	2068t	96	33k	448P	51C	-	A	Omastrand, NO	FR
2	SOLIDOR 4	1064t	87	30k	302P	40C	-	A	Mandal, NO	FR

SOLIDOR 3 Kværner Fjellstrand JumboCat 60m catamaran. Built for *Emeraude Lines* to re-establish fast car ferry services.

SOLIDOR 4 Westamarin W5000CF catamaran. Built for *Gods Trans* of Norway as the ANNE LISE, a high speed frozen fish carrier and used in the North Sea. In 1993 the fish hold was converted to a vehicle deck and an additional passenger accommodation was provided. She was sold to *Brudey Frères* of Guadeloupe renamed the MADIKERA. In 1995 she was sold to *Elba Ferries* and renamed the EXPRESS ELBA; she operated a summer service between Piombino (Italy) and Portoferráio (Elba). In 1999 sold to *Emeraude Lines* and renamed the SOLIDOR 4. After refurbishment, entered service in spring 1999.

FAST PASSENGER FERRIES

3p	COTE DES ISLES	‡199t	76	28k	140P	OC	OL	-	Mandal, NO	FR
4p	NORMANDY EXPRESS	449t	88	38k	306P	OC	OL	-	Öregrund, SW	FR
5p•	TRIDENT 5	211t	74	28k	200P	OC	OL	-	Mandal, NO	FR

COTE DES ISLES Westermoen W86 catamaran built as the FJORDDROTT for *Det Stavangerske D/S* (later *Rogaland Trafikkselskap*) of Norway, operating in the Stavanger area. In 1990 she was renamed the TERNØY (following the delivery of a new FJORDDROTT). In 1991 she was sold to *Channiland* of France and renamed the BRITTANIA; she operated between Granville and St Helier. In 1997 sold to *Alizés* of France, operating between Carteret (France) and Gorey (Jersey) and Portbail (France) and Gorey. In 1999, *Alizés* and *Emeraude Lines* entered into a joint agreement, the COTE DES ISLES taking over *Emeraude Lines'* Carteret – Jersey and Diélette – Guernsey services.

NORMANDY EXPRESS Marinteknik 41 CPV built as the ÖREGRUND for the *Hong Kong Macao Hydrofoil Company* and operated between Hong Kong and Macao. In 1995 she was chartered to *Universal Aboit* of the Philippines, renamed the SUPERCAT 1 and used on inter island services. In 1999 she was chartered to *Emeraude Lines* (with a purchase option) and renamed the NORMANDY EXPRESS.

TRIDENT 5 Westamarin W95 catamaran. Built as the VINGTOR for *Det Stavangereske Dampskibsselskab* of Norway and operated between Stavanger and Bergen. In 1990 sold to *Emeraude Lines* and renamed the TRIDENT 5. In 1998 undertook a charter in the West Indies. In 1999 she ran from St-Laurent-du-Var (near Nice airport) to Cannes and St-Tropez from late-June to September in a joint venture between *Emeraude Ferries* and *Air France*. It is unclear what will happen to her in 2000, although there are currently no plans to operate her on the Channel Islands services.

FJORD LINE

THE COMPANY *Fjord Line* is a Norwegian company, 100% owned by *Bergen-Nordhordland Rutelag AS (BNR)*. It took over the Newcastle – Norway service from *Color Line* in December 1998.

MANAGEMENT Managing Director (UK): Dag Romslo, **Sales Director (UK):** Mike Wood.

ADDRESS Royal Quays, NORTH SHIELDS NE29 6EG.

TELEPHONE Administration: +44 (0)191-296 1313, **Reservations:** +44 (0)191-296 1313, **Fax:** +44 (0)191-296 1540, **Telex:** 537275.

INTERNET Email: fjordline.uk@fjordline.com **Website:** http://www.fjordline.com

ROUTES OPERATED Bergen – Haugesund – Stavanger – Newcastle – Bergen (triangular route), Bergen – Haugesund – Stavanger – Newcastle (Bergen – Stavanger (via 6 hrs), Stavanger – Newcastle (direct: 18 hrs 30 mins, via Bergen: 29 hrs 30 mins), Bergen – Newcastle (21 hrs 15 mins); *(1)*: 3 sailings Norway – Newcastle per week).

Fjord Line also operates between Norway and Denmark; see Section 6.

CONVENTIONAL FERRY

1	JUPITER	20581t	75	19k	1250P	285C	42T	BA	Nantes, FR	NO

JUPITER Built as the WELLAMO for *EFFOA* of Finland for *Silja Line* services between Helsinki and Stockholm. In 1981 sold to *DFDS*, renamed the DANA GLORIA and placed onto the Göteborg – Newcastle and Esbjerg – Newcastle services. In 1983 she was moved to the København – Oslo service. In 1984 she was chartered to *Johnson Line* of Sweden for *Silja Line* service between Stockholm and Turku and renamed the SVEA CORONA – the name previously born by a sister vessel, which had been sold. This charter ended in 1985 and she returned to the København – Oslo service and resumed the name DANA GLORIA. During winter 1988/89 she was lengthened in Papenburg, Germany and in early 1989 she was renamed the KING OF SCANDINAVIA. She returned to the København – Oslo route; in 1990 a Helsingborg call was introduced. In 1994 she was sold to *Color Line* (as part of a deal which involved *DFDS* buying the VENUS from *Color Line*) and renamed the COLOR VIKING. In 1998 she was sold to *Fjord Line* and renamed the JUPITER.

IRISH FERRIES

THE COMPANY *Irish Ferries* is an Irish Republic private sector company, part of the *Irish Continental Group*. It was originally mainly owned by the state owned *Irish Shipping* and partly by *Lion Ferry AB* of Sweden. *Lion Ferry* participation ceased in 1977 and the company was sold into the private sector in 1987. Formerly state owned *B&I Line* was taken over in 1991 and from 1995 all operations were marketed as a single entity.

MANAGEMENT Group Managing Director: Eamon Rothwell, **Group Marketing Director:** Tony Kelly.

ADDRESS 2 Merrion Row, DUBLIN 2, Republic of Ireland.

TELEPHONE Administration: +353 (0)1 855 2222, **Reservations:** *Dublin:* +353 (0)1 638 3333, *Cork:* +353 (0)21 551995, *Rosslare Harbour:* +353 (0)53 33158, *Holyhead:* 0990 329129 (from UK only), *Pembroke Dock:* 0990 329543 (from UK only), *National:* 0990 171717 (from UK only), **Fax:** *Dublin:* +353 (0)1 661 0743, *Cork:* +353 (0)21 504651. *24 hour information:* +353 (0)1 661 0715.

INTERNET Email: info@irishferries.com **Website:** http://www.irishferries.com *(English)*

ROUTES OPERATED Conventional Ferries Dublin – Holyhead (3 hrs 30 mins; *(1)*; 2 per day), Rosslare – Pembroke Dock (4 hrs 15 mins; *(2)*; 2 per day), Rosslare – Cherbourg (17 hrs 30 mins; *(3)*; 1 or 2 per week), Rosslare – Roscoff (16 hrs; *(3)*; 1 or 2 per week) Note: the Rosslare – Cherbourg/Roscoff service operates on a seasonal basis, **Fast Ferry:** Dublin – Holyhead (1 hr 49 min; *(4)*; up to 4 per day). Marketed as 'DUBLIN*Swift*'.

CONVENTIONAL FERRIES

1	ISLE OF INISHMORE	34031t	97	21.3k	2200P	800C	122L	BA2	Krimpen, NL	IR
2	ISLE OF INNISFREE	22365t	95	21.5k	1700P	600C	142T	BA	Krimpen, NL	IR
3	NORMANDY	24872t	82	20.4k	2100P	480C	52L	BA2	Göteborg, SW	IR

ISLE OF INISHMORE Built for *Irish Ferries* to operate on the Holyhead – Dublin service.

ISLE OF INNISFREE Built for *Irish Ferries* to operate on the Holyhead – Dublin. In 1997 transferred to the Rosslare – Pembroke Dock service; for a short period, before modifications at Pembroke Dock were completed, she operated between Rosslare and Fishguard.

NORMANDY One of two vessels ordered by *Göteborg-Frederikshavn-Linjen* of Sweden (trading as *Sessan Linjen*) before the take over of their operations by *Stena Line AB* in 1981. Both were designed for the Göteborg – Frederikshavn route (a journey of about three hours). However, *Stena Line* decided in 1982 to switch the first vessel, the KRONPRINSESSAN VICTORIA (now the STENA EUROPE of *Stena Line AB*), to their Göteborg – Kiel (Germany) route since their own new tonnage for this route, being built in Poland, had been substantially delayed. She was modified to make her more suitable for this overnight route. Work on the second vessel – provisionally called the DROTTNING SILVIA – was suspended for a time but she was eventually delivered, as designed, in late 1982 and introduced onto the Göteborg – Frederikshavn route on a temporary basis pending delivery of new *Stena Line* ordered vessels. She was named the PRINSESSAN BIRGITTA, the existing ex *Sessan Linjen* vessel of the same name being renamed the STENA SCANDINAVICA (see the KING OF SCANDINAVIA, *DFDS Seaways*). In early 1983 she was substantially modified in a similar way to her sister. In June 1983 she was renamed the ST NICHOLAS, re-registered in Great Britain and entered service on five year charter to *Sealink UK* on the Harwich – Hoek van Holland route. In 1988

Jupiter (Matthew Punter)

Isle of Inishmore (Irish Ferries)

Norsea (P&O North Sea)

SuperStar Express (William Mayes)

she was purchased and re-registered in The Bahamas. In 1989 she was sold to *Rederi AB Gotland* of Sweden and then chartered back. In 1991 she was renamed the STENA NORMANDY and inaugurated a new service between Southampton and Cherbourg. She was withdrawn in December 1996, returned to *Rederi AB Gotland* and renamed the NORMANDY. In 1997 she was chartered to *Tallink* and operated between Helsinki and Tallinn; this charter ended at the end of the year. In 1998 she was chartered to *Irish Ferries*. She briefly operated between Rosslare and Pembroke Dock before switching to the their French services. In 1999 she was purchased by *Irish Ferries*.

FAST FERRY

4	JONATHAN SWIFT	5989t	99	39.5k	800P	200C	-	BA	Fremantle, AL	IR

JONATHAN SWIFT Austal Auto-Express 86 catamaran built for *Irish Ferries* for the Dublin – Holyhead route.

Under Construction

5	ULYSSES	c50000t	01	22k	2000P	1300C	340T	BA2	Rauma, FI	IR

ULYSSES Under construction for the Dublin – Holyhead service.

MERCHANT FERRIES/NORSE IRISH FERRIES

THE COMPANY *Merchant Ferries plc* and *Norse Irish Ferries Ltd* are British private sector companies, owned by *Cenargo*. In 1999 the operations of *Belfast Freight Ferries* were integrated into *Merchant Ferries* and *Norse Irish Ferries* was acquired.

MANAGEMENT Managing Director: Philip Shepherd, **Commercial Director:** Richard Harrison.

ADDRESS *Head Office:* Victoria Terminal 2, West Bank Road, BELFAST BT3 9JN Victoria Terminal 2, West Bank Road, BELFAST BT3 9JN, *Liverpool:* North Brocklebank Dock, BOOTLE, Merseyside L20 1BY.

TELEPHONE Administration: *Head Office:* +44 (0)28 9077 9090, **Reservations:** *GB (Liverpool – Dublin):* +44 (0)870 600 4321, *(Liverpool-Belfast):* +44 (0)151 944 1010, *Northern Ireland:* +44 (0)28 9077 9090, *Irish Republic:* +353 (0)1 819 2999, **Fax:** *Head Office:* +44 (0)28 9077 5520, **Fax Reservations:** *GB (Liverpool – Dublin):* +44 (0)151 955 4081, *(Liverpool – Belfast):* +44 (0)151 922 5823, *Northern Ireland:* +44 (0)28 9078 1599, *Irish Republic:* +353 (0)1 819 2942.

INTERNET Email: enquiries@merchant-ferries.com **Websites:** http://www.Norse-Irish-Ferries.com *(English)*

ROUTE OPERATED Liverpool – Dublin (7 hrs; *(1,2)*; 2 per day) (under the name *Merchant Ferries)*, Liverpool – Belfast (8 hrs 30 mins; *(3,4)*; 1 per day (Mon, Wed, Fri, Sun), 2 per day (Tue, Thu, Sat) (under the name *Norse Irish Ferries*; it is intended to operate twice daily services five days per week when a new riverside berth on the Mersey is constructed).

Merchant Ferries also operate a freight-only services between Heysham and Dublin and Heysham and Belfast; see Section 3.

VESSELS

1	BRAVE MERCHANT	22046t	98	22.5k	250P	-	175T	BA	Sevilla, SP	IM
2	DAWN MERCHANT	22152t	98	22.5k	250P	-	175T	BA	Sevilla, SP	IM
3	LAGAN VIKING	21856t	97	24k	340P	100C	164T	A	Donada, IT	IT
4	MERSEY VIKING	21856t	97	24k	340P	100C	164T	A	Donada, IT	IT

BRAVE MERCHANT Built for parent company *Cenargo* and chartered to *Merchant Ferries*. In February 1999 she inaugurated a new service between Liverpool and Dublin.

DAWN MERCHANT Built for parent company *Cenargo* and chartered to *Merchant Ferries*. On delivery in autumn 1998, chartered to *UND RoRo Isletmeri* of Turkey to operate between Istanbul and Trieste. Returned to *Merchant Ferries* in late 1998 and in February 1999, inaugurated a new service between Liverpool and Dublin.

LAGAN VIKING, MERSEY VIKING Built for *Leventina Transport* of Italy and chartered to *Norse Irish Ferries*. In 1999 charter was taken over by *Merchant Ferries*. Charter due to end in 2001.

Under construction

| 5 | MIDNIGHT MERCHANT | 22152t | 00 | 22.5k | 250P | - | 175T | BA | Sevilla, SP | IM |

MIDNIGHT MERCHANT Under construction for parent company *Cenargo*. Initially, at least, to be chartered out. Sister vessel, NORTHERN MERCHANT, is on charter to *Norfolkline* (see Section 3).

P&O IRISH SEA

THE COMPANY *P&O Irish Sea* is the trading name of *P&O European Ferries (Irish Sea) Ltd*, a British private sector company and a subsidiary of the *Peninsular and Oriental Steam Navigation Company*. It was formed in 1998 by the merger of the shipping activities *Pandoro Ltd* and the Cairnryan – Larne services of *P&O European Ferries (Felixstowe) Ltd*.

MANAGEMENT Chairman: Graeme Dunlop, **Managing Director:** J H Kearsley, **Sales Manager:** Philip Simpson.

ADDRESS Compass House, Dock Street, FLEETWOOD, Lancashire FY7 6HP.

TELEPHONE Administration: +44 (0)1253 615700, **Reservations:** 0870 24 24 777 (from UK only), **Fax:** +44 (0)1253 615740.

INTERNET Website: http://www.poirishsea.com *(English)*

ROUTES OPERATED Conventional Ferry: Cairnryan – Larne (2 hrs 15 mins *(1)*, 1 hr 45 min *(4)*; *(1 until late summer, 4 from late summer)*; 3 per day), **Fast Ferry (March – November):** Cairnryan – Larne (1 hr; *(2)*; 6 per day).

CONVENTIONAL FERRY

| 1 | PRIDE OF RATHLIN | 12503t | 73 | 17k | 1041P | 340C | 52L | BA2 | Schiedam, NL | BD |

PRIDE OF RATHLIN Built for *Townsend Thoresen* as the FREE ENTERPRISE VII for Dover – Calais and Dover – Zeebrugge services. After the delivery of new vessels in 1980 she was generally used on the Dover – Zeebrugge service. Extensively rebuilt in Bremerhaven in 1986, through the placing of the existing superstructure and rear part of hull on a new front part of hull. She was renamed the PRIDE OF WALMER in 1988. In summer 1992 she was transferred to the Cairnryan – Larne route and renamed the PRIDE OF RATHLIN. To be withdrawn in late summer 2000.

FAST FERRY

| 2 | SUPERSTAR EXPRESS | 5517t | 97 | 36k | 900P | 175C | - | A | Fremantle, AL | BB |

SUPERSTAR EXPRESS Austal Ships 82 catamaran, built for *Star Cruises* of Malaysia for their service between Butterworth and Langkawi. Built as the SUPERSTAR EXPRESS, she was renamed the SUPERSTAR EXPRESS LANGKAWI later in 1997. She was due, in 1998, to circumnavigate the world and to seek to take the Hales Trophy from HOVERSPEED GREAT BRITAIN. However, these plans did not materialise and instead she was chartered to *P&O European Ferries (Portsmouth)* and placed on the Portsmouth – Cherbourg route. She resumed the name SUPERSTAR EXPRESS. In April 2000 she was transferred to *P&O Irish Sea*.

Under construction

| 3 | EUROPEAN AMBASSADOR | 24500t | 01 | 25k | 405P | 375C | 140T | GB | Shimonoeki , JA | - |
| 4 | EUROPEAN CAUSEWAY | 20800t | 00 | 23k | 410P | 375C | 140T | GB | Shimonoeki , JA | - |

EUROPEAN AMBASSADOR Under construction for *P&O Irish Sea* for the Liverpool – Dublin service (this service is currently shown in Section 3 since, although a small number of passengers is conveyed on some services, it is primarily a freight service).

EUROPEAN CAUSEWAY Under construction for *P&O Irish Sea* for the Cairnryan – Larne service. She is due to enter service in late summer.

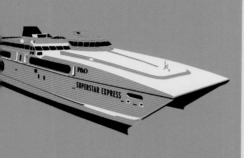

Double Vision

future has never looked so bright at P&O. With two new ships soon to set sail on the Irish Sea.

SuperStar Express - our new fast ferry sailing Larne to Cairnryan in an hour (commences April 2000).

the brand new European Causeway - the fastest conventional crossing on the Irish Sea

mmences August 2000). Our fares are eye catching too. For more information see our brochure or

0870 24 24 777 double quick.

LARNE CAIRNRYAN
DUBLIN FLEETWOOD
LIVERPOOL

P&O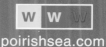
Irish Sea

W W W

poirishsea.com

P&O NORTH SEA FERRIES

THE COMPANY *P&O North Sea Ferries Ltd* is a private sector company, a subsidiary of the *Peninsular and Oriental Steam Navigation Company* of Great Britain. Joint ownership with *The Royal Nedlloyd Group* of The Netherlands ceased in 1996 and the name was changed from *North Sea Ferries* to *P&O North Sea Ferries*. The Felixstowe freight-only operations of *P&O European Ferries* were incorporated into this new company.

MANAGEMENT Managing Director: Peter van den Brandhof, **Passenger Managers:** *UK:* Tony Farrell, *Netherlands:* Michael Amerlaan, *Belgium:* Christian Berkein, *Germany:* Peter Blomberg.

ADDRESS *UK:* King George Dock, Hedon Road, HULL HU9 5QA, *Netherlands:* Beneluxhaven, Rotterdam (Europoort), Postbus 1123, 3180 ROZENBURG ZH, Netherlands, *Belgium:* Leopold II Dam 13, Havendam, B-8380 ZEEBRUGGE, Belgium.

TELEPHONE Administration: *UK:* +44 (0)1482 795141, *Netherlands:* +31 (0)181 25 55 00, *Belgium:* +32 (0)50 54 34 11, **Reservations:** *UK:* +44 (0)1482 377177, *Netherlands:* +31 (0)181 25 55 55, *Belgium:* +32 (0)50 54 34 30, **Fax:** *UK:* +44 (0)1482 706438, *Netherlands:* +31 (0)181 25 52 15, *Belgium:* +32 (0)50 54 71 12.

INTERNET Website: http://www.ponsf.com *(English)*

ROUTES OPERATED Hull – Rotterdam (Europoort) (13 hrs; *(2,4)*; 1 per day), Hull – Zeebrugge (14 hrs; *(1,3)*; 1 per day).

CONVENTIONAL FERRIES

1	NORLAND	26290t	74	18.5k	881P	500C	134T	A	Bremerhaven, GY	GB
2	NORSEA	31785t	87	18.5k	1250P	850C	180T	A	Glasgow, GB	GB
3	NORSTAR	26919t	74	18.5k	881P	500C	134T	A	Bremerhaven, GY	NL
4	NORSUN	31598t	87	18.5k	1250P	850C	180T	A	Tsurumi, JA	NL

NORLAND Built for the Hull – Rotterdam service. In April 1982 she was requisitioned for the Falkland Islands Task Force by the Ministry of Defence. She took part in the invasion of the Islands, disembarking troops and equipment at San Carlos. After the cessation of hostilities, she made trips to Argentina and Uruguay and was then employed on a shuttle service between Port Stanley and Ascension. She returned to Hull on 1st February 1983 and re-entered service on the Rotterdam service on 19th April. In 1987 she was lengthened and refurbished to a similar standard to the NORSEA. She replaced the NORWAVE (3450t, 1965) on the Hull – Zeebrugge service.

NORSEA, NORSUN Built for the Hull – Rotterdam service. The NORSUN was owned by *Nedlloyd* and was sold to *P&O* in 1996 but retains Dutch crew and registry.

NORSTAR Built for *North Sea Ferries* for the Hull – Rotterdam service. In 1987 she was lengthened and replaced the NORWIND (3692t, 1966) on the Hull – Zeebrugge service. She was owned by *Nedlloyd* and was sold to *P&O* in 1996 but retains Dutch crew and registry.

Under construction

5	PRIDE OF HULL	60600t	01	22k	1360P	250C	285T	AS	Venezia, IT	GB
6	PRIDE OF ROTTERDAM	60600t	01	22k	1360P	250C	285T	AS	Venezia, IT	NL

PRIDE OF HULL, PRIDE OF ROTTERDAM On order for *P&O North Sea Ferries* to replace the NORSEA and NORSUN plus the freight vessels NORBAY and NORBANK on the Hull – Rotterdam service. Vessels will also accommodate 125 x 12 metre double stacked containers.

RUISE IN
OMFORT
VERY NIGHT
ROM HULL
O THE
ONTINENT

P&O North Sea Ferries sail every evening from Hull to Rotterdam and Zeebrugge, saving you a tiring trek south. Enjoy a great night out with a five course feast, entertainment, casino, cinema, fantastic shops and fun for the kids. Plus a comfortable bed in a cosy cabin.

Wake up on the Continent with the whole day ahead of you and excellent road links to all parts of Europe.

Ask for our Cruiseferries Brochure – from your Travel Agent or direct from us on 01482 377177.

P&O ✕ **North Sea Ferries**

P&O PORTSMOUTH

THE COMPANY *P&O Portsmouth* is the trading name of *P&O European Ferries (Portsmouth) Ltd,* (until start of 1999 trading as *P&O European Ferries*) a British private sector company, a subsidiary of the *Peninsular and Oriental Steam Navigation Company.*

MANAGEMENT Chairman: Graeme Dunlop, **Managing Director:** Simon Edsall, **Head of Passenger Marketing & Sales:** Paul Barringer, **Head of Freight Sales & Marketing:** Phil Garrett.

ADDRESS Peninsular House, Wharf Road, PORTSMOUTH PO2 8TA.

TELEPHONE Administration: +44 (0)23 9230 1000, **Reservations:** 0870 2424999 (from UK only), **Fax:** +44 (0)23 9230 1134.

INTERNET Email: media@poportsmouth.com **Website:** http://www.poportsmouth.com *(English)*

ROUTES OPERATED Conventional Ferries: Portsmouth – Cherbourg (5 hrs (day), 7 hrs – 8 hrs 15 mins (night); *(1,2,3 (1 once weekly))*; 2 day crossings, one night crossing per day), Portsmouth – Le Havre (5 hrs 30 mins (day), 7 hrs 30 mins – 8 hrs (night); *(4,5)*; 2 day crossings, one night crossing per day), Portsmouth – Bilbao (Santurzi) (35 hrs (UK – Spain), 30 hrs (Spain – UK); *(1)*; 2 per week), **Fast Ferry:** Portsmouth – Cherbourg (2 hrs 45 mins; *(6)*; 3 per day).

CONVENTIONAL FERRIES

1	PRIDE OF BILBAO	37583t	86	22k	2553P	600C	90T	BA	Turku, FI	GB
2	PRIDE OF CHERBOURG	14760t	75	18k	1200P	380C	53L	BA2	Aalborg, DK	GB
3	PRIDE OF HAMPSHIRE	14760t	75	18k	1200P	380C	53L	BA2	Aalborg, DK	GB
4	PRIDE OF LE HAVRE	33336t	89	21k	1600P	575C	118T	BA	Bremerhaven, GY	GB
5	PRIDE OF PORTSMOUTH	33336t	90	21k	1600P	575C	118T	BA	Bremerhaven, GY	GB

PRIDE OF BILBAO Built as the OLYMPIA for *Rederi AB Slite* of Sweden for *Viking Line* service between Stockholm and Helsinki. In 1993 she was chartered to *P&O European Ferries* to inaugurate a new service between Portsmouth and Bilbao. During the summer period she also operates, at weekends, a round trip between Portsmouth and Cherbourg. In 1994 she was purchased by the *Irish Continental Group* and re-registered in the Bahamas. *P&O* have since entered her into the British bareboat register and she is expected to remain on charter to *P&O Portsmouth* until at least 2003.

PRIDE OF CHERBOURG Built as the VIKING VALIANT for Southampton (from 1976 Southampton/Portsmouth and 1984 Portsmouth only) – Cherbourg/Le Havre services. Extensively rebuilt in Bremerhaven in 1986, through the placing of the existing superstructure and rear part of hull on a new front part of hull and from that date generally operated Portsmouth – Le Havre only. In 1989 she was renamed the PRIDE OF LE HAVRE. In 1994 transferred to the Portsmouth – Cherbourg service and renamed the PRIDE OF CHERBOURG.

PRIDE OF HAMPSHIRE Built as the VIKING VENTURER. Details otherwise as the PRIDE OF CHERBOURG. She was renamed the PRIDE OF HAMPSHIRE in 1989. In 1995 she was transferred to the Portsmouth – Cherbourg service.

PRIDE OF LE HAVRE Built as the OLAU HOLLANDIA for *TT-Line* of Germany, to operate for associated company *Olau Line* between Sheerness (Great Britain) and Vlissingen (Netherlands). In May 1994 the service ceased and she was chartered to *P&O European Ferries*, re-registered in Great Britain and renamed the PRIDE OF LE HAVRE. After a brief period on the Portsmouth – Cherbourg service she became a regular vessel on the Portsmouth – Le Havre service.

PRIDE OF PORTSMOUTH Built as the OLAU BRITANNIA for *TT-Line* of Germany, to operate for associated company *Olau Line*. In 1994 she was chartered to *P&O European Ferries*, re-registered in Great Britain and renamed the PRIDE OF PORTSMOUTH. After a brief period on the Portsmouth – Cherbourg service she became a regular vessel on the Portsmouth – Le Havre service from June 1994.

Pride of Le Havre and Pride of Portsmouth (FotoFlite)

FAST FERRY

6	PORTSMOUTH EXPRESS	5902t	98	41k	920P	225C	-	A	Hobart, AL	SP

PORTSMOUTH EXPRESS InCat 91m catamaran. Built as the CATALONIA for *Buquebus* of Argentina and used by *Buquebus España* on their service between Barcelona (Spain) and Mallorca. In April 2000 chartered to *P&O Portsmouth* and renamed the PORTSMOUTH EXPRESS.

P&O STENA LINE

THE COMPANY *P&O Stena Line* is a British private sector company, 60% owned by the *Peninsular and Oriental Steam Navigation Company* and 40% owned by *Stena Line AB* of Sweden. The new company took over the Dover and Newhaven services of *P&O European Ferries* and *Stena Line* in March 1998. Newhaven services ceased at the end of January 1999.

MANAGEMENT Joint Chairmen: Lord Sterling (*P&O*) and Dan Sten Olsson (*Stena Line*), **Managing Director:** Russ Peters, **Passenger Marketing & Sales Director:** John Govett.

ADDRESS Channel House, Channel View Road, DOVER, Kent CT17 9TJ.

TELEPHONE Administration: +44 (0)1304 863000, **Reservations:** 087 0600 0600 (from UK only), **Fax:** +44 (0)1304 863223, **Telex:** 966266.

INTERNET Email: res38@dial.pipex.com **Website:** http://www.posl.com *(English)*

ROUTE OPERATED Dover – Calais (1 hr 15 mins/1 hr 30 mins; *(1,2,3,4,5,6,7)*; up to 35 per day).

CONVENTIONAL FERRIES

1	P&OSL AQUITAINE	28833t	91	21k	2000P	600C	100L	BA2	Temse, BE	GB
2	P&OSL BURGUNDY	28138t	93	21k	1420P	600C	120L	BA2	Bremerhaven, GY	GB
3	P&OSL CALAIS	26433t	87	22k	2290P	650C	100L	BA2	Bremen-Vegesack, GY	GB
4	P&OSL CANTERBURY	25122t	80	19k	1800P	550C	80T	BA2	Malmö, SW	GB
5	P&OSL DOVER	26433t	87	22k	2290P	650C	100L	BA2	Bremen-Vegesack, GY	GB
6	P&OSL KENT	20446t	80	21k	1825P	460C	64L	BA2	Bremerhaven, GY	GB
7•	P&OSL PICARDY	13061t	80	23k	1300P	330C	48L	BA2	Bremerhaven, GY	GB
8	P&OSL PROVENCE	28559t	83	19.5k	2036P	550C	85L	BA2	Dunkerque, FR	GB

P&OSL AQUITAINE Built as the PRINS FILIP for *Regie voor Maritiem Transport (RMT)* of Belgium the Oostende – Dover service. Although completed in 1991, she did not enter service until May 1992. In 1994 the British port became Ramsgate. Withdrawn in 1997 and laid up for sale. In 1998 she was sold to *Northern Maritime*, part of the *Stena Group* and renamed the STENA ROYAL. In November 1998 she was chartered to *P&O Stena Line* to operate as a freight only vessel on the Dover – Zeebrugge route. In spring 1999 it was decided to charter the vessel on a long term basis and she was repainted into *P&O Stena Line* colours and renamed the P&OSL AQUITAINE. In autumn 1999 she was modified to make her suitable to operate between Dover and Calais and was transferred to that route, becoming a passenger vessel.

P&OSL BURGUNDY Built for *P&O European Ferries* for the Dover – Calais service. When construction started she was due to be a sister vessel to the EUROPEAN HIGHWAY, EUROPEAN PATHWAY and EUROPEAN SEAWAY (see Section 3) called the EUROPEAN CAUSEWAY and operate on the Zeebrugge freight route. However, it was decided that she should be completed as a passenger/freight vessel (the design allowed for conversion) and she was launched as the PRIDE OF BURGUNDY. In 1998, transferred to *P&O Stena Line*. In 1998 renamed the P&OSL BURGUNDY.

P&OSL CALAIS Built for *European Ferries* as the PRIDE OF CALAIS for the Dover – Calais service. In 1998, transferred to *P&O Stena Line*. In 1999 renamed the P&OSL CALAIS.

P&OSL CANTERBURY Built as the SCANDINAVIA for *Rederi AB Nordö* of Sweden. After service in the Mediterranean for *UMEF*, she was, in 1981, sold to *SOMAT* of Bulgaria, renamed the TZAREVETZ and used on *Medlink* services between Bulgaria and the Middle East and later on other routes. In 1986 she was chartered to *Callitzis* of Greece for a service between Italy and Greece. In 1988 she

P&OSL Dover (John Hendy)

P&OSL Aquitaine (FotoFlite)

was sold to *Sealink*, re-registered in the Bahamas and renamed the FIESTA. She was then chartered to *OT Africa Line*. During autumn 1989 she was rebuilt in Bremerhaven to convert her for passenger use and in March 1990 she was renamed the FANTASIA and placed her on the Dover – Calais service. Later in 1990 she was renamed the STENA FANTASIA. In 1998, transferred to *P&O Stena Line*. In 1999 she was renamed the P&OSL CANTERBURY.

P&OSL DOVER Built for *European Ferries* as the PRIDE OF DOVER for the Dover – Calais service. In 1998, transferred to *P&O Stena Line*. In 1999 renamed the P&OSL DOVER.

P&OSL KENT Built for *European Ferries (Townsend Thoresen)* as the SPIRIT OF FREE ENTERPRISE for the Dover – Calais service, also operating on the Dover – Zeebrugge service during the winter. She was renamed the PRIDE OF KENT in 1987. Sister vessel of the PRIDE OF BRUGES. During winter 1991/92 she was lengthened in Palermo, Italy to give her similar capacity to the PRIDE OF CALAIS and the PRIDE OF DOVER. Now operates Dover – Calais only. In 1998, transferred to *P&O Stena Line*. Later in 1998 renamed the P&OSL KENT.

P&OSL PICARDY Built for *European Ferries (Townsend Thoresen)* as the PRIDE OF FREE ENTERPRISE for the Dover – Calais service, also operating on the Dover – Zeebrugge service during the winter. She was renamed the PRIDE OF BRUGES in 1988 and, following the delivery of the new PRIDE OF CALAIS, she was transferred all year to the Dover – Zeebrugge service. In 1992, after the closure of that routes to passengers, she returned to the Dover – Calais route. Plans to operate her in a freight-only mode in 1997 were changed and she ran as a full passenger vessel. In 1998, transferred to *P&O Stena Line*. Plans to transfer her to the Newhaven – Dieppe route were dropped and she remained at Dover. In 1999 renamed the P&OSL PICARDY. In early 2000 she was laid up for sale.

P&OSL PROVENCE Built as the STENA JUTLANDICA for *Stena Line* for the Göteborg – Frederikshavn service. In 1996 she was transferred to the Dover – Calais route and renamed the STENA EMPEREUR. In 1998, transferred to *P&O Stena Line*. Later in 1998 renamed the P&OSL PROVENCE.

SEA CONTAINERS FERRIES

THE COMPANY *Sea Containers Ferries Ltd* is a British private sector company, part of the *Sea Containers Group*.

MANAGEMENT Senior Vice President Passenger Transport: David Benson.

ADDRESS Sea Containers House, 20 Upper Ground, LONDON SE1 9PF.

TELEPHONE Administration: +44 (0)20 7805 5000, **Fax:** +44 (0)20 7805 5900.

INTERNET Email: info@seacontainers.com **Website:** http://www.seacontainers.com

Ferry services in the UK are operated through three subsidiaries – *Hoverspeed Ltd*, *Sea Containers Ferries Scotland Ltd* (trading as *SeaCat*) and the *Isle of Man Steam Packet Company* (trading as *Steam Packet*). See also *Silja Line* in Section 6. Because of interchange of fast ferries between companies, they are shown in one section at the end. *IOMSP Co* and *Sea Containers Ferries Scotland* routes are now integrated and are also shown together.

HOVERSPEED

THE COMPANY *Hoverspeed Ltd* is a British private sector company. It was formed in October 1981 by the merger of *Seaspeed*, a wholly owned subsidiary of the *British Railways Board*, operating between Dover and Calais and Dover and Boulogne and *Hoverlloyd*, a subsidiary of *Broström AB* of Sweden, operating between Ramsgate (Pegwell Bay) and Calais. The Ramsgate – Calais service ceased after summer 1982. In early 1984 the company was sold by its joint owners to a management consortium. In 1986 the company was acquired by *Sea Containers*. It was retained by *Sea Containers* in 1990 following the sale of most of *Sealink British Ferries* to *Stena Line*.

MANAGEMENT Managing Director: Geoffrey Ede, **Marketing Controller:** Steve Boffey.

ADDRESS The International Hoverport, Marine Parade, DOVER, Kent CT17 9TG.

TELEPHONE Administration: +44 (0)1304 865000, **Reservations:** 08705 240241 (from UK only), **Fax: Admin:** +44 (0)1304 865087, *Reservations:* +44 (0)1304 240088.

INTERNET Email: info@hoverspeed.co.uk **Website:** http://www.hoverspeed.co.uk *(English)*

ROUTES OPERATED SeaCats: Folkestone – Boulogne (55 mins; *(5)*; 4 per day), Dover – Calais (50 mins; *(5)*; up to 2 per day (up to 1 per day Calais – Dover)), Calais – Folkestone (55 mins; *(5)*; up to 1 per day (no service Folkestone – Calais), Dover – Oostende (2 hrs; *(4,6)*; up to 7 per day), Newhaven – Dieppe (2 hrs; *(9)*; up to 3 per day). **Hovercraft:** Dover – Calais (35 mins; *(12,13)*; up to 14 per day).

ISLE OF MAN STEAM PACKET COMPANY

THE COMPANY The *Isle of Man Steam Packet Company*, trading as *Steam Packet*, is the trading name of an Isle of Man registered company owned by *Sea Containers Ferries Ltd*.

MANAGEMENT Managing Director: Hamish Ross, **Passenger Marketing Manager:** David Morgan.

ADDRESS Imperial Buildings, DOUGLAS, Isle of Man IM1 2BY.

TELEPHONE Administration: +44 (0)1624 645645, **Reservations:** *From UK:* 08705 523523, *From elsewhere:* +44 (0)1624 661661, **Fax: Admin:** +44 (0)1624 645609, *Reservations:* +44 (0)1624 645697.

INTERNET Email: spc@steam-packet.com **Website:** http://www.steam-packet.com *(English)*

ROUTES OPERATED Conventional Ferries: Douglas (Isle of Man) – Heysham (3 hrs 30 mins; *(1,2)*; up to 2 per day), Douglas – Liverpool (4 hrs; *(2)*; irregular), **SeaCats:** Listed with *Sea Containers Ferries Scotland* services below.

CONVENTIONAL FERRIES

1	BEN-MY-CHREE	12504t	98	19k	500P	-	100T	A	Krimpen, NL	IM
2	LADY OF MANN	4482t	76	21k	1000P	130C	0L	S	Troon, GB	IM

BEN-MY-CHREE Built for the *IOMSP Co* and operates between Douglas and Heysham and Christmas period Heysham – Dublin sailings.

LADY OF MANN Built for the *IOMSP Co*. Cars and small vans are side loaded but no ro-ro freight is conveyed. In 1994 replaced by the SEACAT ISLE OF MAN and laid up for sale. She was used in 1995 during the period of the 'TT' motor cycle races between 26th May to 12th June. Later in 1995 she was chartered to *Porto Santo Line* of Madeira for a service from Funchal to Porto Santo. In 1996 she operated throughout the summer, as no SeaCat was chartered. In 1997, she operated for the TT races and then inaugurated a new Liverpool – Dublin service in June, with a weekly Fleetwood – Douglas service until replaced by the SUPERSEACAT TWO in March 1998. In 1998 she operated during the TT race period and was then chartered to *Acor Line*. During winter 1998/99 she provided back-up to the fast ferries on the Liverpool – Dublin and Douglas – Liverpool routes. In summer 2000 she is expected to operate between Douglas and the UK during the TT race period again and also a number of special cruises to Fleetwood and Llandudno.

SEA CONTAINERS FERRIES SCOTLAND

THE COMPANY *Sea Containers Ferries Scotland Ltd* is a subsidiary of *Sea Containers Ferries Ltd.*

MANAGEMENT Managing Director: Hamish Ross, **General Manager, Belfast:** Diane Poole, **General Manager, Liverpool-Dublin:** John Burrows.

ADDRESS 34 Charlotte Street, STRANRAER DG9 7EF.

TELEPHONE Administration: +44 (0)1776 702755, **Reservations:** *From UK:* 087055 523523, *From elsewhere:* +44 (0)28 9031 3543, **Fax:** +44 (0)1776 705894.

INTERNET Email: spc@steam-packet.com **Website:** http://www.steampacket.com *(English)*

ROUTES OPERATED – SEA CONTAINERS' IRISH SEA FAST FERRIES SERVICES – IOMSP & SEA CONTAINERS FERRIES, SCOTLAND Douglas – Liverpool (2 hrs 15 mins; *(7,11)*; up to 2 per day), Douglas – Belfast (2 hrs 45 mins; *(7)*; up to 3 per week), Douglas – Dublin (2 hrs 45 mins; *(7)*; up to 3 per week), Douglas – Heysham (2 hrs; *(7)*; up to 3 per week), Troon – Belfast (2 hrs 30 mins; *(8)*; 3 per day), Liverpool – Dublin; (3 hrs 45 mins); *(11)*; 1 per day, Heysham – Belfast (4 hrs; *(10)*; 1/2 per day).

FAST FERRIES OPERATED BY SEA CONTAINERS COMPANIES IN UK

3•	ATLANTIC II	3012t	90	35k	450P	88C	-	BB	Hobart, AL	BA
4	DIAMANT	3454t	96	37k	654P	140C	-	A	Hobart, AL	LX
5	HOVERSPEED GREAT BRITAIN	3000t	90	37k	577P	80C	-	BA	Hobart, AL	GB
6	RAPIDE	4112t	96	37k	654P	140C	-	A	Hobart, AL	LX
7	SEACAT ISLE OF MAN	3003t	91	37k	500P	80C	-	BA	Hobart, AL	GB
8	SEACAT SCOTLAND	3003t	91	37k	450P	80C	-	BA	Hobart, AL	GB
9	SUPERSEACAT ONE	4462t	97	38k	782P	175C	-	A	La Spézia, IT	IT
10	SUPERSEACAT TWO	4462t	97	38k	782P	175C	-	A	Riva Trigoso, IT	IT
11	SUPERSEACAT THREE	4697t	99	38k	800P	175C	-	A	La Spézia, IT	IT
12	THE PRINCESS ANNE	-	69	50k	360P	55C	-	BA	Cowes, GB	GB
13	THE PRINCESS MARGARET	-	68	50k	360P	55C	-	BA	Cowes, GB	GB

ATLANTIC II Built as SEACAT TASMANIA for *Sea Containers* subsidiary *Tasmanian Ferry Services* of Australia to operate between George Town (Tasmania) and Port Welshpool (Victoria). In 1992 chartered to *Hoverspeed* to operate Dover – Calais and Folkestone – Boulogne services. Returned to Australia after the 1992 summer season but returned to Britain in summer 1993 to operate Dover – Calais and Folkestone – Boulogne services during the summer. She was repainted into *Hoverspeed* livery and renamed the SEACAT CALAIS. In 1994 chartered for five years (with a purchase option)

to *Navegacion Atlantida* for *Ferry Linas Argentinas AS* of Uruguay service between Montevideo (Uruguay) – Buenos Aires (Argentina) service and renamed the ATLANTIC II. The purchase option was not taken up and in 1999 she was returned to *Sea Containers*. In summer 1999 she was used on the Dover – Calais service. At time of going to press, not planned that she will be used on UK routes in 2000.

DIAMANT InCat 81m catamaran. Ordered by *Del Bene SA* of Argentina. In 1996, before completion, purchased by the *Holyman Group* of Australia and named the HOLYMAN EXPRESS. In 1997 she was renamed the HOLYMAN DIAMANT, transferred to *Holyman Sally Ferries* and in March was introduced onto the Ramsgate – Oostende route. In March 1998 transferred to the Dover – Oostende route, operating for the *Hoverspeed – Holyman (UK)* joint venture, and renamed the DIAMANT. In 1999 this became a 100% *Hoverspeed* operation. During winter 1999/2000 she also operated between Dover and Calais at times.

HOVERSPEED GREAT BRITAIN InCat 74m catamaran. Launched as the CHRISTOPHER COLUMBUS but renamed before entering service. During delivery voyage from Australia, she won the Hales Trophy for the 'Blue Riband' of the Atlantic. She inaugurated a car and passenger service between Portsmouth and Cherbourg, operated by *Hoverspeed*. This service was suspended in early 1991 and later that year she was, after modification, switched to a new service between Dover (Eastern Docks) and Boulogne/Calais, replacing hovercraft. In 1992 operated on Channel routes, including services from Folkestone. During winter 1992/3 she was chartered to *Ferry Lineas* of Argentina, operating between Buenos Aires (Argentina) and Montevideo (Uruguay). She now operates mainly between Folkestone and Boulogne; in 2000 she will also cover some Dover – Calais and Boulogne – Folkestone (one way) sailings.

RAPIDE InCat 81m catamaran. Built for the *Holyman Group* as the CONDOR 12. In summer 1996 operated by *Condor Ferries* (at that time part owned by the *Holyman Group*). In 1997 she was renamed the HOLYMAN RAPIDE, transferred to *Holyman Sally Ferries* and in March was introduced onto the Ramsgate – Oostende route. In March 1998 transferred to the Dover – Oostende route, operating for the *Hoverspeed – Holyman (UK)* joint venture, and renamed the RAPIDE. In 1999 this became a 100% *Hoverspeed* operation. During winter 1999/2000 she also operated between Dover and Calais at times.

SEACAT ISLE OF MAN InCat 74m catamaran. Built as the HOVERSPEED FRANCE, the second SeaCat. She inaugurated Dover – Calais/Boulogne service in 1991. In 1992 she was chartered to *Sardinia Express* of Italy and renamed the SARDEGNA EXPRESS; she did not operate on the Channel that year. This charter was terminated at the end of 1992 and in 1993 she was renamed the SEACAT BOULOGNE and operated on the Dover – Calais and Folkestone – Boulogne services. In 1994 she was chartered to *IOMSP Co*, renamed the SEACAT ISLE OF MAN and replaced the LADY OF MANN on services between Douglas (Isle of Man) and Britain and Ireland. During winter 1994/5 operated for *SeaCat Scotland* between Stranraer and Belfast. She returned to *IOMSP Co* in June 1995. During spring 1995 she was chartered to *Condor Ferries*; she then was chartered again to *IOMSP Co* and returned to *Sea Containers* in the autumn. In 1996 she was chartered to *ColorSeaCat KS*, renamed the SEACAT NORGE and inaugurated a new service between Langesund (Norway) and Frederikshavn (Denmark). During winter 1996/97 she operated between Dover and Calais. In early 1997 she was again renamed the SEACAT ISLE OF MAN. During summer 1997 she operated for *IOMSP Co*, serving on Liverpool, Dublin and Belfast seasonal services to Douglas (May to September) plus a weekly Liverpool – Dublin service when the LADY OF MANN operated from Fleetwood. In late 1997 she was transferred to the *Hoverspeed* Dover – Calais route and operated on this route throughout 1998. In 1999 she operated between Douglas and Liverpool and Douglas and Dublin for *IOMSP Co*. In 2000 she will also operate between Douglas and Belfast and Douglas and Heysham.

SEACAT SCOTLAND InCat 74m catamaran, the fifth SeaCat to be built. In 1992 she inaugurated a new high-speed car and passenger service for *SeaCat Scotland* on the Stranraer – Belfast route. In autumn 1994 she was chartered to *Q-Ships* of Qatar for services between Doha (Qatar) and Bahrain and Dubai and renamed the Q-SHIP EXPRESS. In spring 1995 she returned to the Stranraer – Belfast service and resumed the name SEACAT SCOTLAND. In autumn 1997 chartered to *Navegacion Atlantida SA* of Uruguay for service between Colonia (Uruguay) and Buenos Aires (Argentina). She returned to the UK in spring 1998 and operated on to the Stranraer – Belfast route. In 1999 she operated for *Sea Containers Ferries Scotland* between Stranraer and Belfast and Troon and Belfast.

Rapide (Mike Louagie)

SuperSeaCat Two (Gordon Hislip)

Hoverspeed Great Britain (FotoFlite)

Ben-my-Chree (Miles Cowsill)

In 2000 she will operate between Belfast and Troon.

SUPERSEACAT ONE Fincantieri MDV1200 monohull vessel. Built for *Sea Containers*. Between 1997 and 1999 operated for *SeaCat AB* on the Göteborg – Frederikshavn route. In 2000 transferred to *Hoverspeed* to operate on the Newhaven – Dieppe service.

SUPERSEACAT TWO Fincantieri MDV1200 monohull vessel. In 1997 operated on the *Hoverspeed* Dover – Calais route. She was withdrawn from this route at the end of 1997 and in March 1998, she inaugurated a Liverpool – Dublin fast ferry service, operated by *IOMSP Co*. In summer 1999 she operated for *Hoverspeed* between Newhaven and Dieppe. In 2000 she returned to the Irish Sea, operating on the Belfast – Heysham service.

SUPERSEACAT THREE Fincantieri MDV1200 monohull vessel. In 1999 operated on the Liverpool – Dublin service, operated by *Sea Containers Ferries Scotland*, replacing the SUPERSEACAT TWO. In 2000 she will also operate on the Liverpool – Douglas service.

THE PRINCESS ANNE British Hovercraft Corporation SRN4 type hovercraft built for *Seaspeed*. Built to Mark I specification. In 1978 lengthened to Mark III specification. She underwent complete refurbishment at the beginning of 1999. Operated by *Hoverspeed*.

THE PRINCESS MARGARET British Hovercraft Corporation SRN4 type hovercraft built for *Seaspeed*. Built to Mark I specification. In 1979 lengthened to Mark III specification. She underwent complete refurbishment at the beginning of 1999. Operated by *Hoverspeed*.

LAID UP FERRY

14• CLAYMORE	1871t	78	14k	300P	50C	-	AS	Leith, GB		GB

CLAYMORE Built for *Caledonian MacBrayne* for the Oban – Castlebay/ Lochboisdale service, also serving Coll and Tiree between October and May, replacing the IONA (see the PENTALINA B, *Pentland Ferries*). In 1989 she was transferred to the Kennacraig – Port Ellen/Port Askaig (Islay) route, again replacing the IONA. In summer she also operated a weekly service from Port Askaig (Islay) to Colonsay and Oban. She relieved on the Ardrossan – Brodick service during winter 1990. In autumn 1993 she was replaced by the ISLE OF ARRAN and became a spare vessel. Her summer duties in 1994, 1995 and 1996 included Saturday sailings from Ardrossan to Douglas (Isle of Man), returning on Sundays plus standby duties and charter to the *Isle of Man Steam Packet Company* to provide extra sailings between Heysham and Douglas during the TT Season. During the winter she was general relief vessel, spending several months on Islay sailings. In 1997 she was sold to *Sea Containers* to operate for *Sea Containers Ferries Scotland Ltd* (trading as the *Argyll and Antrim Steam Packet Company*) between Campbeltown (Scotland) and Ballycastle (Northern Ireland) (summer only). During the winter she has been chartered back to *Caledonian MacBrayne* to cover during the refit period. The Campbeltown – Ballycastle service will not be operated by *Sea Containers* in 2000 and she is now laid up.

SEAFRANCE

THE COMPANY SeaFrance SA (previously *SNAT (Société Nouvelle Armement Transmanche)*) is a French state owned company. It is jointly owned by *Société Nationale des Chemins de fer Français (French Railways)* and *Compagnie Générale Maritime Français (French National Shipping Company)*. SNAT was established in 1990 to take over the services of *SNCF Armement Naval*, a wholly owned division of *SNCF*. At the same time a similarly constituted body called *Société Proprietaire Navires (SPN)* was established to take over ownership of the vessels; *Sealink British Ferries* (and later *Stena Line Ltd*) also had involvement in this company. Joint operation of services with *Stena Line* ceased at the end of 1995 and *SeaFrance SA* was formed. *Stena Line* involvement in *SPN* ended in 1999.

MANAGEMENT Président du Directoire: M Bonnet, **Directeur Sealink Calais:** M Jachet, **Managing Director (UK):** Robin Wilkins.

ADDRESS *France:* 3 rue Ambroise Paré, 75475, PARIS Cedex 10, France, *UK:* Eastern Docks, DOVER, Kent CT16 1JA.

TELEPHONE Administration: *France:* +33 (0)1 55 31 58 92, *UK:* +44 (0)1304 212696, **Reservations:** *France:* +33 (0)3 21 46 80 79, *UK (Passenger):* 0990 711711 (from UK only), *UK (Freight):* +44 (0)1304 203030, **Fax:** *France:* +33 (0)1 48 74 62 37, *UK:* +44 (0)1304 240033, **Telex:** 280549.

INTERNET Email: wbl@seafrance.fr **Website:** http://www.seafrance.com *(English)*

ROUTE OPERATED Calais – Dover (1 hr 30 mins; *(1,2,4)*; 15 per day).

CONVENTIONAL FERRIES

1	SEAFRANCE CEZANNE	25122t	80	19.5k	1800P	600C	150T	BA2	Malmö, SW	FR
2	SEAFRANCE MANET	15093t	84	18k	1800P	330C	54T	BA2	Nantes, FR	FR
3•	SEAFRANCE MONET	12962t	74	18k	1800P	425C	51L	BA2	Trogir, YU	BA
4	SEAFRANCE RENOIR	15612t	81	18k	1600P	330C	54T	BA2	Le Havre, FR	FR

SEAFRANCE CEZANNE Built as the ARIADNE for *Rederi AB Nordö* of Sweden. Renamed the SOCA before entering service on *UMEF* freight services (but with capacity for 175 drivers) in the Mediterranean. In 1981 she was sold to *SO Mejdunaroden Automobilen Transport (SOMAT)* of Bulgaria and renamed the TRAPEZITZA. She operated on *Medlink* services between Bulgaria and the Middle East. In 1988 she was acquired by *Sealink British Ferries*, re-registered in the Bahamas and in 1989 renamed the FANTASIA. Later in 1989 she was modified in Bremerhaven, renamed the CHANNEL SEAWAY and, in May, she inaugurated a new freight-only service between Dover (Eastern Docks) and Calais. During winter 1989/90 she was modified in Bremerhaven to convert her for passenger service. In spring 1990 she was renamed the FIESTA, transferred to *SNAT*, re-registered in France and replaced the CHAMPS ELYSEES (now the SEAFRANCE MANET) on the Dover – Calais service. In 1996 she was renamed the SEAFRANCE CEZANNE.

SEAFRANCE MANET Built for *SNCF* as the CHAMPS ELYSEES to operate Calais – Dover and Boulogne – Dover services, later operating Calais – Dover only. In 1990 transferred to the Dieppe – Newhaven service. Chartered to *Stena Sealink Line* in June 1992 when they took over the operation of the service. She was renamed the STENA PARISIEN and carried a French crew. In 1997 the charter was terminated; she returned to *SeaFrance* and was renamed the SEAFRANCE MANET. She replaced the SEAFRANCE MONET.

SEAFRANCE MONET Built as the STENA DANICA for *Stena Line AB* of Sweden for their Göteborg – Frederikshavn service. In 1982, in anticipation of the delivery of a new STENA DANICA, she was renamed the STENA NORDICA. In June 1983 she was taken by *RMT* on a three year charter, introduced onto *RMT's* Oostende – Dover service and re-registered in Belgium. In March 1984 she was renamed the STENA NAUTICA. The charter ended in June 1986 when the PRINS ALBERT re-entered service; she returned to *Stena Line* and was re-registered in The Bahamas. In 1987 she was sold to *SNCF*, re-registered in France, renamed the VERSAILLES and introduced onto the Dieppe – Newhaven service. In May 1992 she was chartered to *Stena Sealink Line*, re-registered in The Bahamas, renamed the STENA LONDONER and re-launched that service, which had abandoned by *SNAT* earlier in the year. In April 1996 she was returned to *SeaFrance*, renamed the SEAFRANCE MONET and entered service in July 1996. In 1997 she was replaced by the SEAFRANCE MANET. She spent the summers from 1997 laid up but is used during winters to cover for ships undergoing refits.

SEAFRANCE RENOIR Built for *SNCF* as the COTE D'AZUR for the Dover – Calais service. She also operated Boulogne – Dover in 1985. In 1996 she was renamed the SEAFRANCE RENOIR.

SMYRIL LINE

THE COMPANY *Smyril Line* is a Faroe Islands registered company.

MANAGEMENT Managing Director: Óli Hammer, **Marketing Manager:** Samuel J Arnoldson.

ADDRESS Jonas Bronksgöta 37, PO Box 370, FO-100 TÓRSHAVN, Faroe Islands.

TELEPHONE Administration: +298-315900, **Reservations:** Faroe Islands: +298-315900, *UK:* +44 (0)1224 572615 (*P&O Scottish Ferries*), **Fax:** +298-315707, **Telex:** 81296.

SeaFrance Manet (John Hendy)

INTERNET Email: office@smyril-line.fo **Website:** http://www.smyril-line.fo *(English, Danish, German)*

ROUTES OPERATED Tórshavn (Faroes) – Hanstholm (Denmark) (31 hrs; *(1)*; 1 per week), Tórshavn – Lerwick (Shetland) (14 hrs; *(1)*; 1 per week) – Bergen (Norway) (via Lerwick) (24 hrs – 27 hrs 30 mins; *(1)*; 1 per week), Tórshavn – Seydisfjordur (Iceland) (15 hrs – 18 hrs; *(1)*; 1 per week) (15 May to 10 September only). Note: Lerwick sailings ceased after the 1992 season but resumed in 1998. The service now operates year round but is restricted to Tórshavn – Hanstholm during winter months.

CONVENTIONAL FERRY

1	NORRÖNA	11999t	73	19k	1050P	300C	44L	BA2	Rendsburg, GY	FA

NORRÖNA Built as the GUSTAV VASA for *Lion Ferry AB* of Sweden, a sister vessel of the NILS DACKE (see the QUIBERON, *Brittany Ferries*). In 1982 the Travemünde – Malmö service ceased and in 1983 she was sold to *Smyril Line* and renamed the NORRÖNA. She was rebuilt in Flensburg, Germany, to increase passenger capacity and in the summer took over services from the SMYRIL of *Strandfaraskip Landsins*. In 1993 Esbjerg replaced Hanstholm as the Danish port and calls at Lerwick (Shetland) ceased. Because the service only operated in the summer period, she has, since purchase, undertaken a number of charters and cruises during the winter months. During autumn 1994 she initially served on the short-lived service between Wismar (Germany) and Newcastle for *North Sea Baltic Ferries*. During the early part of 1996 she was chartered to *Stena Line* to operate between Stranraer and Belfast. In 1998 the Danish port became Hanstholm again and Lerwick sailings resumed. She now operates for *Smyril Line* all year round.

Under Construction

2	NEWBUILDING	36000t	02	21k	1500P	644C	152T	BA	Flensburg, GY	FA

NEWBUILDING Under construction for *Smyril Line*, to replace the NORRÖNA.

STENA LINE

THE COMPANY *Stena Line AB* is a Swedish private sector company. Whilst British subsidiary *Stena Line Ltd* and Dutch subsidiary *Stena Line bv* still exist as legal entities, the company is operated on a route management basis, with each Route Director reporting directly to HQ in Göteborg. Some central services are also undertaken by units in UK and Netherlands which report directly to Göteborg.

MANAGEMENT Chief Executive: Bo Severed (*Stena Line AB*, Sweden), **Route Director – Hoek van Holland – Harwich:** Pim de Lange, **Route Director – Fishguard – Rosslare:** Mary Gallagher, **Route Director – Holyhead – Dun Laoghaire/Dublin:** Vic Goodwin, **Route Director – Stranraer – Belfast:** Alan Gordon.

ADDRESS UK: Charter House, Park Street, ASHFORD, Kent TN24 8EX, **Netherlands:** PO Box 2, 3150 AA, HOEK VAN HOLLAND, Netherlands.

TELEPHONE UK: Administration: +44 (0)1233 647022, **Reservations:** 08075 707070 (from UK only), **Fax:** +44 (0)1233 202349, **Netherlands: Administration:** +31 (0)174 38 93 33, **Reservations:** +31 (0)174 31 58 11, **Fax:** +31 (0)174 38 70 45, **Telex:** 31272.

INTERNET Email: info@stenaline.com **Website:** http://www.stenaline.com *(English, Swedish)*

ROUTES OPERATED Conventional Ferries: Stranraer – Belfast (3 hrs; *(2,4)*; 5 per day, (Stranraer – Larne (2hrs 15 mins; *(2,4)*; 6 per day) as from September 2000, Holyhead – Dublin (3 hrs 45 mins; *(3)*; 2 per day); Fishguard – Rosslare (3 hrs 30 mins; *(1)*; 2 per day), **Ro-pax Ferries:** Harwich – Hoek van Holland (Netherlands) (7 hrs 30 mins; *(2,3 from autumn 2000, freight vessels with very limited accommodation (see Section 3) until then)*; 2-3 per day), **Fast Ferries:** Stranraer – Belfast (1 hrs 45 mins; *(8)*; 5 per day), Holyhead – Dun Laoghaire (1 hr 39 mins; *(6)*; up to 4 per day), Fishguard – Rosslare (Summer only) (1 hr 39 mins; *(6)*; up to 4 per day), Harwich – Hoek van Holland – (3 hrs 40 mins; *(5)*; 2 per day).

CONVENTIONAL FERRIES

1	KONINGIN BEATRIX	31189t	86	20k	1800P	500C	75T	BA	Krimpen, NL	GB
2	STENA CALEDONIA	12619t	81	19.5k	1000P	280C	56T	BA2	Belfast, GB	GB
3	STENA CHALLENGER	18523t	91	18k	500P	480C	100T	BA2	Rissa, NO	GB
4	STENA GALLOWAY	12175t	80	19k	1000P	280C	56T	BA2	Belfast, GB	GB

KONINGIN BEATRIX Built for *Stoomvaart Maatschappij Zeeland* of The Netherlands for their Hoek van Holland – Harwich service (trading as *Crown Line*). In 1989 transferred to *Stena Line bv*. In June 1997 chartered by *Stena Line bv* to *Stena Line Ltd* and used on the Fishguard – Rosslare service. In August 1997, transferred to the British flag.

STENA CALEDONIA Built as the ST DAVID for the Holyhead – Dun Laoghaire and Fishguard – Rosslare services. It was originally planned that she would replace the chartered STENA NORMANDICA (5607t, 1975) but it was subsequently decided that an additional large vessel was required for the Irish Sea routes. Until 1985 her normal use was, therefore, to substitute for other Irish Sea vessels as necessary (including the Stranraer – Larne route) and also to operate additional summer services on the Holyhead – Dun Laoghaire route. During the spring of 1983 she operated on the Dover – Calais service while the ST CHRISTOPHER (now the STENA ANTRIM) was being modified. From March 1985 she operated between Dover and Oostende, a service which ceased in December 1985 with the decision of *RMT* to link up with *Townsend Thoresen*. During the early part of 1986 she operated between Dover and Calais and then moved to the Stranraer – Larne route where she became a regular vessel. In 1990 she was renamed the STENA CALEDONIA. In September 1996 she became mainly a freight-only vessel but passengers were carried on certain sailings and when the STENA VOYAGER was unavailable. Cars and passengers are now conveyed on all sailings.

STENA CHALLENGER Built for *Stena Rederi AB* of Sweden and chartered to *Stena Sealink Line* for Dover – Calais and Dover – Dunkerque freight services. Her hull was constructed and launched in Landskrona, Sweden and towed to Norway for fitting out. In 1992 she was switched to the Dover (Eastern Docks) – Dunkerque freight services. From summer 1994 until summer 1996 she operated

Stena Caedonia (Gordon Hislip)

Stena Explorer (Jack Phelan)

passenger services between Dover and Calais. In summer 1996 she was transferred to the Holyhead – Dublin route, then freight-only, replacing sister ship, the STENA TRAVELLER (now the TT-TRAVELLER). Cars and passengers are now carried on all sailings.

STENA GALLOWAY Built as the GALLOWAY PRINCESS for the Stranraer – Larne (now Belfast) service. In 1990 renamed the STENA GALLOWAY. In September 1996 she became mainly a freight-only vessel but passengers were carried on certain sailings and when the STENA VOYAGER was unavailable. Cars and passengers are now conveyed on all sailings.

FAST FERRIES

5	STENA DISCOVERY	19638t	97	40k	1500P	375C	50L	A	Rauma, FI	NL
6	STENA EXPLORER	19638t	96	40k	1500P	375C	50L	A	Rauma, FI	GB
7	STENA LYNX III	4113t	96	35k	620P	181C	-	A	Hobart, AL	GB
8	STENA VOYAGER	19638t	96	40k	1500P	375C	50L	A	Rauma, FI	GB

STENA DISCOVERY Finnyards HSS1500 built for *Stena Line* to replace two conventional ferries on the Harwich – Hoek van Holland service.

STENA EXPLORER Finnyards HSS1500 ('High-speed Sea Service') built for *Stena Line*. Operates on the Holyhead – Dun Laoghaire route.

STENA LYNX III InCat 81m catamaran. Chartered new by *Del Bene* of Argentina to *Stena Line* in June 1996 and named the STENA LYNX III. Initially used on the Dover – Calais service. From summer 1997 until autumn 1998 she operated between Newhaven and Dieppe. In March 1998 she was transferred to *P&O Stena Line* and renamed the ELITE. She was then renamed the P&O STENA ELITE (although only carrying the name ELITE on the bow). In late 1998 she was transferred back to *Stena Line* and renamed the STENA LYNX III. In 1999 she was placed on the Fishguard – Rosslare service, replacing the STENA LYNX (3231t, 1993). Charter due to end October 2000.

STENA VOYAGER Finnyards HSS1500 built for *Stena Line*. Operates on the Stranraer – Belfast route.

Under Construction

9	STENA BRITANNICA	30500t	00	22k	380P	-	200T	BA	Puerto Real, SP	GB
10	STENA HOLLANDICA	30500t	01	22k	380P	-	200T	BA	Puerto Real, SP	NL

STENA BRITANNICA Ro-pax ferry under construction for *Stena Rederi*. To be chartered to *Stena Line bv* to operate between Hoek van Holland and Harwich. She will replace the ro-ro STENA SEARIDER (see section 3).

STENA HOLLANDICA Ro-pax ferry under construction for *Stena Rederi*. To be chartered to *Stena Line bv* to operate between Hoek van Holland and Harwich. She will replace the ro-ro STENA SEATRADER (see section 3). The charter of the ROSEBAY will also end when she is delivered.

SWANSEA CORK FERRIES

THE COMPANY *Swansea Cork Ferries* is a company established in 1987 to re-open the Swansea – Cork service abandoned by *B&I Line* in 1979. It was originally jointly owned by *West Glamorgan County Council, Cork Corporation, Cork County Council* and *Kerry County Council*. The service did not operate in 1989 but resumed in 1990. In 1993 the company was acquired by *Strintzis Lines* of Greece. In 1999 it was purchased from *Strintzis Lines* by a consortium of Irish businessmen.

MANAGEMENT Managing Director: Thomas Hunter McGowan, **Sales Manager:** Alec Maguire.

ADDRESS 52 South Mall, CORK, Republic of Ireland.

TELEPHONE Administration: *Head Office:* +353 (0)21 276000, *Cork Ferry Port:* +353 (0)21 378036, **Reservations:** *IR:* +353 (0)21 271166, *UK:* +44 (0)1792 456116, **Fax:** *IR – Admin:* +353 (0)21 275814, *IR – Reservations:* +353 (0)21 275061, *UK:* +44 (0)1792 644356.

INTERNET Email: scf@iol.ie **Website:** http://www.swansea-cork.ie *(English)*

ROUTE OPERATED *In 2000 March – November:* Cork – Swansea (10 hrs; *(2)*; 1 per day or alternate days, according to season. Due to tidal restrictions at Swansea, the service operates to Pembroke Dock on a few days each year).

CONVENTIONAL FERRY

1	SUPERFERRY	14797t	72	21k	1400P	350C	50L	BA2	Hashihama, JA	GR

SUPERFERRY Built as the CASSIOPEIA for *Ocean Ferry KK* of Japan. In 1976 the company became *Ocean Tokyu Ferry KK* and she was renamed the IZU NO 3. She was used on the service between Tokyo (Honshu) – Tokushima (Shikoku) – Kokura (Kyshu). In 1991 she was sold to *Strintzis Lines* and briefly renamed the IONIAN EXPRESS. Following major rebuilding, she was renamed the SUPERFERRY and used on their services between Greece and the Greek islands. In 1993 time chartered to *Swansea Cork Ferries*. The charter has continued following the sale of *SCF* by *Strintzis Lines*. In winter returns to *Strintzis Lines* in Greece for refit and has also operated for them on Mediterranean routes.

Caledonian MacBrayne

Section 2 – DOMESTIC SERVICES

ARGYLL AND BUTE COUNCIL

THE COMPANY *Argyll and Bute Council* is a British local government authority.

MANAGEMENT Head of Transportation Services: D Duthie.

ADDRESS Manse Brae, LOCHGILPHEAD, Argyll PA31 8RD.

TELEPHONE Administration: +44 (0)1546 603749, **Fax:** +44 (0) 1546 604420.

INTERNET Email: dave.duthie@argyll/bute.gov.uk

ROUTES OPERATED Seil – Luing (5 mins; *(1)*; frequent service), Port Askaig (Islay) – Feolin (Jura) (5 mins; *(2)*; approx hourly).

VESSELS

1	BELNAHUA	35t	72	8k	40P	5C	1L	BA	Campbeltown, GB	GB
2	EILEAN DHIURA	86t	98	9k	50P	13C	1L	BA	Bromborough, GB	GB

BELNAHUA Built for *Argyll County Council* for the Seil – Luing service. In 1975, following local government reorganisation, transferred to *Strathclyde Regional Council*. In 1996, transferred to *Argyll and Bute Council*.

EILEAN DHIURA Built for *Argyll County Council* to replace the *Western Ferries (Argyll)* SOUND OF GIGHA on the Islay – Jura route. *Serco-Denholm Ltd* manage and operate this vessel on behalf of the *Argyll and Bute Council*.

ARRANMORE ISLAND FERRY SERVICES

THE COMPANY *Arranmore Island Ferry Services* is an Irish Republic company, supported by *Údarás na Gaeltachta (The Gaeltacht Authority)*, a semi-state owned body responsible for tourism and development in the Irish speaking areas of The Irish Republic. The operation is also known as *Maoin-Na-Farraige* (literally 'sea treasure' or 'sea wealth').

MANAGEMENT Managing Director: Cornelius Bonner.

ADDRESS Bridge House, Leabgarrow, ARRANMORE, County Donegal, Republic of Ireland.

TELEPHONE Administration & Reservations: +353 (0)75 20532, **Fax:** + 353 (0)75 20750.

ROUTE OPERATED Burtonport (County Donegal) – Leabgarrow (Arranmore Island) (20 mins; *(1,2,3,4)*; up to 8 per day (summer), 5 per day (winter)) (Note: only one vessel is usually in use at any one time).

VESSELS

1	ÁRAINN MHÓR	64t	72	8k	138P	4C	-	B	Port Glasgow, GB	GB
2	COLL	69t	74	8k	152P	6C	-	B	Port Glasgow, GB	GB
3	MORVERN	64t	73	8k	138P	4C	-	B	Port Glasgow, GB	GB
4	RHUM	69t	73	8k	164P	6C	-	B	Port Glasgow, GB	GB

ÁRAINN MHÓR Built as the KILBRANNAN for *Caledonian MacBrayne*. Used on a variety of routes until 1977, she was then transferred to the Scalpay (Harris) – Kyles Scalpay service. In 1990 she was replaced by the CANNA and, in turn, replaced the CANNA in her reserve/relief role. In 1992 sold to *Arranmore Island Ferry Services* and renamed the ÁRAINN MHÓR.

COLL Built for *Caledonian MacBrayne*. For several years she was employed mainly in a relief capacity. In 1986 she took over the Tobermory (Mull) – Kilchoan service from a passenger only vessel; the conveyance of vehicles was not inaugurated until 1991. In 1996 she was transferred to the Oban – Lismore route. In 1998 she was sold to *Arranmore Island Ferry Services*.

MORVERN Built for *Caledonian MacBrayne*. After service on a number of routes she was, after 1979, the main vessel on the Fionnphort (Mull) – Iona service. In 1992 replaced by the LOCH BUIE and became a spare vessel. In 1995 sold to *Arranmore Island Ferry Services*.

RHUM Built for *Caledonian MacBrayne*. Until 1987, she was used primarily on the Claonaig – Lochranza (Arran) service. After that time she served on various routes. In 1994 she inaugurated a new service between Tarbert (Loch Fyne) and Portavadie. In 1997 operated between Kyles Scalpay and Scalpay until the opening of the new bridge on 16th December 1997. In 1998 she was sold to *Arranmore Island Ferry Services*.

BERE ISLAND FERRIES

THE COMPANY *Bere Island Ferries Ltd* is an Irish Republic private sector company.

MANAGEMENT Operator: Colm Harrington.

ADDRESS Ferry Lodge, West End, BERE ISLAND, County Cork, Republic of Ireland.

TELEPHONE Administration: +353 (0)27 75009, **Reservations:** Not applicable.

INTERNET Email: tjb@indigo.ie

ROUTE OPERATED Castletownbere (County Cork) – Bere Island (10 mins; *(1,2)*; up to 10 per day).

VESSELS

1	F.B.D. DUNBRODY	139t	60	8k	107P	18C	-	BA	Hamburg, GY	IR
2	MISNEACH	30t	78	7k	80P	4C	-	B	New Ross, IR	IR

F.B.D. DUNBRODY Built as the BERNE-FARGE for the service between Berne and Farge, across the River Weser in Germany. Subsequently she was sold to *Elbe Clearing* of Germany, renamed the ELBE CLEARING 12 and used as a floating platform for construction works in the Elbe. In 1979 she was sold to *Passage East Ferry Company* and renamed the F.B.D. DUNBRODY. Withdrawn in January 1998 and became a spare vessel. Later in 1998 she was sold to *Bere Island Ferries*.

MISNEACH Built for *Arranmore Island Ferry Services* of the Irish Republic and used on the Burtonport – Arranmore service. In 1992 sold to *Bere Island Ferries*. In 1993 inaugurated a car ferry service between Castletownbere and Bere Island. Now reserve vessel.

CALEDONIAN MACBRAYNE

THE COMPANY *Caledonian MacBrayne Limited* is a British state owned company, the responsibility of the First Minister of Scotland. Until 1990 it was part of the state owned *Scottish Transport Group* (formed in 1969). *Caledonian MacBrayne Limited* as such was formed in 1973 by the merger of the *Caledonian Steam Packet Company Ltd* (which had been formed in 1889) and *David MacBrayne Ltd* (whose origins go back to 1851). The company has more vessels sailing under the British flag than any other.

MANAGEMENT Managing Director: Capt J A B Simkins, **Marketing Manager:** Mike Blair.

ADDRESS The Ferry Terminal, GOUROCK PA19 1QP.

TELEPHONE Administration: +44 (0)1475 650100, **Vehicle Reservations:** 08705 650000 (from UK only), **Fax: *Admin:*** +44 (0)1475 637607, ***Vehicle Reservations:*** +44 (0)1475 635235.

INTERNET Email: mike.blair@calmac.co.uk **Website:** http://www.calmac.co.uk

ROUTES OPERATED *All year vehicle ferries (frequencies are for summer):* Ardrossan – Brodick (Arran) (55 mins; *(2)*; up to 6 per day), Largs – Cumbrae Slip (Cumbrae) (10 mins; *(13,20)*; every 30 or 15 mins), Wemyss Bay – Rothesay (Bute) (35 mins; *(11,12,26,28)*; up to 22 per day), Colintraive – Rhubodach (Bute) (5 mins; *(16)*; frequent service), Tarbert (Loch Fyne) – Portavadie (20 mins; *(8)*; up to 11 per day), Gourock – Dunoon (20 mins; *(11,12, 28)*; hourly service with extras at peaks), Kennacraig – Port Ellen (Islay) (2 hrs 15 mins; *(7)*; 1 or 2 per day), Kennacraig – Port Askaig (Islay) (2 hrs; *(7)*; 1 or 2 per day), Tayinloan – Gigha (20 mins; *(19)*; hourly with some gaps), Oban – Lismore (50 mins; *(5)*; up to 4 per day), Oban – Colonsay (2 hrs 10 mins; *(4,7,10)*; 3 per

Isle of Arran (Colin Smith)

Loch Linnhe (Dominic McCall)

week), Oban – Craignure (Mull) (40 mins; *(9)*; two hourly), Oban – Coll (2 hrs 45 mins (direct), 4 hrs 50 mins (via Tiree); *(4 (summer), 25 (winter))*; up to 5 per week), Oban – Tiree (3 hrs 30 mins (direct), 4 hrs 15 mins (via Coll); *(4 (summer), 25 (winter))*; up to 5 per week), Oban – Castlebay (Barra) (5 hrs (direct); *(4 (summer), 25 (winter))*; 4 per week), Oban – Lochboisdale (South Uist) (5 hrs (direct), 7 hrs (via Barra); *(4 (summer), 25 (winter))*; up to 5 per week)5 per week), Otternish (North Uist) – Leverburgh (Harris) (1 hr 10 mins; *(14)*; 3-4 per day), Lochaline – Fishnish (Mull) (15 mins; *(17)*; up to 16 per day), Mallaig – Armadale (Skye) (30 mins; *(4 (summer), 24 (winter))*; up to 7 per day), Sconser (Skye) – Raasay (15 mins; *(21)*; up to 10 per day), Uig (Skye) – Tarbert (Harris) (1 hr 45 mins; *(6)*; 1 or 2 per day), Uig (Skye) – Lochmaddy (North Uist) (1 hr 45 mins; *(6)*; 1 or 2 per day), Ullapool – Stornoway (Lewis) (2 hrs 40 mins; *(6)*; up to 3 per day).

All year passenger and restricted vehicle ferries (frequencies are for summer): Fionnphort (Mull) – Iona (5 mins; *(15)*; frequent), Ballycastle (Northern Ireland) – Rathlin Island (40 mins; *(3)*; 2 per day),Mallaig – Eigg – Muck – Rum – Canna – Mallaig (round trip 7 hrs (all islands); *(24)*; at least 1 sailing per day – most islands visited daily). Note: although these services are operated by vehicle ferries, special permission is required to take a vehicle and tourist vehicles are not conveyed.

Summer only vehicle ferries: Claonaig – Lochranza (Arran) (30 mins; *(22)*; up to 10 per day), Kennacraig – Port Askaig – Colonsay – Oban (3 hrs 35 mins; *(6)*; 1 per week), Tobermory (Mull) – Kilchoan (35 mins; *(18)*; up to 11 per day), Mallaig – Lochboisdale (3 hrs 15 mins); *(25)*; 1 per week), Mallaig – Castlebay (3 hrs 45 mins); *(25)*; 1 per week. ***Winter only vehicle ferries:*** Tarbert – Lochranza (1 hr; *(varies)*; 1 per day).

Clyde Cruising In addition to car and passenger services, the following cruises are operated in the Clyde between May and September; parts of these cruises are sometimes normal car/passenger services: Gourock – Dunoon – Largs – Rothesay – Tighnabruaich – Tarbert (Loch Fyne); *(11,12,28)*; 4 per week (only one per week to Tarbert)).

VESSELS

1	BRUERNISH	69t	73	8k	164P	6C	-	B	Port Glasgow, GB	GB
2	CALEDONIAN ISLES	5221t	93	15k	1000P	120C	-	BA	Lowestoft, GB	GB
3	CANNA	69t	73	8k	140P	6C	-	B	Port Glasgow, GB	GB
4	CLANSMAN	5499t	98	16.5k	634P	90C	-	BA	Appledore, GB	GB
5	EIGG	69t	75	8k	44P	6C	-	B	Port Glasgow, GB	GB
6	HEBRIDEAN ISLES	3040t	85	15k	507P	68C	-	BAS	Selby, GB	GB
7	ISLE OF ARRAN	3296t	84	15k	659P	68C	-	BA	Port Glasgow, GB	GB
8	ISLE OF CUMBRAE	169t	77	8.5k	138P	15C	-	BA	Troon, GB	GB
9	ISLE OF LEWIS	6753t	95	18k	680P	123C	-	BA	Port Glasgow, GB	GB
10	ISLE OF MULL	4719t	88	15k	1000P	80C	-	BA	Port Glasgow, GB	GB
11	JUNO	902t	74	14k	531P	40C	-	AS	Port Glasgow, GB	GB
12	JUPITER	898t	74	14k	531P	40C	-	AS	Port Glasgow, GB	GB
13	LOCH ALAINN	396t	97	10k	150P	24C	-	BA	Buckie, GB	GB
14	LOCH BHRUSDA	246t	96	10k	150P	18C	-	BA	Bromborough, GB	GB
15	LOCH BUIE	295t	92	9k	250P	9C	-	BA	St Monans, GB	GB
16	LOCH DUNVEGAN	549t	91	9k	200P	36C	-	BA	Port Glasgow, GB	GB
17	LOCH FYNE	549t	91	9k	200P	36C	-	BA	Port Glasgow, GB	GB
18	LOCH LINNHE	206t	86	9k	203P	12C	-	BA	Hessle, GB	GB
19	LOCH RANZA	206t	87	9k	203P	12C	-	BA	Hessle, GB	GB
20	LOCH RIDDON	206t	86	9k	203P	12C	-	BA	Hessle, GB	GB
21	LOCH STRIVEN	206t	86	9k	203P	12C	-	BA	Hessle, GB	GB
22	LOCH TARBERT	211t	92	9k	149P	18C	-	BA	St Monans, GB	GB
23	LOCHMOR	175t	79	11k	130P	-	-	C	Troon, GB	GB
24	LOCHNEVIS	750t	00	-	200P	14C	-	A	Troon, GB	GB
25	LORD OF THE ISLES	3504t	89	16k	506P	56C	-	BAS	Port Glasgow, GB	GB
26	PIONEER	1088t	74	16k	356P	33C	-	AS	Leith, GB	GB

| 27 | RAASAY | 69t | 76 | 8k | 75P | 6C | - | B | Port Glasgow, GB | GB |
| 28 | SATURN | 899t | 78 | 14k | 531P | 40C | - | AS | Troon, GB | GB |

BRUERNISH Until 1980 she served on a variety of routes. In 1980 she inaugurated ro-ro working between Tayinloan and the island of Gigha and served this route until June 1992 when she was replaced by the LOCH RANZA and became a relief vessel. In summer 1994 she operated as secondary vessel on the Tobermory (Mull) – Kilchoan service for one season only. In December 1996 she started a vehicle ferry service between Ballycastle (on the North West coast of Northern Ireland) and Rathlin Island under charter; the route became a *Caledonian MacBrayne* operation in April 1997 – see the CANNA. In 1997 she operated on the Tarbert – Portavadie service and in 1998 on the Oban – Lismore service. In 1999 she was a spare vessel and this is likely to be repeated in 2000.

CALEDONIAN ISLES Built for the Ardrossan – Brodick (Arran) service.

CANNA She was the regular vessel on the Lochaline – Fishnish (Mull) service. In 1986 she was replaced by the ISLE OF CUMBRAE and until 1990 she served in a relief capacity in the north, often assisting on the Iona service. In 1990 she replaced the KILBRANNAN (see the ÁRAINN MHÓR, *Arranmore Island Ferry Services*) on the Kyles Scalpay (Harris) – Scalpay service (replaced by a bridge in autumn 1997). In spring 1997 she was transferred to the Ballycastle – Rathlin Island route.

CLANSMAN Built to replace the LORD OF THE ISLES on the Oban – Coll and Tiree and Oban – Castlebay and Lochboisdale service in the summer. She also serves as winter relief vessel on the Stornoway, Tarbert, Lochmaddy, Mull, Islay and Brodick routes.

EIGG Since 1976 she was employed mainly on the Oban – Lismore service. In 1996 she was transferred to the Tobermory (Mull) – Kilchoan route, very occasionally making special sailings to the Small Isles (Canna, Eigg, Muck and Rum) for special cargoes. In 1999 her wheelhouse was raised to make it easier to see over taller lorries and she returned to the Oban – Lismore route, on which she is expected to continue in 2000.

HEBRIDEAN ISLES Built for the Uig – Tarbert/Lochmaddy service. She was used initially on the Ullapool – Stornoway and Oban – Craignure/Colonsay services pending installation of link-span facilities at Uig, Tarbert and Lochmaddy. She took up her regular role in May 1986. Since May 1996 she has no longer operated direct services between Tarbert and Lochmaddy, this role being taken on by the new Harris – North Uist services of the LOCH BHRUSDA. In 2000 to be replaced by the HEBRIDES; she will probably become the fleet spare vessel.

ISLE OF ARRAN Built for the Ardrossan – Brodick service. In 1993 transferred to the Kennacraig – Port Ellen/Port Askaig service, also undertaking the weekly Port Askaig – Colonsay – Oban summer service. Until 1997/98 she also relieved on the Brodick, Coll/Tiree, Castlebay/Lochboisdale, Craignure and Tarbert/Lochmaddy routes in winter.

ISLE OF CUMBRAE Built for the Largs – Cumbrae Slip (Cumbrae) service. In 1986 she was replaced by the LOCH LINNHE and the LOCH STRIVEN and transferred to the Lochaline – Fishnish (Mull) service. She used to spend most of the winter as secondary vessel on the Kyle of Lochalsh – Kyleakin service; however this ceased following the opening of the Skye Bridge in 1995. In 1997 she was transferred to the Colintraive – Rhubodach service. In summer 1999 she was transferred to the Tarbert – Portavadie service.

ISLE OF LEWIS Built to replace the SUILVEN on the Ullapool – Stornoway service. Largest vessel ever to operate on Clyde or Western Isles routes and has never operated on any other service.

ISLE OF MULL Built for the Oban – Craignure (Mull) service. She also operates the Oban – Colonsay service and until 1997/98 was the usual winter relief vessel on the Ullapool – Stornoway service. She has also deputised on the Oban – Castlebay/Lochboisdale and Oban – Coll/Tiree routes.

JUNO, JUPITER, SATURN Built for the Gourock – Dunoon, Gourock – Kilcreggan and Wemyss Bay – Rothesay services. The JUPITER has been upgraded to Class III standard for the Ardrossan – Brodick service. Before 1986, the JUNO and JUPITER operated mainly on the Gourock – Dunoon and Gourock – Kilcreggan (now withdrawn) services and the SATURN on the Wemyss Bay – Rothesay service. Since 1986 they have usually rotated on a three weekly basis on the three services. They are all used on the summer cruise programme.

Caledonian MacBrayne

Scotland's Enchanted Isles

Caledonian MacBrayne is the name synonymous with sea travel to the islands off the West Coast of Scotland. The company operates services on the Firth of Clyde and the Hebrides.
In total, we sail to 22 Scottish Islands, using 52 different ports or terminals.

"Island Hopscotch®" and "Island Rover" tickets are available for tourists who wish to visit several islands in their holiday programme.
Go for a full holiday, a short break or even just a day trip, to explore some of the finest scenic locations in Europe.

Why not try one of our Evening Dinner Cruises from Ardrossan or Oban enjoying the delights of a Hebridean sunset, while sitting down to a three course meal served at your table.

For a holiday brochure giving details of times and fares, contact:

Caledonian MacBrayne

The Ferry Terminal, Gourock, PA19 1QP
Tel: 01475 650100 Fax: 01475 637607
Vehicle Reservations : (08705) 650000
Brochure Line: (01475) 650288
www.calmac.co.uk

SECTION 2 – DOMESTIC SERVICES

LOCH ALAINN Built for the Lochaline – Fishnish service. Launched as the LOCH ALINE but renamed the LOCH ALAINN before entering service. After a brief period on the service she was built for, she was transferred to the Colintraive – Rhubodach route. In summer 1998 she was transferred to the Largs – Cumbrae Slip service.

LOCH BHRUSDA Built to inaugurate a new Otternish (North Uist) – Berneray – Leverburgh (Harris) service. Note: 'Bhrusda' is pronounced "Vroosda".

LOCH BUIE Built for the Fionnphort (Mull) – Iona service to replace the MORVERN (see *Arranmore Island Ferry Services*) and obviate the need for a relief vessel in the summer. Due to height restrictions, loading arrangements for vehicles taller than private cars are bow only. Only islanders' cars and service vehicles (eg mail vans, police) are carried; no tourist vehicles are conveyed.

LOCH DUNVEGAN Built for the Kyle of Lochalsh – Kyleakin service. On the opening of the Skye Bridge in October 1995 she was withdrawn from service and put up for sale. In autumn 1997, returned to service on the Lochaline – Fishnish route. In 1998 she was due to be transferred to the Colintraive – Rhubodach route but this was delayed due to problems in providing terminal facilities. She operated on the Clyde and between Mallaig and Armadale during the early summer and spent the rest of the summer laid up. In 1999 she was transferred to the Colintraive – Rhubodach route.

LOCH FYNE Built for the Kyle of Lochalsh – Kyleakin service (see the LOCH DUNVEGAN). In autumn 1997, she also served on the Lochaline – Fishnish route and was transferred to this route as regular vessel in 1998.

LOCH LINNHE Until 1997 she was used mainly on the Largs – Cumbrae Slip (Cumbrae) service and until winter 1994/95 she was usually used on the Lochaline – Fishnish service during the winter. Since then she had relieved on various routes in winter. In summer 1998 she operated mainly on the Tarbert – Portavadie route. In 1999 she was transferred to the summer only Tobermory – Kilchoan service.

LOCH RANZA Built for the Claonaig – Lochranza (Arran) seasonal service and used a relief vessel in the winter. In 1992 she was replaced by the LOCH TARBERT and transferred to the Tayinloan – Gigha service.

LOCH RIDDON Until 1997 she was used almost exclusively on the Colintraive – Rhubodach service. In 1997, she was transferred to the Largs – Cumbrae Slip service.

LOCH STRIVEN Used mainly on the Largs – Cumbrae Slip service until 1997. In winter 1995/6 and 1996/67 she was used on the Tarbert – Portavadie and Claonaig – Lochranza routes. In 1997 she took over the Sconser – Raasay service.

LOCH TARBERT Built for the Claonaig – Lochranza service. She has been the regular winter vessel on the Largs – Cumbrae Slip route since winter 1994/5 and is also the winter relief vessel for the Otternish – Leverburgh route.

LOCHMOR Built for the passenger only 'Small Isles' service from Mallaig to Eigg, Muck, Rum and Canna with, until 1997, weekly summer cruises to Kyle of Lochalsh. She also maintained the winter restricted passenger-only service between Mallaig and Armadale. In spring 2000, replaced by the LOCHNEVIS and withdrawn.

LOCHNEVIS Built to replace the LOCHMOR on the Mallaig – Small Isles service and the winter Mallaig – Armadale service. Although a vehicle ferry, cars are not normally be carried to the small isles. The ro-ro facility is used for the carriage of agricultural machinery and livestock and it is possible to convey a vehicle on the ferry from which goods can be unloaded directly onto local transport rather than transhipping at Mallaig. Ramps are being provided at each island and, when complete, the practice of tendering at Eigg, Muck and Rum will cease, the ULVA being disposed of.

LORD OF THE ISLES Built to replace the CLAYMORE on the Oban – Castlebay and Lochboisdale services and also the COLUMBA (1420t, 1964) on the Oban – Coll and Tiree service. She took over Mallaig – Armadale and Mallaig – Outer Isles service in July 1998 but returned to her previous routes during the winter period. In summer 1999 will again operate from Mallaig.

PIONEER Built to operate on the West Loch Tarbert – Port Ellen service (see the PENTALINA B,

Glenbrook (Miles Cowsill)

Freedom 90 (Andrew Cooke)

Pentland Ferries). When the IONA was at last able to operate this service in 1978 (following the move to Kennacraig) the PIONEER was transferred to the Mallaig – Armadale service, operating as a relief vessel in the winter on Upper Clyde and Small Isles routes. In 1989 she was replaced at Mallaig by the IONA and became the company's spare vessel, replacing the GLEN SANNOX (1269t, 1957). Since summer 1995 she has undertaken Wemyss Bay – Rothesay and Rothesay – Largs – Brodick sailings. She serves as a Clyde and Small Isles relief vessel in the winter replacing the JUNO, JUPITER, SATURN and LOCHMOR for annual overhaul. In 1998 she opened the Mallaig – Armadale/Outer Isles service and temporarily operated between Oban and Craignure before returning to the Clyde in July. In summer 2000 she is expected to operate on the Clyde, solely on the Wemyss Bay – Rothesay route, after which she may be withdrawn.

RAASAY Built for and used primarily on the Sconser (Skye) – Raasay service. In 1997 she was replaced by the LOCH STRIVEN and became a spare/relief vessel. She is likely to continue in this role in 2000.

SATURN As the JUNO and JUPITER. In earlier days operated mainly on the Wemyss Bay – Rothesay service.

Under Construction

29	HEBRIDES		5500t	00	16.5k	650P	110C	-	BA	Port Glasgow, GB	GB

HEBRIDES Under construction for the Uig – Tarbert and Uig – Lochmaddy services.

Caledonian MacBrayne also operates the ULVA, a 35 ft motor vessel built in 1958 and carrying up to 28 passengers. She tenders to the LOCHNEVIS at Eigg. She will be withdrawn when a ramp is built on the island.

COMHAIRLE NAN EILEAN SIAR

THE COMPANY *Comhairle Nan Eilean Siar* (formerly the *Western Isles Council*) is a British municipal authority.

ADDRESS Council Offices, Sandwick Road, STORNOWAY, Isle of Lewis HS1 2BW.

TELEPHONE Administration: +44 (0)1851 703773, Extn 440 **Reservations:** +44 (0)1878 720261, **Fax:** +44 (0)1851 706426.

INTERNET   **Email:**   calum-mcleod@cne-siar.gov.uk   **Website:** http://www.open.gov.uk/westile/wiichome.htm *(English)*

ROUTES OPERATED Car Ferries: Ludaig (South Uist) – Eriskay (30 mins; *(3)*; 3 per day (minimum)) (additional services operate during the summer), **Passenger Only Ferry:** Ludaig (South Uist) – Eriskay (15 mins; *(1)*; 3 per day), Ludaig (South Uist) – Eoligarry (Barra) (40 mins; *(1)*; 2 per day).

VESSELS

1p	ALLASDALE LASS	-	98	12k	50P	0C	0T	-	Stornoway, GB	GB
2●	EILEAN BHEARNARAIGH	67t	83	7k	35P	4C	1T	BA	Glasgow, GB	GB
3	EILEAN NA H-OIGE	69t	80	7k	35P	4C	1T	BA	Stornoway, GB	GB

ALLASDALE LASS Owned and operated by *G V MacLeod Ltd* on behalf of *Comhairle Nan Eilean Siar*. Operates passenger only sailings between Ludaig and Eriskay and Barra.

EILEAN BHEARNARAIGH Built for *Western Isles Islands Council* for their Otternish (North Uist) – Berneray service. From 1996 until 1999 she was operated by *Caledonian MacBrayne* in conjunction with the LOCH BHRUSDA on the service between Otternish and Berneray and during the winter she was laid up. Following the opening of a causeway between North Uist and Berneray in early 1999 the ferry service ceased and she is now relief vessel for the Ludaig – Eriskay route.

EILEAN NA H-OIGE Built for *Western Isles Islands Council* (from 1st April 1996 the *Western Isles Council* and from 1st January 1998 *Comhairle Nan Eilean Siar*) for their Ludaig – Eriskay service.

CROSS RIVER FERRIES

THE COMPANY *Cross River Ferries Ltd* is an Irish Republic company, jointly owned by *Marine Transport Services Ltd* of Cobh and *Arklow Shipping Ltd* of Arklow, County Wicklow.

MANAGEMENT Operations Manager: Edward Perry.

ADDRESS Atlantic Quay, COBH, County Cork, Republic of Ireland.

TELEPHONE Administration: +353 (0)21 811223, **Reservations:** Not applicable, **Fax:** +353 (0)21 812645.

ROUTE OPERATED Carrigaloe (near Cobh, on Great Island) – Glenbrook (Co Cork) (4 mins; *(1,2)*; frequent service (one or two vessels used according to demand).

VESSELS

1	CARRIGALOE	‡225t	70	8k	200P	27C	-	BA	Newport (Gwent), GBIR
2	GLENBROOK	‡225t	71	8k	200P	27C	-	BA	Newport (Gwent), GBIR

CARRIGALOE, GLENBROOK Built as the KYLEAKIN and the LOCHALSH for *Caledonian Steam Packet Company* (later *Caledonian MacBrayne*) for the Kyle of Lochalsh – Kyleakin service. In 1991 replaced by the LOCH DUNVEGAN and the LOCH FYNE and sold to *Marine Transport Services Ltd* who renamed them the CARRIGALOE and the GLENBROOK respectively. They entered service in March 1993.

GLENELG – KYLERHEA FERRY

THE COMPANY The *Glenelg – Kylerhea Ferry* is privately operated.

MANAGEMENT Ferry Master: R MacLeod.

ADDRESS Corriehallie, Inverinate, KYLE IV40 8HD.

TELEPHONE Administration & Reservations: +44 (0)1599 511302, **Fax:** +44 (0)07070 600845.

ROUTE OPERATED *Easter – October only:* Glenelg – Kylerhea (Skye) (10 mins; *(1)*; frequent service).

VESSEL

1	GLENACHULISH	44t	69	9k	12P	6C	-	BSt	Troon, GB	GB

GLENACHULISH Built for the *Ballachulish Ferry Company* for the service between North Ballachulish and South Ballachulish, across the mouth of Loch Leven. In 1975 the ferry was replaced by a bridge and she was sold to *Highland Regional Council* and used on a relief basis on the North Kessock – South Kessock and Kylesku – Kylestrome routes. In 1984 she was sold to the operator of the Glenelg – Kylerhea service. She is the last turntable ferry in operation.

THE HIGHLAND COUNCIL

THE COMPANY The *Highland Council* (previously *Highland Regional Council*) is a British local government authority.

MANAGEMENT Area Road & Transport Manager: James C Tolmie, **Ferry Manager:** J McAuslane.

ADDRESS *Area Office:* Lochybridge Deport, Carr's Corner Industrial Estate, FORT WILLIAM PH33 6TQ, *Ferry Office:* Ferry Cottage, Ardgour, FORT WILLIAM.

TELEPHONE Administration: *Area Office:* +44 (0)1397 703701, *Corran:* +44 (0)1855 841243, *Fort William:* +44 (0)1397 772483, **Reservations:** Not applicable, **Fax:** *Area Office:* +44 (0)1397 705735, *Corran:* +44 (0)1855 841243.

ROUTES OPERATED Vehicle Ferries: Corran – Ardgour (5 mins; *(2,3)*; half hourly), **Passenger Only Ferry:** Fort William – Camusnagaul (10 mins; *(1)*, frequent).

VESSELS

1p	CAILIN AN AISEAG	-	80	7.5k	26P	0C	0L	-	Buckie, GB	GB
2	MAID OF GLENCOUL	‡166t	75	8k	116P	16C	-	BA	Ardrossan, GB	GB
3	ROSEHAUGH	150t	67	8.5k	150P	18C	-	BA	Berwick on Tweed, GB	GB

CAILIN AN AISEAG Built for *Highland Regional Council* and used on the Fort William – Camusnagaul service.

MAID OF GLENCOUL Built for *Highland Regional Council* for the service between Kylesku and Kylestrome. In 1984 the ferry service was replaced by a bridge and she was transferred to the Corran – Ardgour service. In April 1996, ownership transferred to *The Highland Council*.

ROSEHAUGH Built for *Ross and Cromarty County Council* for the service between South Kessock and North Kessock (across the Beauly Firth, north of Inverness). In 1975, ownership was transferred to *Highland Regional Council*. In 1982 a bridge was opened and she was transferred to the Corran – Ardgour route. Following the arrival of the MAID OF GLENCOUL in 1984 she has been the reserve vessel. In April 1996, ownership transferred to *The Highland Council*.

Under construction

4	NEWBUILDING	-	01	8k	150P	30C	-	BA	Hull, GB	GB

NEWBUILDING Under construction for *The Highland Council*. To replace the MAID OF GLENCOUL as main vessel. This vessel will become the reserve and the ROSEHAUGH withdrawn.

ISLES OF SCILLY STEAMSHIP COMPANY

THE COMPANY *Isles of Scilly Steamship Company* is a British private sector company.

MANAGEMENT Group Operations Manager: R Johns, **Marketing Manager:** J Hoelen.

ADDRESS *Scilly:* PO Box 10, Hugh Town, ST MARY'S, Isles of Scilly TR21 0LJ, *Penzance:* Steamship House, Quay Street, PENZANCE, Cornwall, TR18 4BD.

TELEPHONE Administration & Reservations: *Scilly:* +44 (0)1720 422357, *Penzance:* +44 (0)1736 334220, **Fax: *Scilly:*** +44 (0)1720 422192, *Penzance:* +44 (0)1736 351223.

INTERNET Email: sales@islesofscilly-travel.co.uk **Website:** http://www.islesofscilly-travel.co.uk *(English)*

ROUTES OPERATED *Passenger service:* Penzance – St Mary's (Isles of Scilly) (2 hrs 40 mins; *(1,3)*; 1 per day), ***Freight services:*** St Mary's – Tresco/St Martin's/St Agnes/Bryher; *(2)*; irregular).

VESSELS

1	GRY MARITHA	590t	81	10.5k	12P	5C	1L	C	Kolvereid, NO	GB
2	LYONESSE LADY	50t	91	9k	12P	1C	0L	A	Fort William, GB	GB
3p	SCILLONIAN III	1256t	77	15.5k	600P	-	-	C	Appledore, GB	GB

GRY MARITHA Built for *Gjofor* of Norway. In design she is a coaster rather than a ferry. In 1990 sold to *Isles of Scilly Steamship Company*. She operates a freight and passenger service all year (conveying all residents' cars and other vehicles to and from the islands – tourist cars are not conveyed). During the winter she provides the only sea passenger service to the islands, the SCILLONIAN III being laid up.

LYONESSE LADY Built for inter-island ferry work.

SCILLONIAN III Built for the Penzance – St Mary's service. She operates from Easter to late autumn and is laid up in the winter. Last major conventional passenger/cargo ferry built for UK waters and probably Western Europe. Extensively refurbished during winter 1998/99.

KERRERA FERRY

THE COMPANY The *Kerrera Ferry* is privately operated.

MANAGEMENT Ferry Master: Duncan MacEachen.

ADDRESS The Ferry, Isle of Kerrera, By OBAN PA34 4SX

TELEPHONE Administration: +44 (0)1631 563665.

INTERNET Email: kerrera_ferry@hotmail.com

ROUTE OPERATED Gallanach (Argyll) – Kerrera.

CONVENTIONAL FERRY

1	GYLEN LADY		9t	99	8k	12P	1C	-	B	Corpach, GB		GB

GYLEN LADY Built to inaugurate a vehicle ferry service to the Isle of Kerrera, replacing open passenger boat.

ORKNEY FERRIES

THE COMPANY *Orkney Ferries Ltd* (previously the *Orkney Islands Shipping Company*) is a British company, owned by *The Orkney Islands Council*.

MANAGEMENT Operations Director: R S Moore, **Ferry Services Manager:** A Learmonth.

ADDRESS Shore Street, KIRKWALL, Orkney KW15 1LG.

TELEPHONE Administration: +44 (0)1856 872044, **Reservations:** +44 (0)1856 872044, **Fax:** +44 (0)1856 872921, **Telex:** 75475.

INTERNET Website: http://www.orkneyislands.com/travel/orkfer *(English)*

ROUTES OPERATED Kirkwall (Mainland) to Eday (1 hr, 15 mins), Westray (1 hr 25 mins), Sanday (1 hr 25 mins), Stronsay (1 hr 35 mins), Papa Westray (1 hr 50 mins), North Ronaldsay (2 hrs 30 mins) ('North Isles service') (timings are direct from Kirkwall – sailings via other islands take longer; *(1,2,9)*; 1 per day except Papa Westray which is twice weekly and North Ronaldsay which is weekly), Pierowall (Westray) – Papa Westray (25 mins; *(4)*; up to six per day (passenger only)), Kirkwall – Shapinsay (25 mins; *(7)*; 6 per day), Houton (Mainland) to Lyness (Hoy) (35 mins; *(6)*; 5 per day), Flotta (35 mins; *(6)*; 4 per day) and Graemsay (25 mins; *(6)*; weekly) ('South Isles service') (timings are direct from Houton – sailings via other islands take longer), Tingwall (Mainland) to Rousay (20 mins; *(3)*; 6 per day), Egilsay (30 mins; *(3)*; 5 per day) and Wyre (20 mins; *(3)*; 5 per day) (timings are direct from Tingwall – sailings via other islands take longer), Stromness (Mainland) to Moaness (Hoy) (25 mins; *(5)*; 2/3 per day) and Graemsay (25 mins; *(5)*; 2/3 per day) (passenger/cargo service – cars not normally conveyed).

VESSELS

1	EARL SIGURD	771t	90	12k	190P	26C	-	BA	Bromborough, GB	GB
2	EARL THORFINN	771t	90	12k	190P	26C	-	BA	Bromborough, GB	GB
3	EYNHALLOW	79t	87	9.5k	95P	8C	-	BA	Bristol, GB	GB
4p	GOLDEN MARIANA	33t	73	9.5k	40P	0C	-	-	Bideford, GB	GB
5	GRAEMSAY	82t	96	10k	73P	1C	-	C	Troon, GB	GB
6	HOY HEAD	358t	94	9.8k	125P	18C	-	BA	Bideford, GB	GB
7	SHAPINSAY	199t	89	9.5k	91P	12C	-	BA	Hull, GB	GB
8	THORSVOE	400t	91	10.5k	96P	16C	-	BA	Campbeltown, GB	GB
9	VARAGEN	950t	89	12k	144P	33C	5L	BA	Selby, GB	GB

EARL SIGURD, EARL THORFINN Built to inaugurate ro-ro working on the 'North Isles' service (see above).

EYNHALLOW Built to inaugurate ro-ro services from Tingwall (Mainland) to Rousay, Egilsay and

Earl Sigurd (Colin Smith)

St Ola (P&O)

Wyre. In 1991 she was lengthened by 5 metres, to increase car capacity.

GOLDEN MARIANA Passenger only vessel. Generally operates feeder service between Pierowall (Westray) and Papa Westray.

GRAEMSAY Built to operate between Stromness (Mainland), Moaness (Hoy) and Graemsay. Designed to offer an all year round service to these islands, primarily for passengers and cargo.

HOY HEAD Built to replace the THORSVOE on the 'South Isles' service (see above).

SHAPINSAY Built for the service from Kirkwall (Mainland) to Shapinsay.

THORSVOE Built for the 'South Isles' service (see above). In 1994 replaced by new HOY HEAD and became the main reserve vessel for the fleet.

VARAGEN Built for *Orkney Ferries*, a private company established to start a new route between Gills Bay (Caithness, Scotland) and Burwick (South Ronaldsay, Orkney). However, due to problems with the terminals it was not possible to maintain regular services. In 1991, the company was taken over by *OISC* and the VARAGEN became part of their fleet, sharing 'North Isles' services with the EARL SIGURD and the EARL THORFINN and replacing the freight vessel ISLANDER (494t, 1969).

P&O SCOTTISH FERRIES

THE COMPANY *P&O Scottish Ferries* is British private sector company, a subsidiary of the *Peninsular and Oriental Steam Navigation Company*. The name was changed from *P&O Ferries* to *P&O Scottish Ferries* in 1989.

MANAGEMENT Managing Director: Terry Cairns, **Marketing Director:** Scott Colegate.

ADDRESS PO Box 5, Jamieson's Quay, ABERDEEN AB9 8DL.

TELEPHONE Administration: +44 (0)1224 589111 **Reservations:** +44 (0)1224 572615, **Fax:** +44 (0)1224 574411.

INTERNET Email: passenger@poscottishferries.co.uk **Website:** http://www.poscottishferries.co.uk *(English)*

ROUTES OPERATED Scrabster – Stromness (Orkney) (1 hr 45 mins; *(2)*; up to 3 per day)), Aberdeen – Lerwick (Shetland) (direct) (14 hrs; *(1,3)*; up to 4 per week), Aberdeen – Stromness (8 hrs (day), 14 hrs (night)) – Lerwick (8 hrs; *(3)*; 1 per week (2 per week June, July and August)).

VESSELS

1	ST CLAIR	8696t	71	19k	600P	160C	30L	A	Bremerhaven, GY	GB
2	ST OLA	4833t	71	16k	500P	140C	12L	BA	Papenburg, GY	GB
3	ST SUNNIVA	6350t	71	16k	400P	199C	28L	A	Helsingør, DK	GB

ST CLAIR Built as the TRAVEMÜNDE for *Gedser-Travemünde Ruten* for their service between Gedser (Denmark) and Travemünde (Germany). In 1981 she was sold to *Prekookeanska Plovidba* of Yugoslavia, renamed the NJEGOS and used on their services between Yugoslavia, Greece and Italy. In 1984 chartered to *Sally Line* for use on their Ramsgate – Dunkerque service. In 1985 she was taken on a two year charter by *Brittany Ferries*, renamed the TREGASTEL and moved to the Plymouth – Roscoff service. In 1987 she was purchased and re-registered in France. In 1989 she was replaced by the QUIBERON and transferred to *Truckline Ferries* for their Poole – Cherbourg service. In 1991 she was renamed the TREG and sold to *P&O Scottish Ferries*. Following a major refit she was, in 1992, renamed the ST CLAIR and in March 1992 introduced onto the Aberdeen – Lerwick service, replacing the previous ST CLAIR (4468t, 1965). In addition to operating between Aberdeen and Lerwick, in 1993 she inaugurated a weekly peak season Lerwick – Bergen (Norway) service; this service last operated in 1997.

ST OLA Built as the SVEA SCARLETT for *Stockholms Rederi AB Svea* of Sweden and used on the *SL (Skandinavisk Linjetrafik)* service between København (Tuborg Havn) and Landskrona (Sweden). In 1980 she was sold to *Scandinavian Ferry Lines* of Sweden and *Dampskibsselskabet Øresund A/S* of Denmark (jointly owned). Initially she continued to serve Landskrona but later that year the Swedish

terminal became Malmö. In 1981 she operated on the Helsingborg – Helsingør service for a short while, after which she was withdrawn and laid up. In 1982 she was sold to *Eckerö Linjen* of Finland, renamed the ECKERÖ and used on services between Grisslehamn (Sweden) and Eckerö (Åland Islands). In 1991 she was sold to *P&O Scottish Ferries* and renamed the ST OLA. In March 1992 she replaced the previous ST OLA (1345t, 1974) on the Scrabster – Stromness service.

ST SUNNIVA Built as the DJURSLAND for *Jydsk Færgefart* of Denmark for their service between Grenaa (Jylland) and Hundested (Sjælland). In 1974 she was replaced by a larger vessel called DJURSLAND II (4371t, 1974) and switched to the company's other route, between Juelsminde (Jylland) and Kalundborg (Sjælland), being renamed the LASSE II. In 1979 she was sold to *P&O Ferries*, renamed the N F PANTHER ('N F' standing for *'Normandy Ferries'*) and became the third vessel on the Dover – Boulogne service. Sold to *European Ferries* in 1985 and in summer 1986 replaced (with sister vessel NF TIGER (4045t, 1972)) by the FREE ENTERPRISE IV (5049t, 1969) and FREE ENTERPRISE V (5044t, 1970). In 1987 sold to *P&O Scottish Ferries*, renamed the ST SUNNIVA, converted to an overnight ferry and introduced onto the Aberdeen – Lerwick service, supplementing ST CLAIR and also providing a weekly Aberdeen – Stromness – Lerwick and return service (twice weekly in high summer).

PASSAGE EAST FERRY

THE COMPANY *Passage East Ferry Company Ltd* is an Irish Republic private sector company.

MANAGEMENT Managing Director: Derek Donnelly. **Operations Manager:** Conor Gilligan.

ADDRESS Barrack Street, PASSAGE EAST, Co Waterford, Republic of Ireland.

TELEPHONE Administration: +353 (0)51 382480, **Reservations:** Not applicable, **Fax:** +353 (0)51 382598.

INTERNET Email: passageferry@eircom.net **Website:** http://www.passageferry.com

ROUTE OPERATED Passage East (County Waterford) – Ballyhack (County Wexford) (7 mins; *(1)*; frequent service).

VESSEL

1	EDMUND D		300t	68	9k	143P	30C	-	BA	Dartmouth, GB	IR

EDMUND D Built as the SHANNON HEATHER for *Shannon Ferry Ltd* and used on their service between Killimer (County Clare) and Tarbert (County Kerry). Withdrawn from regular service in 1996 and, in 1997, sold to *Passage East Ferry* and renamed the EDMUND D. She entered service in January 1998.

PENTLAND FERRIES

THE COMPANY *Pentland Ferries* is a UK private sector company.

ADDRESS St Margaret's Hope, SOUTH RONALDSAY, Orkney.

TELEPHONE Administration: +44 (0)1856 831226.

ROUTE OPERATED Summer only: Gills Bay (Scotland) – Burwick (South Ronaldsay, Orkney) (service not yet started; start in summer 2000 is subject to confirmation).

CONVENTIONAL FERRY

1	PENTALINA B	1908t	70	16k	250P	47C	-	BAS	Troon, GB	GB

PENTALINA B Built for *David MacBrayne*. She was actually built to operate the Islay service. However, shortly after the order was placed, plans to build a new pier at Redhouse, near the mouth of West Loch Tarbert, were abandoned, so she was not able to operate on this route until *Caledonian MacBrayne* acquired the *Western Ferries'* pier in deeper water at Kennacraig in 1978. She operated on the Gourock – Dunoon service in 1970 and 1971, between Mallaig and Kyle of Lochalsh and Stornoway in 1972 and between Oban and Craignure in 1973. From 1974 until 1978 she operated mainly on the Oban to Castlebay/Lochboisdale service and in addition the winter Oban – Coll/Tiree route. From 1978 until 1989 she operated mainly on the Islay service. In 1989 she was replaced by the CLAYMORE and then replaced the PIONEER as the summer Mallaig – Armadale vessel. Full ro-ro working was introduced on the route in 1994 and she also operated a twice weekly sailing between Mallaig, Lochboisdale and Castlebay and, in 1997, a weekly Mallaig – Coll and Tiree sailing. She was withdrawn in October 1997 and sold to *Pentland Ferries*. In 1998 she was renamed the PENTALINA B. In spring 1998 she was chartered back to *Caledonian MacBrayne* to operate between Oban and Craignure following the breakdown of the ISLE OF MULL. Services have not yet started.

RED FUNNEL FERRIES

THE COMPANY *Red Funnel Ferries* is the trading name of the *Southampton Isle of Wight and South of England Royal Mail Steam Packet Public Limited Company*, a British private sector company. The company was acquired by *Associated British Ports* (owners of Southampton Docks) in 1989.

MANAGEMENT Managing Director: A M Whyte, **Marketing Director:** Ms O H Glass.

ADDRESS 12 Bugle Street, SOUTHAMPTON SO14 2JY.

TELEPHONE Administration: +44 (0)23 8033 3042, **Reservations:** +44 (0)23 8033 4010, **Fax:** +44 (0)23 8063 9438.

INTERNET Email: admin@redfunnel.co.uk **Website:** http://www.redfunnel.co.uk *(English)*

ROUTES OPERATED Conventional Ferries: Southampton – East Cowes (55 mins; *(1,2,3)*; hourly), **Fast Passenger Ferries:** Southampton – Cowes (20 mins; *(4,5,6)*; every half hour).

CONVENTIONAL FERRIES

1	RED EAGLE	3028t	96	13k	900P	140C	16L	BA	Port Glasgow, GB	GB
2	RED FALCON	2881t	94	13k	900P	140C	16L	BA	Port Glasgow, GB	GB
3	RED OSPREY	2881t	94	13k	900P	140C	16L	BA	Port Glasgow, GB	GB

RED EAGLE, RED FALCON, RED OSPREY Built for the Southampton – East Cowes service.

FAST PASSENGER FERRIES

4p	RED JET 1	168t	91	34k	138P	0C	0L	-	Cowes, GB	GB
5p	RED JET 2	168t	91	34k	138P	0C	0L	-	Cowes, GB	GB
6p	RED JET 3	213t	98	34k	190P	0C	0L	-	Cowes, GB	GB
7p•	SHEARWATER 5	62t	80	32k	67P	0C	0L	-	Messina, IT	GB
8p•	SHEARWATER 6	62t	82	32k	67P	0C	0L	-	Messina, IT	GB

RED JET 1, RED JET 2, RED JET 3 FBM Marine catamarans built for the Southampton – Cowes service.

SHEARWATER 5 Rodriquez RHS40 hydrofoil built for the Southampton – Cowes service. Now laid up.

SHEARWATER 6 Rodriquez RHS40 hydrofoil built for the Southampton – Cowes service. In 1998 withdrawn and laid up.

SEABOARD MARINE (NIGG)

THE COMPANY *Seaboard Marine (Nigg) Ltd* is a British private company.

MANAGEMENT Managing Director: Andrew Thoms, **Marketing Manager:** Robert McCrae.

ADDRESS Cliff House, Cadboll, TAIN, Ross-shire.

INTERNET Email: seaboard@zetnet.co.uk

TELEPHONE Administration: +44 (0)1862 871254, **Reservations:** +44 (0)1862 871254, **Fax:** +44 (0)1862 871231.

ROUTE OPERATED Cromarty – Nigg (Ross-shire) (10 mins; *(1)*; half hourly).

Red Jet 1 (Andrew Cooke)

St Faith (Andrew Cooke)

VESSEL

| 1 | CROMARTY ROSE | 28t | 87 | 8k | 50P | 2C | - | B | Ardrossan, GB | GB |

CROMARTY ROSE Built for *Seaboard Marine (Nigg) Ltd.*

SHANNON FERRY LTD

THE COMPANY *Shannon Ferry Ltd* is an Irish Republic private company owned by six families on both sides of the Shannon Estuary.

MANAGEMENT Managing Director: J J Meehan.

ADDRESS Ferry Terminal, KILLIMER, County Clare, Republic of Ireland.

TELEPHONE Administration: +353 (0)65 9053124, **Reservations:** Not applicable, **Fax:** +353 (0)65 9053125.

INTERNET Email: sferry@iol.ie **Website:** http://www.shannonferries.com *(English, German, French, Italian)*

ROUTE OPERATED Killimer (County Clare) – Tarbert (County Kerry) (20 mins; *(1,2)*; hourly (half hourly during July and August).

VESSELS

| 1 | SHANNON DOLPHIN | 501t | 95 | 10k | 350P | 52C | - | BA | Appledore, GB | IR |
| 2 | SHANNON WILLOW | 360t | 78 | 10k | 300P | 44C | - | BA | Bowling, GB | IR |

SHANNON DOLPHIN, SHANNON WILLOW Built for *Shannon Ferry Ltd.*

SHETLAND ISLANDS COUNCIL

THE COMPANY *Shetland Islands Council* is a British Local Government authority.

MANAGEMENT Director of Marine Operations: Capt G H Sutherland, FNI, MRIN, **Divisional Manager – Ferry Operations:** Capt M J Hogan.

ADDRESS Port Administration Building, Sella Ness, MOSSBANK, Shetland ZE2 9QR.

TELEPHONE Administration: +44 (0)1806 244216, 244262, 244252, **Reservations:** +44 (0)1957 722259, **Fax:** +44 (0)1806 242237, **Voice Banks:** +44 (0)1426 980317 (Bressay), +44 (0)1426 983633 (Fair Isle, Foula), +44 (0)1426 980209 (Unst/Fetlar), +44 (0)1426 983633 (Whalsay), +44(0)1426 980735 (Yell), **Telex:** 75142 Sulvoe G.

INTERNET Emails: marine.ferries@shetland.gov.uk Mike.Hoga@sic.shetland.gov.uk

Lara.Jamieson@sic.shetland.gov.uk   **Website:**   http://www.shetland-news.co.uk/tourism/time.html#one *(English)*

ROUTES OPERATED Toft (Mainland) – Ulsta (Yell) (20 mins; *(1,5)*; up to 26 per day), Gutcher (Yell) – Belmont (Unst) (10 mins; *(3)*; 30 per day), Gutcher (Yell) – Oddsta (Fetlar) (25 mins; *(4)*; 6 per day), Lerwick (Mainland) – Maryfield (Bressay) (5 mins; *(10)*; 19 per day), Laxo (Mainland) – Symbister (Whalsay) (30 mins; *(8,12)*; 17 per day), Vidlin (Mainland) – Symbister (Whalsay) (30-45 mins; *(8,12)*; operates when weather conditions preclude using Laxo), Lerwick (Mainland) – Out Skerries (3 hrs; *(2)*; 2 per week), Vidlin (Mainland) – Out Skerries (1 hrs 30 mins; *(2)*; 7 per week), Grutness (Mainland) – Fair Isle (3 hrs; *(6)*; 2 per week), West Burrafirth (Mainland) – Papa Stour (40 mins; *(9)*; 7 per week), Foula – Walls (Mainland) (3 hrs; *(11)*; 2 per week).

VESSELS

1	BIGGA	274t	91	11k	96P	21C	4L	BA	St Monans, GB	GB
2	FILLA	130t	83	9k	12P	6C	1T	A	Flekkefjord, NO	GB
3	FIVLA	230t	85	11k	95P	15C	4L	BA	Troon, GB	GB
4	FYLGA	147t	75	8.5k	93P	10C	2L	BA	Tórshavn, FA	GB

5	GEIRA	226t	88	10.8k	95P	15C	4L	BA	Hessle, GB	GB
6	GOOD SHEPHERD IV	76t	86	10k	12P	1C	0L	C	St Monans, GB	GB
7	GRIMA	147t	74	8.5k	93P	10C	2L	BA	Bideford, GB	GB
8	HENDRA	225t	82	11k	100P	18C	4L	BA	Bromborough, GB	GB
9	KOADA	35t	69	8k	12P	1C	0L	C	Bideford, GB	GB
10	LEIRNA	420t	92	9k	100P	20C	4L	BA	Port Glasgow, GB	GB
11	NEW ADVANCE	21t	96	8.7k	12P	1C	-	C	Penryn, GB	GB
12	THORA	147t	75	8.5k	93P	10C	2L	BA	Tórshavn, FA	GB

BIGGA Used on the Toft (Mainland) – Ulsta (Yell) service.

FILLA Used on the Lerwick (Mainland) – Out Skerries and Vidlin (Mainland) – Out Skerries services. At other times she operates freight and charter services around the Shetland Archipelago. She resembles a miniature oil rig supply vessel. Passenger capacity is 20 from 1 April to 31 October inclusive.

FIVLA Used on the Gutcher (Yell) – Belmont (Unst) service.

FYLGA Used on the Gutcher (Yell) – Oddsta (Fetlar) service.

GEIRA Used on the Toft (Mainland) – Ulsta (Yell) service.

GOOD SHEPHERD IV Used on the service between Grutness (Mainland) and Fair Isle. Vehicles conveyed by special arrangement and generally consist of agricultural vehicles.

GRIMA Used on the Lerwick (Mainland) – Maryfield (Bressay) service until 1992 when she was replaced by the LEIRNA and became a spare vessel.

HENDRA Used on the Laxo (Mainland) – Symbister (Whalsay) service.

KOADA Built as an inshore trawler and bought by the shareholders on Fair Isle to operate to Shetland and named the GOOD SHEPHERD III. In 1986 the service was taken over by *Shetland Islands Council* and she was replaced by GOOD SHEPHERD IV. She was however acquired by the *Shetland Islands Council* and renamed the KOADA. She now operates between West Burrafirth (Mainland) and Papa Stour (operation to Foula having ceased following the delivery of the NEW ADVANCE). Car carrying capacity used occasionally.

LEIRNA Built for *Shetland Islands Council* for the Lerwick – Maryfield (Bressay) service.

NEW ADVANCE Built for the Foula service. Although built in Penryn, she was completed at Stromness in Orkney. She has a Cygnus Marine GM38 hull and is based on the island where she can be lifted out of the water. Vehicle capacity is to take new vehicles to the island – not for tourist vehicles. Mainland ports used are Walls and Scalloway.

THORA Sister vessel to the FYLGA and the GRIMA. After a period as a spare vessel, in 1998 she took over the Laxo – Symbister service from the withdrawn KJELLA.

Shetland Islands Council is at present undertaking feasibility studies for a major fleet and terminal replacement programme.

STRANGFORD LOUGH FERRY SERVICE

THE COMPANY The *Strangford Lough Ferry Service* is operated by the *DRD (Department for Regional Development)*, a Northern Ireland Government Department (formerly operated by *DOE (Northern Ireland)*).

MANAGEMENT Ferry Manager: D Pedlow.

ADDRESS Strangford Lough Ferry Service, STRANGFORD, Co Down BT30 7NE.

TELEPHONE Administration: +44 (0)1396 881637, **Reservations:** Not applicable, **Fax:** +44 (0)1396 881249.

ROUTE OPERATED Strangford – Portaferry (County Down) (10 mins; *(1,2)*; half hourly).

VESSELS

1	PORTA FERRY	151t	62	9k	200P	18C	-	BA	Pembroke, GB	GB
2	STRANGFORD FERRY	186t	69	10k	263P	20C	-	BA	Cork, IR	GB

PORTA FERRY Built as the CLEDDAU KING for *Pembrokeshire County Council* (from 1974 *Dyfed County Council*) for their service between Hobbs Point (Pembroke Dock) and Neyland. Following the opening of a new bridge, the service ceased and, in 1976, she was sold to *DOE (Northern Ireland)* and renamed the PORTA FERRY.

STRANGFORD FERRY Built for *Down County Council*. Subsequently transferred to the *DOE (Northern Ireland)*.

C TOMS & SON LTD

THE COMPANY *C Toms & Son Ltd* is a British private sector company.

MANAGEMENT Managing Director: Mr Alan Toms.

ADDRESS East Street, Polruan, FOWEY, Cornwall PL23 1PB.

TELEPHONE Administration: +44 (0)1726 870232, **Fax:** +44 (0)1726 870318.

ROUTE OPERATED Fowey – Bodinnick (Cornwall) (5 mins; *(1,2)*; frequent).

VESSELS

1	JENACK	60t	4-5k	00	50P	15C	-	BA	Fowey, GB	GB
2	NO 4	-	-	75	48P	8C	-	BA	Fowey, GB	-

JENACK Built by *C Toms & Sons Ltd*. Self propelled and steered.

NO 4 Built by *C Toms & Son Ltd*. Float propelled by motor launch.

VALENTIA ISLAND FERRIES

THE COMPANY *Valentia Island Ferries Ltd* is an Irish Republic private sector company.

MANAGEMENT Manager: Richard Foran.

ADDRESS VALENTIA ISLAND, County Kerry, Republic of Ireland.

TELEPHONE Administration: +353 (0)66 76141, **Reservations:** Not applicable, **Fax:** +353 (0)66 76377.

INTERNET Email: reforan@indigo.ie **Website:** http://www.euroka.com/ferries/valentia.html *(English)*

ROUTE OPERATED Reenard (Co Kerry) – Knightstown (Valentia Island) (5 minutes; *(1)*; frequent service, 1st April – 30th September).

VESSEL

1	GOD MET ONS III	95t	63	-	95P	18C	-	BA	Millingen, NL	IR

GOD MET ONS III Built for *FMHE Res* of the Netherlands for a service across the River Maas between Cuijk and Middelaar. In 1987 a new bridge was opened and the service ceased. She was latterly used on contract work in the Elbe and then laid up. In 1996 acquired by *Valentia Island Ferries* and inaugurated a car ferry service to the island. Note: this island has never had a car ferry service before. A bridge was opened at the south end of the island in 1970; before that a passenger/cargo service operated between Reenard Point and Knightstown.

Thora (Miles Cowsill)

King Harry Ferry (John Hendy)

WESTERN FERRIES

THE COMPANY *Western Ferries (Clyde) Ltd* is a British private sector company.

MANAGEMENT Managing Director: Kenneth C Cadenhead.

ADDRESSES Hunter's Quay, DUNOON PA23 8HJ.

TELEPHONE Administration: +44 (0)1369 704452, **Reservations:** Not applicable, **Fax:** +44 (0)1369 706020.

INTERNET Email: kcadenhead@western-ferries.co.uk

ROUTE OPERATED McInroy's Point (Gourock) – Hunter's Quay (Dunoon) (20 mins; *(1,2,3,4,5)*; half hourly).

VESSELS

1	SOUND OF SANDA	403t	61	10k	220P	37C	-	BA	Arnhem, NL	GB
2	SOUND OF SCALPAY	403t	61	10k	220P	37C	-	BA	Arnhem, NL	GB
3	SOUND OF SCARBA	175t	60	7k	200P	22C	-	BA	Åmål, SW	GB
4	SOUND OF SHUNA	244t	62	7k	200P	25C	-	BA	Åmål, SW	GB
5	SOUND OF SLEAT	466t	61	10k	296P	30C	-	BAS	Hardinxveld, NL	GB

SOUND OF SANDA Built as the G24 for *Amsterdam City Council* and operated from Centraal Station to the other side of the River IJ. In 1996 purchased by *Western Ferries* and renamed the SOUND OF SANDA.

SOUND OF SCALPAY Built as the G23 for *Amsterdam City Council*. In 1995 sold to *Western Ferries* and renamed the SOUND OF SCALPAY.

SOUND OF SCARBA Built as the ÖLANDSSUND III for *Rederi AB Ölandssund* of Sweden for service between Revsudden on the mainland and Stora Rör on the island of Öland. Following the opening of a new bridge near Kalmar, about 4 miles to the South, the ferry service ceased. In 1973 she was sold to *Western Ferries*, renamed the SOUND OF SCARBA and joined the SOUND OF SHUNA their McInroy's Point – Hunter's Quay service. Now relief vessel and also used on contract work in the Clyde estuary.

SOUND OF SHUNA Built as the ÖLANDSSUND IV for *Rederi AB Ölandssund* of Sweden (see the SOUND OF SCARBA above). In 1973 she was sold to *Western Ferries*, renamed the SOUND OF SHUNA and, with the SOUND OF SCARBA, inaugurated the McInroy's Point – Hunter's Quay service.

SOUND OF SLEAT Built as the DE HOORN for the service between Maassluis and Rozenburg, across the 'Nieuwe Waterweg' (New Waterway) in The Netherlands. In 1988 she was purchased by *Western Ferries* and renamed the SOUND OF SLEAT.

WIGHTLINK

THE COMPANY *Wightlink* is a British private sector company, owned by *CINVen Ltd*, a venture capital company. The routes and vessels were previously part of *Sealink* but were excluded from the purchase of most of the *Sealink* operations by *Stena Line AB* in 1990. They remained in *Sea Containers* ownership until purchased by *CINVen*.

MANAGEMENT Chairman: Michael Aiken, **Head of Marketing:** Janet Saville.

ADDRESS PO Box 59, PORTSMOUTH PO1 2XB.

TELEPHONE Administration: +44 (0)23 9281 2011, **Reservations:** 0870 582 7744 (from UK only), +44 (0)23 9281 2011 (from overseas), **Fax:** +44 (0)23 9285 5257, **Telex:** 86440 WIGHTLG.

INTERNET Email: info@wightlink.co.uk **Website:** http://www.wightlink.co.uk *(English)*

ROUTES OPERATED Conventional Ferries: Lymington – Yarmouth (Isle of Wight) (approx 30 mins; *(1,2,3)*; half hourly), Portsmouth – Fishbourne (Isle of Wight) (approx 35 mins; *(4,5,6,7)*; half hourly or hourly depending on time of day), **Fast Passenger Ferries:** Portsmouth – Ryde (Isle of

Wight) (passenger only) (approx 15 mins; *(8,9)*; half hourly/hourly).

CONVENTIONAL FERRIES

1	CAEDMON	‡763t	73	9.5k	512P	58C	6L	BA	Dundee, GB	GB
2	CENRED	‡761t	73	9.5k	512P	58C	6L	BA	Dundee, GB	GB
3	CENWULF	‡761t	73	9.5k	512P	58C	6L	BA	Dundee, GB	GB
4	ST CATHERINE	2036t	83	12.5k	771P	142C	12L	BA	Leith, GB	GB
5	ST CECILIA	2986t	86	12.5k	771P	142C	12L	BA	Selby, GB	GB
6	ST FAITH	3009t	90	12.5k	771P	142C	12L	BA	Selby, GB	GB
7	ST HELEN	2983t	83	12.5k	771P	142C	12L	BA	Leith, GB	GB

CAEDMON Built for Portsmouth – Fishbourne service. In 1983 transferred to the Lymington – Yarmouth service.

CENRED, CENWULF Built for Lymington – Yarmouth service.

ST CATHERINE, ST CECILIA, ST FAITH, ST HELEN Built for the Portsmouth – Fishbourne service.

FAST PASSENGER FERRIES

| 8p | OUR LADY PAMELA | 313t | 86 | 28.5k | 410P | 0C | 0L | - | Hobart, AL | GB |
| 9p | OUR LADY PATRICIA | 313t | 86 | 28.5k | 410P | 0C | 0L | - | Hobart, AL | GB |

OUR LADY PAMELA, OUR LADY PATRICIA InCat 30 m catamarans. Built for the Portsmouth – Ryde service.

WOOLWICH FREE FERRY

THE COMPANY The *Woolwich Free Ferry* is operated by the *London Borough of Greenwich*, a British municipal authority.

MANAGEMENT Ferry Manager: Capt P Deeks.

ADDRESS New Ferry Approach, Woolwich, LONDON SE18 6DX.

TELEPHONE Administration: +44 (0)20 8312 5583, **Reservations:** Not applicable, **Fax:** +44 (0)20 8316 6096.

ROUTE OPERATED Woolwich – North Woolwich (free ferry) (5 mins; *(1,2,3)*; every 9 mins (weekdays – two ferries in operation), every 16 mins (weekends – one ferry in operation)). Note: one ferry always in reserve/under maintenance.

VESSELS

1	ERNEST BEVIN	738t	63	8k	310P	32C	6L	BA	Dundee, GB	GB
2	JAMES NEWMAN	738t	63	8k	310P	32C	6L	BA	Dundee, GB	GB
3	JOHN BURNS	738t	63	8k	310P	32C	6L	BA	Dundee, GB	GB

ERNEST BEVIN, JAMES NEWMAN, JOHN BURNS Built for the *London County Council* who operated the service in 1963. In 1965 ownership was transferred to the *Greater London Council*. Following the abolition of the *GLC* in April 1986, ownership was transferred to the *Department of Transport*. The *London Borough of Greenwich* operate the service on their behalf. An alternative loading is 6 x 18m articulated lorries cars and 14 cars; lorries of this length are too long for the nearby northbound Blackwall Tunnel.

European Seaway (Mike Louagie)

AN SEAWAY

Section 3 – FREIGHT ONLY FERRIES
ARGOMANN FERRY SERVICE

THE COMPANY *ArgoMann Ferry Service GmbH* is a joint venture between *Argo Reederei* of Germany and *Mann & Son (London) Ltd* of Great Britain.

MANAGEMENT Joint Managing Directors: Mr D R Adler (Germany), Mr A W S Binks (UK), **Marketing Director (UK):** Roger G Gibbs.

ADDRESS *Germany:* Argo Reederei RA&S, 2800 BREMEN 1, Am Wall 187/189, Germany, *UK:* Mann & Son (London) Ltd, The Naval House, Kings Quay Street, HARWICH CO12 3JJ.

TELEPHONE Administration & Reservations: *(Germany):* +49 (0)421 36 30 70, *(UK):* +44 (0)1255 245200, **Fax:** *(Germany):* +49 (0)421 32 15 75, *(UK):* +44 (0)1255 24 52 19, **Telex:** *(UK):* 98229.

INTERNET Email: argomann@manngroup.co.uk **Website:** http://www.ArgoMann.com *(English)*

ROUTE OPERATED Harwich (Navyard) *(dep: 22.00 Fri:)* – Cuxhaven *(arr: 17.00 Sat, dep: 19.00 Sat)* – Tallinn *(arr: 15.00 Mon, dep: 21.00 Mon)* – Turku *(arr: 08.00 Tue, dep: 17.30 Tue)* – Bremerhaven *(arr: 18.00 Thu, dep: 21.00 Thu)* – Harwich *(arr: 16.00 Fri)*; *(1)*; one per week.

VESSEL

1	AMAZON	18205t	99	20k	12P	130C	160T	A	Rauma, FI		FI

Built as the ESTRADEN for *Rederi Ab Engship* of Finland and chartered to *ArgoMann*. Later in 1999 renamed the AMAZON.

CCTL

THE COMPANY *CCTL (CargoConnect Transport + Logistics Ltd)* is a UK company.

MANAGEMENT Managing Director: Joachim Dirks, **Marketing Manager:** John Richmond.

ADDRESS CCTL, 2 Crusader Business Park, Stephenson Road, CLACTON-ON-SEA, Essex CO15 4XA.

TELEPHONE Administration *(Clacton):* +44 (0)1255 476947, **Reservations** *(Hull):* +44 (0)1482 701584, **Fax** *(Hull):* +44 (0) 1482 701594.

INTERNET Email: service@cctl.de

ROUTE OPERATED Hull *(dep: 21.00 Mon, 20.00 Wed, 09.00 Fri, 21.00 Sat)* – Hamburg (Germany) *(dep: 21.00 Mon, 20.00 Wed, 09.00 Fri, 22.00 Sat)* (30 – 33 hrs; *(1,2)*; 4 per week).

VESSELS

1	CCTL HAMBURG	8454t	77	16.5k	12P	-	72T	A	Rauma, FI	MA
2	PASEWALK	10243t	83	14k	12P	-	90T	A	Wismar, GE	LB

CCTL HAMBURG Built as the MEKHANIK FEDOROV for *Latvian Shipping* of the former Soviet Union. In 1991 renamed the MEHANIKIS FJODOROVS (the same name but in Latvian rather than Russian). She was generally used on services from Latvia to North West Europe. In 1999 she was chartered to *CCTL*, renamed the CCTL HAMBURG and placed on their Hamburg – Hull service.

PASEWALK Built as the AUERSBERG for *DSR RORO* of Germany (DDR) and used on various services. Following the unification of Germany, she was in 1993 transferred to subsidiary *Euroseabridge*. She was then placed on services between Germany and Lithuania and Denmark and Lithuania. In 1999 she was chartered *CCTL* and placed on a new service between Hull and Hamburg.

Dart 4 (Mike Louagie)

Clementine (Mike Louagie)

COBELFRET FERRIES

THE COMPANY *Cobelfret Ferries nv* is a Belgian private sector company, a subsidiary of *Cobelfret nv* of Antwerpen.

MANAGEMENT Operations Manager (Belgium): Marc Vandersteen, **UK:** *Purfleet, Dagenham and Sheerness services:* Cobelfret Ferries UK Ltd – **General Manager, Line & Agency Division:** Phil Tomkins, *Immingham Services:* Exxtor Shipping Services Ltd – **Director & General Manager:** Jeffe Baker.

ADDRESS *Belgium:* Sneeuwbeslaan 14, B-2610 ANTWERP, Belgium, *UK Purfleet:* Purfleet Thames Terminal, London Road, PURFLEET, Essex RM19 1RP, *UK Immingham:* Exxtor Shipping Services Ltd, PO Box 40, Manby Road, IMMINGHAM, South Humberside DN40 3EG.

TELEPHONE Administration: *Belgium:* +32 (0)3 829 90 11, *UK:* +44 (0)1708 865522, **Reservations:** *Belgium:* +32 (0)50 54 72 00, *UK (Purfleet Services):* +44 (0)1708 891199, *(Immingham Services):* +44 (0)1469 551341, **Fax:** *Belgium – Admin:* +32 (0)3 237 7646, *Belgium – Reservations:* +32 (0)50 54 53 48, *UK – Admin:* +44 (0)1708 866418, *UK – Reservations (Purfleet):* +44 (0)1708 890853, *UK – Reservations (Immingham):* +44 (0)1469 573739.

INTERNET Email: *Zeebrugge:* pur.cobzee@cobelfretferries.be   *Purfleet:* cobferry1@aol.com **Website:** http://www.cobelfret.com *(Not yet active)*

ROUTES OPERATED

Zeebrugge *(dep: 04.00, 10.00, 16.00, 22.00)* – Purfleet *(dep: 06.00, 12.00, 18.00, 23.00)* (8 hrs; *(2,4,5,6,8,13,14,15,16)*, 4 per day), Zeebrugge *(dep: 07.00, 19.00)* – Dagenham *(dep: 10.00, 22.00)* (contract service for Ford Motor Company) (8 hrs 30 mins; *(2,4,5,8,13,14,15,16)*), Zeebrugge *(dep: 18.00)* – Immingham *(dep: 18.00)* (14 hrs; *(3,10,12)*; 1 per day), Rotterdam (Europoort) *(dep: 17.30)* – Immingham *(dep: 17.30)* (14 hrs; *(1,7)*; 1 per day), Zeebrugge – Göteborg (36 hrs; *(9,11,17)*; 4 per week at present) (this service is operated by *Wagenborg* of the Netherlands for the *Stora-Enso* paper and board group, primarily for the conveyance of their products. *Cobelfret Ferries* act as handling agents at Zeebrugge and market the surplus capacity on the vessels, which is available for general ro-ro traffic. Although this route is strictly outside the scope of this book it is included for the sake of completeness).

VESSELS

1	AMANDINE	14715t	78	14.5k	12P	-	150T	A	Kiel, GY	GB
2	CELANDINE	23986t	00	18k	12P	635C	188T	A	Sakaide, JA	GB
3	CLEMENTINE	23986t	97	17.8k	24P	654C	156T	A	Sakaide, JA	LX
4	CYMBELINE	11866t	92	14.5k	10P	790C	130T	A2	Dalian, CH	LX
5	EGLANTINE	10035t	89	14.5k	10P	790C	120T	A2	Dalian, CH	LX
6	LOVERVAL	10931t	78	17k	12P	675C	112T	A2	Lödöse, SW	LX
7	LYRA	12817t	78	15k	12P	-	145T	A	Kiel, GY	AT
8	MELUSINE	23987t	99	18k	12P	635C	188T	A	Sakaide, JA	LX
9	SCHIEBORG	18500t	00	17k	12P	-	156T	A	Lübeck, GY	NL
10	SOUTHERN CARRIER	16947t	78	15k	12P	180C	183T	A	Landskrona, SW	SW
11	SPAARNEBORG	18500t	00	17k	12P	-	156T	A	Lübeck, GY	NL
12	STENA SHIPPER	12337t	79	18.5k	12P	-	70T	A2	Papenburg, GY	BA
13	SYMPHORINE	10030t	88	14.5k	10P	790C	130T	A2	Dalian, CH	LX
14	UNDINE	11854t	91	14.5k	10P	790C	130T	A2	Dalian, CH	LX
15	VALENTINE	23987t	99	18k	12P	635C	188T	A	Sakaide, JA	GB
16	VICTORINE	23987t	00	18k	12P	635C	188T	A	Sakaide, JA	GB

AMANDINE Built as the MERZARIO PERSIA for *Merzario Line* of Italy and used on services between Italy and the Middle East. In 1986 she was chartered to *Grimaldi* of Italy and renamed the PERSIA, continuing on Middle East services. In 1988 she was sold to *Eimskip* of Iceland and renamed the BRUARFOSS. She was used on their service between Reykjavik, Immingham, Hamburg and

Rotterdam. In 1996, the ro-ro service was replaced by a container only service and she was withdrawn. She was renamed the VEGA and was placed a number of short term charters including *Suardiaz* of Spain and *Fred. Olsen Lines*. In 1998, she was sold to *Cobelfret* and renamed the AMANDINE.

CELANDINE, MELUSINE, VALENTINE, VICTORINE Built for *Cobelfret*. Similar to the CLEMENTINE. The CELANDINE was originally to be called the CATHERINE and the VICTORINE the CELANDINE. The names were changed before delivery.

CLEMENTINE Built for *Cobelfret*. Currently used on the Zeebrugge – Immingham service. Sister vessel, delivered as the CELESTINE, is currently on charter to the British *Ministry of Defence* as the SEA CRUSADER.

CYMBELINE, EGLANTINE, SYMPHORINE, UNDINE Built for *Cobelfret*. Currently used on the Zeebrugge – Purfleet and Zeebrugge – Dagenham (Ford) services.

LOVERVAL Built as the VALLMO for the *Johansson Group* of Sweden and undertook a variety of charters. In 1982 she was sold to *Cobelfret* and renamed the MATINA. In 1984 renamed the LOVERVAL. In recent years has been chartered out but she is currently used on the Zeebrugge – Purfleet service.

LYRA Built as the MERZARIO ARABIA for *Merzario Line* of Italy and used on services between Italy and the Middle East. In 1986 she was chartered to *Ignazio Messina* of Italy and renamed the JOLLY OCRA, continuing on Middle East services. In 1987, she was chartered to *Lloyd Triestino Line* of Italy and renamed the DUINO. In 1988 she was sold to *Eimskip* of Iceland, renamed the LAXFOSS and used on their services from Iceland to the UK, Netherlands and Germany. In 1996, the ro-ro service was replaced by a container only service and she was withdrawn. She was chartered to *Nordana Line* of Denmark and renamed the SILKEBORG. In 1997 she was renamed the LYRA and briefly chartered to *Dart Line* and used on their Dartford – Zeebrugge service. Later in 1997 she was chartered to *Exxtor Ferries* to operate between Immingham and Rotterdam. When the service was taken over by *Cobelfret* later in the year, the charter was transferred to them and she continues to operate between Immingham and Rotterdam.

SCHIEBORG, SPAARNEBORG Built for *Wagenborg* of the Netherlands and time chartered to *Stora-Enso* to operate between Zeebrugge and Göteborg .

SOUTHERN CARRIER Built as the ANNA ODEN for *AB Norsjöfrakt* of Sweden and chartered to *Oden Line* of Sweden for North Sea services, in particular associated with the export of Volvo cars and trucks from Göteborg. In 1980 *Oden Line* was taken over by *Tor Lloyd AB*, a joint venture between *Tor Line* and *Broströms AB* and the charter transferred to them, moving to *Tor Line* in 1981 when *DFDS* took over. In 1987 she was lengthened and on re-entry into service in early 1988 was renamed the TOR FLANDRIA and became regular vessel on the Göteborg – Ghent (Belgium) service, largely operated for Volvo. In 1999 the charter was ended and she was renamed the SOUTHERN CARRIER. Chartered to *Cobelfret Ferries*.

STENA SHIPPER Built as the NESTOR for *Nestor Reederei* of Germany and chartered out. In 1984 she was renamed the NESTOR 1 but in 1985 she resumed the name NESTOR. In 1986 she was chartered to *Nile Dutch Line* and operated between Northern Europe and West Africa. In 1989 the charter terminated and she was renamed the NESTOR; the following year she was chartered to *Stream Line*, renamed the CARIBBEAN STREAM and placed on service between Europe and South America. This charter ended in 1991 and she resumed the name NESTOR. In 1994 she was purchased by *Stena Rederi AB*, renamed the STENA SHIPPER and chartered to *Cobelfret*. Generally used on the Zeebrugge – Immingham service. In September 1999 inaugurated the Zeebrugge – Göteborg service, pending the delivery of purpose built ships in 2000. Now returned to the Zeebrugge – Immingham service.

Under construction

| 17 | SLINGEBORG | 18500t | 00 | 17k | 12P | - | 156T | A | Lübeck, GY | NL |

SLINGEBORG Under construction for *Wagenborg* of the Netherlands. To be time chartered to *Stora-Enso* to operate between Zeebrugge and Göteborg.

COMMODORE FERRIES

THE COMPANY *Commodore Ferries (CI) Ltd* is a Guernsey private sector company.

MANAGEMENT & ADDRESS See Section 1.

TELEPHONE Administration & Reservations: +44 (0)1481 728620, **Fax:** +44 (0)1481 728521.

INTERNET Email: JVidamour@CommodoreFerries.com

ROUTE OPERATED Portsmouth *(dep: 09.30*, 20.30)* – Guernsey *(dep: 04.00, 18.00*)* (6 hrs 30 min) – Jersey *(dep: 08.00, 22.00*)* (10 hrs 30 min; *(1.)*; 2 per day). **operated by ro-pax ferry* COMMODORE CLIPPER – see Section 1. Also Saturday charter from Jersey to St Malo for *Morvan Fils*: Jersey *(dep: 11.00 Sat)* – St Malo *(arr: 14.00 Sat, dep: 17.00 Sat)* – Jersey *(arr: 06.00 Sun)* *((1)*; 1 per week).

VESSEL

1	COMMODORE GOODWILL	11166t	96	18.3k	12P	-	95T	A	Vlissingen, NL	BA

COMMODORE GOODWILL Built for *Commodore Ferries.*

DART LINE

THE COMPANY *Dart Line Ltd* is a British private sector company owned by *Jacobs Holdings plc.* It took over the Dartford – Vlissingen service from *Sally Ferries* in 1996.

MANAGEMENT Managing Director: Stephen Hepplewhite, **Marketing Director:** Kevin Miller.

ADDRESS Crossways Business Park, Thames Europort, DARTFORD, Kent DA2 6QB.

TELEPHONE Administration & Reservations: +44 (0)1322 281122, **Fax:** +44 (0)1322 281133.

INTERNET Email: sales@dartline.co.uk **Website:** http://www.dartline.co.uk *(English)*

ROUTES OPERATED Dartford *(dep: 09.00 Tue-Fri & Sun, 21.00 Sun, Tue-Sat, 20.00 Mon)* – Vlissingen *(dep: 10.00 Tue-Fri, Sun, 22.00 Tue-Sat, 21.00 Mon)* (9 hrs 30 mins; *(2,3)*; 2 per day). Dartford *(dep: 03.30 Tue-Fri, 05.00 Sat, 08.30 Tue-Fri, 20.30 daily)* – Zeebrugge *(dep: 09.30 Tue-Fri, 16.30 Mon-Sat, 21.30 Sun-Fri)* (8 hrs 30 mins – 9 hrs; *(1,4,5)*; 3 per day).

VESSELS

1	DART 2	9082t	84	15k	12P	-	100T	A	Galatz, RO	BA
2	DART 3	9088t	85	15k	12P	-	100T	A	Galatz, RO	BA
3	DART 4	9088t	85	16.5k	12P	-	100T	A	Galatz, RO	BA
4	DART 8	22748t	80	18k	12P	-	190T	A	Sakaide, JA	BA
5	DART 9	22748t	80	18k	12P	-	190T	A	Sakaide, JA	BM

DART 2 Built as the BALDER HAV for *K/S A/S Balder RO/RO No 2* of Norway. In 1985 acquired by *Navrom* of Romania, renamed the BAZIAS 2 and used on Mediterranean services. In 1995 chartered to *Dart Line* and renamed the DART 2. Operations began in 1996. Later in 1996 she was sold to *Jacobs Holdings.* Now operates on the Dartford – Zeebrugge route.

DART 3 Built as the BALDER STEN for *K/S A/S Balder RO/RO No 2* of Norway (part of the *Parley Augustsson* group). In 1995 acquired by *Navrom* of Romania and renamed the BAZIAS 3. In 1991 chartered to *Sally Ferries* for the Ramsgate – Oostende freight service and subsequently purchased by a joint *Sally Ferries/Romline* company. In 1993 renamed the SALLY EUROROUTE and re-registered in The Bahamas. In October 1996 chartered to *Belfast Freight Ferries* and renamed the MERLE. In 1997 *Sally Ferries'* interests in her were purchased by *Jacobs Holdings.* In January 2000 joined *Dart Line* and was placed on the Vlissingen service, being renamed the DART 3.

DART 4 Built as the BALDER BRE for *K/S A/S Balder RO/RO No 2* of Norway. Later in 1985 acquired by *Navrom* of Romania and renamed the BAZIAS 4. In 1991 chartered to *Sally Ferries* for the Ramsgate – Oostende freight service and subsequently purchased by *Rosal SA*, a joint *Sally*

Commodore Ferries has now introduced a new RoPax vessel "Commodore Clipper" on their well established and efficient twice daily Roll-on Roll-off service between Portsmouth and the Channel Islands.

This new vessel not only maintains the present freight carrying capacity but in addition, in partnership with **Condor Ferries**, offers a new all weather route connecting Portsmouth to Jersey and Guernsey.

Commodore Clipper has quality facilities for 500 passengers and their cars.

SECTION 3 – FREIGHT ONLY FERRIES

Ferries/Romline company. In 1993 renamed the SALLY EUROLINK and re-registered in The Bahamas. In 1997 *Sally Ferries'* interests in her were purchased by *Jacobs Holdings*. She was later transferred to *Dart Line* and renamed the DART 4. In 1998 she was chartered to *Belfast Freight Ferries*. She returned to *Dart Line* in February 1999. She now operates on the Dartford – Vlissingen route.

DART 8 Built as the XI FENG KOU, a deep sea ro-ro/container ship for *China Ocean Shipping Company* of the People's Republic of China for service between the USA, Australia and New Zealand. In 1999, purchased by *Jacobs Holdings*. After delivery, she was converted in Nantong, China to short sea ro-ro specification, including the fitting of a stern ramp (replacing the quarter ramp) and luxury accommodation for 12 drivers and entered service in August 1999 on the Dartford – Zeebrugge service.

DART 9 Built as the GU BEI KOU. As the DART 8. She entered service in September 1999 on the Dartford – Zeebrugge service.

Dart Line also owns the MONT VENTOUX, on charter to *Sudcargos* of France; she is the former ZHANG JIA KOU, a sister of the DART 8 and DART 9 and was rebuilt as the DART 10. It is possible she will be transferred to the Dartford – Zeebrugge service in due course.

DFDS TOR LINE

THE COMPANY *DFDS Tor Line Group A/S* is the freight division of *DFDS A/S*, a Danish private sector company. *North Sea Line* (previously owned by *Fred. Olsen*) were taken over in January 1999, now marketed as *NorBridge*. Later in 1999 *DFDS Tor Line* was merged with *DFDS Liner Division* (Denmark – UK services), taking the name of the former but with HQ in Denmark. The joint service with *Stena Line AB* between Göteborg and Harwich is marketed as *Stena Tor Line*.

MANAGEMENT Managing Director: Oddbjörn Fastesson, **Marketing Director:** Eric Nilsson, **Managing Director UK:** Ebbe K. Pedersen.

ADDRESS *Denmark (Head Office):* Sankt Annæ Plads 30, DK-1295 KØBENHAVN K, Denmark, *UK:* Nordic House, Western Access Road, Immingham Dock, IMMINGHAM, South Humberside DN40 2LZ.

TELEPHONE Administration & Reservations: *Denmark (Head Office):* +45 33 42 33 00, *UK:* +44 (0)1469 575231, **Fax: *Denmark:*** +45 33 42 33 01, *UK:* +44 (0)1469 552690.

INTERNET Email: info@dfdstorline.com **Website:** http://www.dfdstorline.com *(English)*

ROUTES OPERATED Immingham *(dep: 15.00 Mon, 22.00 Tue, 00.01 Thu, 11.00 Fri, 23.00 Sat)* – Esbjerg *(dep: 19.00 Mon, 21.00 Tue, 01.00 Thu, 19.00 Fri, 16.00 Sat)* (21 hrs; *(3,5)*; 5 per week), Immingham *(dep: 10.00 Sun, 21.30 Tue, 03.00 Fri)* – Cuxhaven *(dep: 19.00 Mon, 01.00 Thu, 08.00 Sat)* (22 hrs; *(1)*; 3 per week), Esbjerg *(dep: 20.00 Tue, 21.00 Thu, 23.00 Sat)* – Harwich *(dep: 23.00 Sun, 20.00 Wed, 20.00 Fri)* (20 hrs; *(6)*; 3 per week (complemented by sailings from passenger vessel DANA ANGLIA giving 6 per week), Göteborg *(dep: 19.00 Tue, 19.00 Thu, 18.00 Sat)* – Harwich *(dep: 19.00 Tue, 19.00 Thu, 16.00 Sat)* (36 hrs; *(8,11 (4 not 11 until third newbuilding delivered))*; 3 per week), **Phasing-in schedule pending delivery of third newbuilding:** Göteborg *(dep: 23.59 Sun, 19.00 Mon-Fri, 14.00 Sat)* – Immingham *(dep: 23.59 Sun, 20.00 Mon-Fri, 13.00 Sat)* – (38 hrs; *(11,12,19,20)*; 7 per week), **Final schedule after delivery of third newbuilding:** Göteborg *(dep: 21.00 Sun-Mon)* – Immingham *(dep: 04.00 Sun-Fri, 10.00 Sat)* – (26 hrs; *(19,20,21)*; 7 per week), Immingham *(dep: 19.00 Mon, 17.00 Tue-Fri, 17.30 Sat)* – Rotterdam *(dep: 19.00 Mon, 18.00 Tue-Sat)* (14 hrs 30 mins); *(7,9)*, 6 per week), Göteborg *(dep: 03.00 Sun, Tue-Sat)* – Gent (Belgium) *(dep: 03.00 Sun, Tue-Sat)* (42 hrs; *(10,12,13,18 (chartered vessel not 18 until final newbuilding delivered)*; 6 per week), Fredericia *(dep. 01.00 Sat (via København), 21.00 Tue (direct))* – Klaìpeda (Lithuania) *(dep. 21.30 Sun (via København), 12.30 Thu (direct)) (2)*; 2 per week), København *(dep. 14.00 Sat (direct), 21.00 Mon (via Fredericia)* – Klaìpeda (Lithuania) *(21.30 Sun (direct), 12.30 Thu (via Fredericia) ((2)*; 2 per week), **Norway – Bremerhaven/Hamburg:** Oslo *(dep: 19.00 Wed)* – Fredrikstad *(arr: 07.00 Thu, dep: 12.00 Thu)* – Voldsfjorden *(arr: 16:00 Thu, dep: 00.01 Fri)* – Kristiansand *(arr: 07.00 Fri, dep: 13.00 Fri)* – Bremerhaven *(arr: 07.00 Sun, dep: 12.00 Sun)* – Hamburg *(arr: 01.00 Mon, dep: 23.00 Mon)* – Oslo *(arr: 07.00 Wed)* (currently operated by container ship but could be replaced by ro-ro at some stage), **Norway – Rotterdam:** Oslo *(dep: 16.00 Tue)* –

Tor Selandia (Mike Louagie)

Commodore Goodwill (Miles Cowsill)

Brevik (arr: 22.00 Tue, dep: 03.00 Wed) – Kristiansand *(arr: 09.00 Wed, dep: 11.00 Wed)* – Rotterdam *(arr: 15.00 Thu, dep: 21.00 Thu)* – Kristiansand *(arr: 23:59 Sat, dep: 02.00 Sat)* – Brevik *(arr 08.00 Sat dep: 10.00 Sat)* – Oslo *(arr: 16.00 Sat, dep: 21.00 Sat)* – Rotterdam *(arr: 07.00 Mon, dep: 16.00 Tue)* – Brevik *(arr: 01.00 Thu, dep: 05.00 Thu)* – Oslo *(arr: 11.00 Thu, dep: 17.00 Thu)* – Rotterdam *(arr: 07.00 Sat, dep: 14.00 Sat)* – Kristiansand *(arr: 18.00 Sun, dep: 20.00 Sun)* – Oslo *(arr: 08.00 Mon)* (14,17), **Norway – the UK:** Oslo *(dep: 14.00 Sun)*, Kristiansand *(arr: 00:01 Mon, dep: 03.00 Mon)* Immingham *(arr: 08:00 Tue, dep: 18.30 Tue)*, – Oslo *(arr: 08:00 Thu, dep 16:00 Thu)* – Brevik *(arr: 22:00 Thu, dep: 02:00 Fri)* Immingham *(arr: 08.00 Sat, dep: 16.00 Sat)* – Herøya *(arr: 23.00 Sun, dep: 02.00 Mon)* – Oslo *(arr: 08.00 Mon, dep: 12.00 Tue)* – Brevik *(arr: 18:00 Tue, dep: 22.00 Tue)* – Kristiansand *(arr: 04.00 Wed, dep: 07.00 Wed)* – Immingham *(arr: 10:00 Thu, dep: 18.00 Thu)* – Felixstowe *(arr: 08.00 Fri, dep: 16:00 Fri)* – Oslo *(arr: 07:00 Sun)* (15,16).

Space is also used for freight on *DFDS Seaways'* passenger vessels between Hamburg – Harwich (3 per week), Gothenburg – Kristiansand/Newcastle (2-3 per week) and IJmuiden – Newcastle (daily as from 20th April).

Note: Non-UK routes shown above are strictly outside the scope of this book but are shown for the sale of completeness.

VESSELS

1	DANA CIMBRIA	12189t	86	17k	12P	-	150T	A	Frederikshavn, DK	DK
2	DANA CORONA	12110t	72	16.5	12P	-	105T	A2	Rauma, FI	DK
3	DANA FUTURA	18469t	96	20k	12P	-	170T	AS	Donada, IT	IT
4	DANA HAFNIA	11125t	79	16k	12P	400C	121T	A2	Lödöse, SW	DK
5	DANA MAXIMA	17068t	78	17k	12P	-	210T	A	Osaka, JA	DK
6	DANA MINERVA	21213t	78	18k	0P	-	171T	A	Oskarshamn, SW	DK
7	NORSE MERSEY	14820t	95	19.5k	61P	-	160T	A	Donada, IT	IT
8	STENA GOTHICA	14406t	75	16k	12P	-	150T	A	Sandefjord, NO	SW
9	TOR ANGLIA	17492t	77	15k	12P	-	206T	A	Kiel, GY	SW
10	TOR BELGIA	21491t	78	18k	12P	200C	224T	AS	Dunkerque, FR	SW
11	TOR CALEDONIA	14424t	77	16k	12P	-	160T	A	Frederikstad, NO	DK
12	TOR DANIA	21850t	78	18k	12P	200C	224T	AS	Dunkerque, FR	DK
13	TOR FLANDRIA	33652t	82	19k	12P	300C	240T	A	Malmö, SW	SW
14	TOR GOTHIA	12259t	71	17k	12P	-	130T	A	Sandefjord, NO	GB
15	TOR HOLLANDIA	12254t	73	15.5k	12P	-	130T	A	Sandefjord, NO	GB
16	TOR HUMBRIA	20165t	78	18.5k	0P	-	178T	A	Oskarshamn, SW	SW
17	TOR NORVEGIA	12494t	75	19k	12P	-	142T	A	Florø, NO	NO
18	TOR SCANDIA	33652t	82	19k	12P	300C	240T	A	Malmö, SW	SW
19	TOR SELANDIA	24196t	98	21.1k	12P	-	230T	A	Ancona, IT	SW
20	TOR SUECIA	24200t	99	21.1k	12P	-	230T	A	Ancona, IT	SW

DANA CIMBRIA Launched as the MERCANDIAN EXPRESS II and immediately bare-boat chartered to *DFDS* for their North Sea freight services, being renamed the DANA CIMBRIA. Purchased by *DFDS* in 1989. Until 1996, generally used on Immingham and North Shields – Esbjerg services; between 1996 and 1998 she operated between Immingham and Esbjerg. In 1998 she was transferred to the Immingham – Cuxhaven service.

DANA CORONA Built as the ANTARES for *Finska Ångfartygs A/B* of Finland and used on services between Finland and Germany. In 1975 she was renamed the RHEINFELS. In 1977 she was sold to *Nedlloyd* of the Netherlands and renamed the NEDLLOYD ROCKANJE. In the early eighties she was chartered to *Constellation Line* of the USA for services between the USA and Europe. In 1983 she was sold to *Kotka Line* of Finland, renamed the KOTKA LILY and used on their services between Finland, UK and West Africa. In 1985 she was chartered to *Jahre Line* of Norway, renamed the JALINA and operated freight services between Oslo and Kiel. Two years later, she returned to Baltic waters, being chartered to *Finncarriers* and renamed the FINNROVER. In 1988 she was chartered to *Kent Line*, renamed the SEAHORSE and used on their Dartford – Zeebrugge service. In 1991 she was chartered to *DFDS* and in 1992 she was renamed the DANA CORONA. She was initially used on the service between the Immingham and Cuxhaven (Germany) but in 1995 she was transferred to the Fredericia – København – Klaìpeda (Lithuania) service.

DANA FUTURA Built for *DFDS*. Initially operated mainly between Esbjerg and Harwich, in 2000 she is expected to operate mainly between Esbjerg and Immingham.

DANA HAFNIA Built as the LINNÉ and chartered to *OT Africa Line* for services between Italy and Libya. In 1985 sold and renamed the BELINDA; she was employed on a variety of charters including *DFDS* and *Stena Line* until 1988 when she was sold to *Dannebrog* of Denmark and renamed the NORDBORG. Chartering continued, including *Kent Line* and *DFDS* again, and in 1993 she was chartered to *Cobelfret*. In 1994 she was sold to *DFDS* and renamed the DANA HAFNIA. Initially operated on *Tor Line* services but in 1995 transferred to *DFDS* to operate between Harwich and Esbjerg. Following delivery of the DANA FUTURA in 1996 she was transferred to the Immingham – Cuxhaven service. In 1998 she was replaced by the DANA CIMBRIA and was due to be transferred to *DFDS Baltic Line* to operate between Fredericia (Denmark) – København – Klaìpeda (Lithuania). However, following the collapse of the Russian economy, she was, instead, chartered to *Cobelfret Ferries*. In 1999 she was transferred to *DFDS Tor Line* and used on Norway services. Later in 1999 she was chartered to *Århus-Kalundborg Linien* of Denmark to operate between Århus and Kalundborg as the KATTEGAT SYD. However, this venture only lasted a few weeks and she was returned to *DFDS Tor Line* and resumed the name DANA HAFNIA. She initially returned to the Norway service and was then transferred to the Göteborg – Harwich route. It is not at present clear what will happen to her when the third newbuilding enters service as it is currently planned to replace her with the TOR CALEDONIA.

DANA MAXIMA Built for *DFDS* for their North Sea services. Until 1996, generally used on Esbjerg – Grimsby and North Shields. Now mainly operates between Esbjerg and Immingham. In summer 1995 she was lengthened to increase trailer capacity.

DANA MINERVA Built as the BANDAR ABBAS EXPRESS for *A/S Skarhamns Oljetransport* of Norway and chartered out. In 1980 renamed the SAUDI EXPRESS. During the early eighties she undertook a number of charters including *Mideastcargo* for services between Europe and the Middle East, *Atlanticargo* for services from Europe to USA and Mexico and *OT West Africa Line* from Europe to West Africa. In 1983 she was chartered to *Ignazio Messina* of Italy, renamed the JOLLY AVORIO and used on services from Italy to the Middle East. In 1986 this charter ended and she briefly reverted to the name the SAUDI EXPRESS before being chartered again to *OT West Africa Line* and renamed the KARAWA. In 1987 she was sold to *Fred. Olsen Lines* who renamed her the BORACAY; she operated between Norway and Northern Europe. In 1998 she was sold to *DFDS*, renamed the DANA MINERVA and placed on the Esbjerg – Immingham route. In 2000 she is expected to operate mainly on the Esbjerg – Harwich route.

NORSE MERSEY Built for Italian interests for charter. On delivery, chartered to *Norse Irish Ferries* and named the NORSE MERSEY. In July 1997 she was replaced by the MERSEY VIKING and was chartered to *P&O Ferrymasters*. In 1999 she was chartered to *DFDS Tor Line* and placed on their Immingham – Rotterdam service.

STENA GOTHICA Built as the MELBOURNE TRADER for *Australian National Line* for services in Australia. She was of the same design as *Tor Line's* TOR GOTHIA class. In 1987 sold to *Forest Shipping*. In 1988 she was chartered to *Elbe-Humber RoLine* and renamed the RAILRO 2. Later in 1988 she was sold to *Stena Line*, renamed the STENA PROJECT and was then chartered by them to *CoTuNav* of Tunisia and renamed the MONAWAR L. In 1990, following the start of a joint *Stena Line/DFDS TorLine* service between Göteborg and Harwich (operated by *DFDS Tor Line*) she was renamed the STENA GOTHICA, lengthened by 31m and chartered to *DFDS Tor Line*, operating on a combined Göteborg -Immingham/Harwich service. In 1999 the Immingham and Harwich services were separated. She initially operated between Göteborg and Immingham but was then transferred to the Göteborg – Harwich service.

TOR ANGLIA Built as the MERZARIO GALLIA and chartered to *Merzario Line* of Italy for services between Italy and Saudi Arabia. In 1981 she was chartered to *Wilhelmsen*, renamed the TANA and used between USA and West Africa. In 1983 she was chartered to *Salenia AB* of Sweden and renamed the NORDIC WASA. In 1987 she had a brief period on charter to *Atlantic Marine* as the

AFRICAN GATEWAY and in 1988 she was sold to *Tor Line* and renamed the TOR ANGLIA. In 1989 an additional deck was added. In recent years she has operated on the Göteborg – Gent service but in late 1998 she was switched to the Immingham – Rotterdam service.

TOR BELGIA Built as the VILLE DU HAVRE for *Société Française de Transports Maritimes* of France. Between 1979 and 1981 she was chartered to *Foss Line*, renamed the FOSS HAVRE and operated between Europe and the Middle East. In 1987 she was renamed the KAMINA. In 1990 she was chartered to *Maersk Line* of Denmark, renamed the MAERSK KENT and used on *Kent Line* services between Dartford and Zeebrugge. In 1992 she was chartered to and later purchased by *Tor Line*, placed on the Göteborg – Immingham route and renamed the TOR BRITANNIA. In 1994 she was lengthened by 23.7m. In 1999 she was renamed the TOR BELGIA and was later transferred to the Göteborg – Gent route.

TOR CALEDONIA Built for charter to *Tor Line* for freight service between Sweden and UK/Netherlands. She was a lengthened version of the TOR GOTHIA class, these vessels being lengthened in the same year. In 1982 she served with the British Falkland islands Task Force. In 1984 she was chartered to *Grimaldi* of Italy, renamed the GOTHIC WASA. Later that year she was renamed the GALLOWAY but in 1985 she was returned to *Tor Line* and renamed the TOR CALEDONIA. In 1988 she was purchased by *DFDS* and in 1990 she was lengthened by 26m. Generally operated on the Göteborg – Immingham/Harwich route. In 1999 the Immingham and Harwich services were separated and since then she has operated between Göteborg and Immingham. When the third newbuilding enters service, she is to be transferred to the Göteborg – Harwich service.

TOR DANIA Built as the VILLE DE DUNKERQUE for *Société Française de Transports Maritimes* of France. Between 1979 and 1981 she was chartered to *Foss Line*, renamed the FOSS DUNKERQUE and operated between Europe and the Middle East. In 1986 she was chartered to *Grimaldi* of Italy and renamed the G AND C EXPRESS. In 1988 she was briefly chartered to *Elbe-Humber RoLine* and renamed the RAILRO. She was then chartered to *DFDS* where she was renamed the DANIA HAFNIA. The following year she was chartered to *Maersk Line* of Denmark, renamed the MAERSK ESSEX and used on *Kent Line* services between Dartford and Zeebrugge. In 1992 she was chartered to and later purchased by *DFDS* and renamed the TOR DANIA. In 1993 she was renamed the BRIT DANIA but later in the year reverted to her original name. She was generally used on the Harwich – Esbjerg service, working in consort with the passenger ferry DANIA ANGLIA (see *DFDS Seaways*). In 1994 she was lengthened by 23.7m. and chartered to *Tor Line* and placed on the Göteborg – Immingham route. When the third newbuilding enters service she is to be transferred to the Göteborg – Gent route.

TOR FLANDRIA Built as the FINNCLIPPER for the *Johansson Group* of Sweden and chartered out. In 1983 she was sold to *Zenit Shipping* and renamed the ZENIT CLIPPER. She was chartered to *Foss Line* and used on services between Northern Europe and the Middle East. In 1986 she was sold to *Crowley American Transport* of the USA and chartered to the US Military. She was renamed the AMERICAN FALCON and used for military transport purposes across the world. In 1998 sold to *Stena Rederi* and was renamed the STENA PARTNER. She was then chartered to *Tor Line* and renamed the TOR SCANDIA; part of her charter conditions are that she be purchased at the end of the five year charter period. She is used on the Göteborg – Gent route.

TOR GOTHIA Built for *Tor Line*. Lengthened in 1977. She was usually used on the Immingham – Rotterdam service. In 1999 transferred to the Norway – UK service and in 2000 to the Norway – Netherlands service.

TOR HOLLANDIA Built as the TOR DANIA for charter to *Tor Line*. In 1975 she was chartered to *Salenrederierna* for service in the Middle East and renamed the BANDAR ABBAS EXPRESS. In 1977 she was lengthened and, in 1978, returned to *Tor Line* and resumed the name TOR DANIA. Purchased by *Tor Line* in 1986. In 1992 she was renamed the TOR DAN and in 1993 the TOR HOLLANDIA. She was usually used on the Immingham – Rotterdam service. In 1999 transferred to the Norway – UK service.

TOR HUMBRIA Built as the EMIRATES EXPRESS for *A/S Skarhamns Oljetransport* of Norway and chartered to *Mideastcargo* for services between Europe and the Middle East. In 1981 chartered to

OT West Africa Line for services between Europe and West Africa and renamed the ABUJA EXPRESS. In 1983 chartered to Foss Line, renamed the FOSSEAGLE and returned to Middle East service. In 1985 she was renamed the FINNEAGLE, chartered briefly to Finncarriers and then to Fred. Olsen Lines. In 1987 they purchased her and renamed her the BORAC. In 1999 purchased by DFDS Tor Line and renamed the TOR HUMBRIA. She is now generally used on the Norway – UK service.

TOR NORVEGIA Built as the BALDUIN for Fred. Olsen Lines. 1999 purchased by DFDS Tor Line and renamed the TOR NORVEGIA. She is now used on the Norway – Netherlands service.

TOR SCANDIA Built as the KUWAIT EXPRESS for the Johansson Group of Sweden and chartered to NYK Line of Japan for services between Japan and the Arabian Gulf. In 1983 she was sold to Zenit Shipping and renamed the ZENIT EXPRESS. She was chartered to Foss Line and used on services between Northern Europe and the Middle East. In 1984 she was sold to Crowley American Transport of the USA and chartered to the US Military. She was reamed the AMERICAN CONDOR and used for military transport purposes across the world. In 1998 sold to Stena Rederi and was renamed the STENA PORTER. She was sold to Tor Line and renamed the TOR SCANDIA. She is used on the Göteborg – Gent route.

TOR SELANDIA, TOR SUECIA Built for DFDS Tor Line. They operate on the Göteborg – Immingham route.

Under Construction

| 21 | NEWBUILDING 6022 | 24200t | 00 | 21.1k | 12P | - | 230T | A | Ancona, IT | DK |

NEWBUILDING 6022 Under construction to operate on the Göteborg – Immingham service. Expected to be called the TOR BRITANNIA on entry to service.

FALCON SEAFREIGHT

THE COMPANY Falcon Seafreight is operated by Falcon Marfreight Limited, a UK company.

MANAGEMENT Managing Director: Ian Longdon.

ADDRESS The Freight Office, Folkestone Harbour, FOLKESTONE, Kent CT20 1QH.

TELEPHONE Administration & Reservations: +44 (0)1303 221456, **Fax:** +44 (0)1303 248709.

ROUTES OPERATED Folkestone (dep: 01.30 Mon-Sat, 05.15 Mon-Sat, 10.00 Mon-Fri, 13.00 Daily, 17.00 (Sun-Fri), 20.45 Sun-Fri) – Boulogne (dep: 02.00 Mon-Sat, 06.45 Mon-Fri, 10.15 Mon-Sat, 14.15 Mon-Fri, 18.00 Daily, 22.00 Sun-Fri (2 hrs 15 mins; (1,2); 6 per day). See Late News.

VESSELS

| 1 | NEPTUNIA | 8547t | 77 | 17k | 150P | - | 62T | BA | Korneuburg, AU | MA |
| 2 | PURBECK | 6507t | 78 | 17.5k | 58P | - | 57T | BA | Le Havre, FR | BA |

NEPTUNIA Built as the STENA TOPPER, a ro-ro freight vessel for Stena Line AB of Sweden. Built in sections which were welded together at Galatz in Romania. Purchased by James Fisher of Barrow in 1978 and renamed the DARNIA. Chartered to Sealink UK for use on the Stranraer – Larne route. In 1982 passenger capacity was increased from 92 to 412 in order to operate on passenger/car ferry services. In 1991 she was sold to Nordström & Thulin, renamed the NORD NEPTUNUS and used generally on a freight-only role on their Gotlandslinjen service between Sweden and Gotland. She also operated for associated company EstLine and has been chartered to TT-Line. Later in 1997 she was acquired by ESCO on long-term bareboat charter, renamed the NEPTUNIA and placed on the Stockholm – Tallinn route as a ro-pax vessel. Following the introduction of the BALTIC KRISTINA as second passenger vessel she, for a time, continued to provide freight back up on the route but was later switched to ESCO's freight only routes. In February 2000 she was time chartered to Falcon Seafreight to operate as second vessel between Folkestone and Boulogne.

PURBECK Built for Truckline Ferries for their Cherbourg – Poole service. In 1986 she was lengthened to increase vehicle capacity by 34%. In 1992 transferred to the Roscoff – Plymouth and

Finnbirch (Philippe Holthof)

SeaFrance Nord-pas-de-Calais (Miles Cowsill)

Santander – Plymouth services. In 1994 she was sold to *Channel Island Ferries* (parent company of *British Channel Island Ferries*) to operate freight services between Poole and The Channel Islands. Later in 1994, chartered to *Commodore Ferries* following the cessation of *BCIF's* operations. In 1995 she was chartered to *Sally Ferries* for use on their Dartford – Vlissingen service until replaced by the DART 5 later in the year. During summer 1996 she was chartered to *Irish Ferries* to operate supplementary freight services between Dublin and Holyhead. In autumn 1996 she returned to *Sally Ferries* and in 1997 she was transferred to *Holyman Sally Ferries*. In summer 1997 she was chartered to *Truckline Ferries* to operate between Portsmouth and Caen. Later in 1997, she was chartered to *Gaelic Ferries* to inaugurate a new Cork – Cherbourg service. During the French truckers' blockade in late 1997, she operated between Cork and Santander (Spain). In 1998 she was chartered to *Falcon Seafreight*. In 2000 chartered to Truckline - See Late News.

FARMERS' FERRY

THE COMPANY *Farmers' Ferry Ltd* is a British private sector company. No other information is available.

ROUTE OPERATED Dunkerque – Dover (3 hrs; *(1)*; irregular). Services operate for the carriage of livestock only.

VESSEL

1	CAP AFRIQUE	‡1583t	78	13.5k	12P	-	50T	A	Niigata, JA	KE

CAP AFRIQUE Built as the CATHERINE SCHIAFFINO for *Schiaffino Line* of France and chartered out, generally operating on services in the Mediterranean. In 1983 she was transferred to the company's own service between Dover and Oostende; in 1984 the British terminal moved to Ramsgate. In 1989 she was renamed the SAINT CHARLES and in 1990 she was chartered to *Sally Ferries*, who took over the service. She was later sold to *Delom* and in 1991 she was renamed the CAP AFRIQUE. She undertook a number of charters and was also used on *Delom's* own services between France and Tunisia. In 1996 she was moved to Dunkerque and began a number of charters conveying livestock from Dover. In 1997 she returned to Mediterranean service but returned to *Farmers' Ferry* in autumn 1998.

FERRYWAYS

THE COMPANY *Ferryways nv* is a Belgian company.

MANAGEMENT Managing Director: J Dewilde, **Marketing Manager:** Martin Gouwy.

ADDRESS *Oostende:* Esplanadestraat 10, B-8400 OOSTENDE, Belgium. ***Ipswich:*** Waratah House, West Bank Terminal, Wherstead Road, IPSWICH IP2 8NB.

TELEPHONE Administration & Reservations : *Oostende:* +32 (0)59 34 22 20, ***Ipswich:*** +44 (0)1473 696200, **Fax: *Oostende:*** +32 (0)59 34 22 29, ***Ipswich:*** +44 (0)1473 696201.

INTERNET Email: *Oostende:* info@ferryways.com ***Ipswich:*** info@ferryways.co.uk

ROUTE OPERATED Oostende *(dep: 10.30 Mon-Sat, 22.00 Mon-Fri, 21.00 Sun)* – Ipswich *(dep:10.00 Mon-Fri, 21.00 Mon-Fri, 11.00 Sat, 20.00 Sun)* (6 hrs 30 min – 7 hrs; *(1,2)*; 2 per day)

VESSELS

1	GABRIELE WEHR	7635t	78	15k	12P	55C	80T	A	Bremerhaven, GY	TV
2	THOMAS WEHR	7628t	77	16k	12P	55C	91T	A	Bremerhaven, GY	TV

GABRIELE WEHR Built for *Wehr Transport* of Germany and chartered to several operators. In 1982, chartered to *Tor Lloyd* (later *Tor Line*) for North Sea service and renamed the TOR ANGLIA. This charter terminated in 1985 when she resumed her original name and, in early 1986, she was chartered to *North Sea Ferries* for their Hull – Zeebrugge service. This charter ended in summer 1987 when the lengthened NORLAND and NORSTAR entered service. Subsequent charters included *Kent Line* and *Brittany Ferries*. In 1989 she was chartered to *P&O European Ferries* for the Portsmouth – Le Havre freight service. Her charter was terminated following the transfer of the

EUROPEAN TRADER to the route in late 1992 but in 1993 it was renewed, following the transfer of the EUROPEAN CLEARWAY (now the EUROPEAN PATHFINDER) to *Pandoro*. In 1996, she was transferred to the Felixstowe – Zeebrugge service. In autumn 1999 the charter was ended. In 2000 she was chartered to *Ferryways*.

THOMAS WEHR Built for *Wehr Transport* of Germany as THOMAS WEHR but on delivery chartered to *Wacro Line* and renamed the WACRO EXPRESS. In 1978 charter ended and she was renamed the THOMAS WEHR. Over the next few years she was chartered to several operators. In 1982 she was chartered to *Tor Lloyd* (later *Tor Line*) for North Sea service and renamed the TOR NEERLANDIA. In 1985 the charter was transferred to *DFDS* and she was renamed the DANA GERMANIA. This charter terminated in 1985 and she resumed her original name. In early 1986 she was chartered to *North Sea Ferries* for their Hull – Zeebrugge service. This charter ended in summer 1987. Subsequent charters included *Cobelfret* and *Elbe-Humber RoLine* and a twelve month period with *North Sea Ferries* again – this time on the Hull – Rotterdam and Teesport – Zeebrugge routes. In 1993 she was renamed the MANA, then the SANTA MARIA and finally chartered to *TT-Line* and renamed the FULDATAL. 1994 she was chartered to *Horn Line* for service between Europe and the Caribbean and renamed the HORNLINK. Later that year she was chartered to *P&O European Ferries* for the Portsmouth – Le Havre freight service and resumed the name THOMAS WEHR. In late 1995 transferred to the Felixstowe – Zeebrugge freight service. In autumn 1999 the charter was ended. In 2000 she was chartered to *Ferryways*.

FINANGLIA FERRIES

THE COMPANY *Finanglia Ferries* is a joint operation between *Finncarriers Oy Ab*, a Finnish private sector company and *Andrew Weir Shipping*, (owners of the *United Baltic Corporation*), a British private sector company.

MANAGEMENT Managing Director: John Ashley, **Sales Manager:** Caroline Cotton.

ADDRESSES *UK:* 8 Heron Quay, LONDON E14 4JB, *Finland:* PO Box 197, Porkkalankatu 7, FIN-00181 HELSINKI, Finland.

TELEPHONE Administration & Reservations: *UK:* +44 (0)20 7519 7300, *Finland:* +358 (0)10 34350, **Fax:** *UK:* +44 (0)20 7536 0255, *Finland:* +358 (0)10 3435200, **Telex:** *Finland:* 1001743.

INTERNET Email: marketing.faf-london@finanglia.com **Website:** http://www.finanglia.co.uk

ROUTES OPERATED Felixstowe *(arr:/dep: Tues, Sat)* – Helsinki (Finland) *(arr: Tue, Fri, dep: Mon, Fri)* – Hamina (Finland) *(arr: Wed, Sat, dep: Tue, Sat)* (3/4 days; *(1,4,5,6);* 2 per week), Hull *(arr: Tue, dep: Fri)* – Helsinki *(arr: Tue, dep Fri)* – Hamina *(arr: Wed, dep: Thu)* (5 days; *(2,3);* 1 per week).

VESSELS

1	BALTIC EIDER	20865t	89	19k	OP	-	180T	A	Ulsan, SK	IM
2	FINNBIRCH	15396t	78	17k	OP	-	174T	A	Ulsan, SK	SW
3	FINNFOREST	15525t	78	17k	OP	-	174T	A	Ulsan, SK	SW
4	FINNRIVER	20172t	79	16.5k	OP	-	136T	Q	Ichihara, JA	SW
5	FINNROSE	20169t	78	19k	OP	-	136T	Q	Ichihara, JA	SW
6	TRANSBALTICA	21224t	90	19k	OP	-	182T	A	Ulsan, SK	CY

BALTIC EIDER Built for *United Baltic Corporation.*

FINNBIRCH Laid down as the STENA PROSPER and completed as the ATLANTIC PROSPER for *Stena Rederi* and chartered to *ACL* of Great Britain for service between Britain and Canada. In 1981 chartered to *Merzario Line* of Italy for services between Italy and Saudi Arabia and renamed, initially, the STENA IONIA and then the MERZARIO IONIA. Later the same year she reverted to the name STENA IONIA and was chartered to *OT West Africa Line* for services between Europe and Nigeria. In 1985 she was renamed the STENA GOTHICA and used on *Stena Portlink* services. In 1988 she was chartered to *Bore Line* of Finland and renamed the BORE GOTHICA. In 1992 chartered to *Finncarriers*. In 1996 renamed the FINNBIRCH. In 1997 she began operating a service between Hull and Zeebrugge on charter to *P&O North Sea Ferries* in the course of her normal two week circuit from Finland. This ceased in 1999.

FINNFOREST Laid down as the STENA PROJECT and completed as ATLANTIC PROJECT for *Stena Rederi* and chartered to *ACL* (see above). In 1981 chartered to *Merzario Line* of Italy for services between Italy and Saudi Arabia and renamed the MERZARIO HISPANIA. In 1983 returned to *Stena Line* and renamed the STENA HISPANIA. In 1984 chartered to *Kotka Line* of Finland, renamed the KOTKA VIOLET and used on their services between Finland, UK and West Africa. This charter ended in 1985 and she was again named the STENA HISPANIA. In 1986 she was renamed the STENA BRITANNICA and used on *Stena Portlink* (later *Stena Tor Line*) service between Sweden and Britain. In 1988 she was chartered to *Bore Line* of Finland, renamed the BORE BRITANNICA and used on services between Finland and Britain. In 1992 chartered to *Finncarriers*. In 1997 renamed the FINNFOREST. In 1997 she began operating a service between Hull and Zeebrugge on charter to *P&O North Sea Ferries* in the course of her normal two week circuit from Finland. This ceased in 1999.

FINNRIVER Built as the VASALAND for *Boström AB* of Sweden and chartered to *EFFOA* of Finland for services between Scandinavia and Mediterranean ports. In 1983 chartered to *Swedish Orient Line* for similar services and renamed the HESPERUS. In 1986 chartered to *Finncarriers* and renamed the CELIA. In 1996 the charter was extended for a further five years and she was renamed the FINNROVER.

FINNROSE Built as the TIMMERLAND for *Boström AB* of Sweden and chartered to *EFFOA* of Finland for services between Scandinavia and Mediterranean ports. In 1984 chartered to *Swedish Orient Line* for similar services and renamed the HEKTOS. In 1986 chartered to *Finncarriers* and renamed the CORTIA. In 1996 the charter was extended for a further five years and she was renamed the FINNROSE.

TRANSBALTICA Built as the AHLERS BALTIC the for *Ahlers Line* and chartered to *Finncarriers*. In 1995 acquired by *Poseidon Schiffahrt AG* of Germany and renamed the TRANSBALTICA. She continued to be chartered to *Finncarriers* and was acquired by them when they purchased *Poseidon Schiffahrt AG* in 1997.

Under Construction

8	NEWBUILDING 1	11400t	00	20k	0P	-	158T	A	Jinling, CH	-
9	NEWBUILDING 2	11400t	00	20k	0P	-	158T	A	Jinling, CH	-

NEWBUILDING 1, NEWBUILDING 2 Under construction for *Nordic Forest Terminals* of Sweden to operate for *Finncarriers* on UK routes.

MERCHANT FERRIES

THE COMPANY *Merchant Ferries* is a British private sector company, owned by *Cenargo*. In 1999, *Belfast Freight Ferries*, acquired by *Cenargo* in 1998, was mated with *Merchant Ferries*.

MANAGEMENT Managing Director: Philip Shepherd, **Route Manager, Belfast – Heysham:** Diane Parry, **Route Manager, Dublin – Liverpool/Heysham:** Gerard Macken.

ADDRESS *Belfast:* Victoria Terminal 1, Dargan Road, BELFAST BT3 9LJ, *Heysham:* North Quay, Heysham Harbour, MORECAMBE, Lancs LA3 2UL, *Dublin:* Alexandra Road Extension, Dublin Port, Dublin 1.

TELEPHONE Administration: *Belfast:* +44 (0)28 9076 6000, *Heysham:* +44 (0)1524 865000, **Reservations:** *Belfast:* +44 (0)28 9078 6050, *Heysham:* +44 (0)1524 865050, *Dublin:* +353 (0)1 819 2955, **Fax Admin:** *Belfast:* +44 (0)28 9078 1217, *Heysham:* +44 (0)1524 865072, **Fax Reservations:** *Belfast:* +44 (0)28 9078 1217, *Heysham:* +44 (0)1524 865070, *Dublin:* +353 (0)1 819 2942.

INTERNET Website: http://www.merchant-ferries.com **Email:** enquiries@merchant-ferries.com

ROUTES OPERATED Heysham *(dep: 06.30, 24.00)* – Dublin *(dep: 12.00, 19.00)* (8 hrs; *(5,7)*; 2 per day), Heysham *(dep: 06.30, 10.30, 18.30, 22.30)* – Belfast *(dep: 06.30, 10.30, 18.30, 22.30)*; (8 hrs; *(1,2,3,4)*; 4 per day). *Merchant Ferries* also operate a passenger/freight service from Liverpool to Dublin. See Section 1.

Stena Challenger (Miles Cowsill)

Lagan Viking (Mike Louagie)

VESSELS

1	MERCHANT BRAVERY	9368t	78	17k	12P	-	106T	A	Oslo, NO	BA
2	MERCHANT BRILLIANT	9368t	79	17k	12P	-	106T	A	Kyrksæterøra, NO	BA
3	MERCHANT VENTURE	6056t	79	17k	12P	-	55T	A	Castelo, PL	IM
4	RIVER LUNE	7765t	83	15k	12P	-	100T	A	Galatz, RO	BA
5	SAGA MOON	7746t	84	15k	12P	-	75T	A	Travemünde, GY	GI
6•	SPHEROID	7171t	71	16k	12P	-	55T	A	Sharpsborg, NO	IM
7	VARBOLA	7800t	98	17k	12P	-	88T	A	Huelva, SP	ES

MERCHANT BRAVERY Launched as the STEVI for *Steineger & Wiik* of Norway and, on delivery, chartered to *Norient Line* of Norway, being renamed the NORWEGIAN CRUSADER. In 1980 chartered to *Ignazio Messina* of Italy for Mediterranean service and renamed the JOLLY GIALLO. In 1982 the charter ended and she was briefly renamed the NORWEGIAN CRUSADER before being purchased by *Ignazio Messina* and resuming the name JOLLY GIALLO. In 1993 sold to *Merchant Ferries*, renamed the MERCHANT BRAVERY and placed on the Heysham – Warrenpoint (Dublin since 1995) service. In 1999 transferred to *Belfast Freight Ferries'* Heysham – Belfast service.

MERCHANT BRILLIANT Built as the NORWEGIAN CHALLENGER *for Steineger & Wiik* of Norway and chartered to *Norient Line* of Norway. In 1982, chartered to *Ignazio Messina* of Italy for Mediterranean service and renamed the JOLLY BRUNO. Later in 1982 she was purchased by *Ignazio Messina*. In 1993 sold to *Merchant Ferries*, renamed the MERCHANT BRILLIANT and placed on the Heysham – Warrenpoint (Dublin since 1995) service. In 1999 transferred to *Belfast Freight Ferries'* Heysham – Belfast service.

MERCHANT VENTURE Built as the FARMAN and chartered to *GNMTC* of Italy for Mediterranean services. In 1982 she was sold to *Medlines* for similar service and renamed the MED ADRIATICO. In 1985 she was sold, renamed the ARGENTEA and chartered to *SGMAT*, continuing to operate in the Mediterranean. In 1987 sold to *Cenargo* and chartered to *Merchant Ferries* who renamed her first the MERCHANT ISLE and then the MERCHANT VENTURE. She was purchased by *Merchant Ferries* in 1993. Until 1993 she was used on the Fleetwood – Warrenpoint service; in 1993 the UK terminal was moved to Heysham and in 1995 the Irish terminal was moved to Dublin. In autumn 1998 she was placed on the charter market. In Autumn 1999 she was chartered to *P&O Irish Sea* and used on the Fleetwood – Larne service. In 2000 to operate between Heysham and Belfast.

RIVER LUNE Built for *Almira Shipping* of Liberia (part of the Norwegian *Balder* group) as the BALDER VIK and initially used on services between Italy and the Middle East. Subsequently she was employed on a number of charters including *North Sea Ferries* and *Norfolk Line*. In 1986 she was acquired by *Navimpex* of Romania, renamed the BAZIAS 7 and initially used on Mediterranean and Black Sea services. In 1987 she was chartered to *Kent Line* for service between Chatham and Zeebrugge. In 1988 she was sold to *Stena Rederi AB* of Sweden and chartered for service between Finland and Germany. In 1989 she was briefly renamed the STENA TOPPER before being further renamed the SALAR. During the ensuing years she undertook a number of charters. In 1993 she briefly resumed the name STENA TOPPER before being chartered to *Belfast Freight Ferries* and renamed the RIVER LUNE. In October 1996 she was sold to *Belfast Freight Ferries*. In 1999 she was transferred to *Merchant Ferries'* Heysham – Dublin service. In 2000 she returned to the Heysham – Belfast route.

SAGA MOON Built as the LIDARTINDUR for *Trader Line* of the Faroe Islands for services between Tórshavn and Denmark. In 1986 chartered to *Belfast Freight Ferries* renamed the SAGA MOON. In 1990 she was sold to *Belfast Freight Ferries*. In 1995 she was lengthened by 18m to increase trailer capacity from 52 to 72 units and trade cars from 25 to 50; the lift was replaced by an internal fixed ramp. In 1998 she was transferred to *Merchant Ferries'* Heysham – Dublin service.

SPHEROID Built as the STARMARK for *Avermoi Oy* of Finland. In 1981 sold to *Manta Line* of Greece for Mediterranean and deep sea service and renamed the RORO TRADER. In 1985 she was sold to *Oceanwide Shipping* for charter and renamed the NIEKIRK. In 1986 chartered to *Belfast Freight Ferries* and in 1987 sold to them and renamed the SPHEROID. In 2000 laid up for sale or charter.

VARBOLA Built as the for *Estonian Shipping Company*. On completion, chartered to *Dart Line* and placed on the Dartford – Vlissingen route. In 1999 she was renamed the DART 6. At the end of August 1999, the charter was terminated and she was renamed the VARBOLA. She undertook a number of short term charters, including *Merchant Ferries*. In 2000 chartered to *Merchant Ferries* to operate between Heysham and Dublin.

NOR-CARGO

THE COMPANY *Nor-Cargo AS* is a Norwegian company jointly owned by *Ofotens og Vesteraalen Dampskipsselskab, Det Stavangerske Dampskipsselskab* and *Troms Fylkes Dampskipsselskab*. *Nor-Cargo Ltd* is a British registered subsidiary company.

ADDRESS *Norway:* Pir-Senteret, N-7005 TRONDHEIM, Norway, *UK:* 1 Prince Albert Gardens, GRIMSBY DN31 3HT.

TELEPHONE Administration & Bookings: *Norway:* +47 73 54 50 00, *UK:* +44 (0)1472 240241, **Fax:** *Norway:* +47 73 54 50 01, *UK:* +44 (0)1472 240250.

INTERNET Email: Info@Nor-Cargo.com **Website:** http://www.nor-cargo.demon.co.uk/

ROUTES OPERATED Circuit 1: Bergen *(dep: Sat)* – Tananger *(dep: Sun)* – Stavanger *(dep: Sun)* – Aberdeen *(arr: Mon)* – Grimsby *(arr/dep: Tue)* – Aberdeen *(dep: Wed)* – Tananger *(arr: Thu)* / Stavanger *(arr: Thu)* – Sandnes *(arr: Thu)* – Håvik *(arr: Fri)* – Haugesund *(arr: Fri)* – Bergen *(arr: Sat)* (1 week; *(1)*; weekly), **Circuit 2:** Grimsby *(dep: Wed)* – Amsterdam *(dep: Thu)* – Grimsby *(dep: Fri)* – Tanager *(dep: Sun)* – Haugesund *(dep: Sun)* – Bergen *(dep: Sun)* – Aagotnes *(dep: Sun)* (on request) – Haavik *(dep: Mon)* – Tanager *(dep: Mon)* – Stord *(dep: Mon)* (on request) – Grimsby *(arr: Wed)* (1 week; *(2)*; weekly), **Circuit 3:** Bergen *(dep: Mon)* – Håvik *(dep: Tue)* – Stavanger *(dep: Tue)* – Amsterdam *(arr: Thu/dep: Fri)* – Aberdeen *(arr/dep: Sat)* – Stavanger *(arr: Sun)* – Bergen *(arr: Mon)* (1 week; *(3)*; weekly).

VESSELS

1	COMETA	4610t	81	16k	0P	-	26T	AS	Rissa, NO	NO
2	NORDHAV	5846t	80	15k	12P	-	67T	A	Kraljevica, YU	NO
3	TUNGENES	4234t	79	15.5k	0P	-	29T	AS	Rissa, NO	NO

COMETA Built for *Nor-Cargo*.

NORDHAV Built as the CRES for *Losinjska Plovidba* of Yugoslavia (later Croatia) and used on Mediterranean services. In 1998 she was sold to *Nor-Cargo* and renamed the NORDHAV.

TUNGENES Built for *Nor-Cargo*. Launched as the ERIC JARL but renamed the ASTREA before entering service. In 1986 she sank and, after raising and refitting she was, in 1992, renamed the TUNGENES.

Nor-Cargo also operate a lo-lo service between Grimsby and the West Coast of Norway using cargo vessels NORDJARL (3698t, 1985 (ex ICE PEARL, 1995)), NORDKYN (2503t, 1979) and NORDVÆR (2731t, 1986 (ex VICTORIAHAMN, 1993)). The service leaves Grimsby every Saturday, arriving back on Friday three weeks later.

NORFOLKLINE

THE COMPANY *Norfolkline* (before 1 January 1999 *Norfolk Line*) is a Dutch private sector company owned by *A P Møller Finance* of Denmark.

MANAGEMENT Managing Director: D G Sloan, **Deputy Managing Director:** D V J M Blom, **Marketing Manager:** R A Meijer, **Managing Director UK:** E J Green, **Manager Dover:** Wayne Bullen, **Manager Dunkerque:** Alain Declerq.

ADDRESS *Netherlands:* Kranenburgweg 211, 2583 ER SCHEVENINGEN, Netherlands. *UK:* Norfolk House, The Dock, FELIXSTOWE, Suffolk IP11 8UY, *Dover:* Export Freight Plaza, Eastern Docks, DOVER, Kent CT16 1JA.

TELEPHONE Administration: *Netherlands:* +31 (0)70 352 74 00, *UK:* +44 (0)1394 673676,

Reservations: *Netherlands:* +31 (0)70 352 74 71, *Felixstowe:* +44 (0)1394 603630, *Immingham:* +44 (0)1469 571122, *Dover:* +44 (0)1304 208528, **Fax:** *Netherlands:* +31 (0)70 352 74 35, *Felixstowe:* +44 (0)1394 603673, *Dover:* +44 (0)1304 208517.

INTERNET Email: info@norfolkline.com   dover@norfolkline.com   dunkerque@norfolkline.com
Website: http://www.norfolkline.com *(English)*

ROUTES OPERATED Felixstowe *(dep: 06.00, 12.00, 18.00, 23.50)* – Scheveningen *(dep: 07.00, 14.00, 19.30, 23.59)* (7 hrs; *(1,2,3,4)*; 4 per day), Scheveningen *(dep: 14.00 Sat, 19.00 Sat)* – Esbjerg *(dep: 13.00 Sat, 20.00 Sun)* (20 hrs; *(1,4)*; 2 per week), Dover *(dep: 05.00, 13.00, 21.00)* – Dunkerque *(dep: 02.00, 10.00, 18.00)* (2 hrs; *(5)*; 3 per day), Immingham – Esbjerg (22 hrs; 5 per week), Harwich – Esbjerg (21 hrs; 6/7 per week). UK – Denmark services operated in conjunction with *DFDS Tor Line* who provide all vessels.

VESSELS

1	MAERSK EXPORTER	13017t	96	18.6k	12P	-	122T	A	Shimizu, JA	NL
2	MAERSK FLANDERS	13017t	99	18.6k	12P	-	122T	A	Guangzhou, CH	NL
3	MAERSK FRIESLAND	7199t	78	15k	12P	-	80T	A	Tokyo, JA	NL
4	MAERSK IMPORTER	13017t	96	18.6k	12P	-	122T	A	Shimizu, JA	NL
5	NORTHERN MERCHANT	22152t	00	22.5k	250P	-	175T	BA	Sevilla, SP	GB

MAERSK EXPORTER, MAERSK IMPORTER, MAERSK FLANDERS Built for *Norfolkline*. Used on the Felixstowe – Scheveningen service.

MAERSK FRIESLAND Built as the ADMIRAL ATLANTIC for *Admiral Shipping* of the USA for Caribbean service. In 1983 she was chartered to *Portlink* for North Sea services. In 1984 sold to Swedish interests and renamed the ROMIRA. In 1986 she was sold to *Norfolkline*, renamed the DUKE OF FLANDERS and used on their services between Great Yarmouth and Esbjerg (Denmark), Immingham and Esbjerg and Immingham and Cuxhaven. In 1990 she was renamed MAERSK FLANDERS. In 1999 she was renamed the MAERSK FRIESLAND. Due to be replaced by NEWBUILDING in June 2000.

NORTHERN MERCHANT Built for *Cenargo* (owners of *Merchant Ferries*). On delivery, chartered to *Norfolkline* to inaugurate a Dover – Dunkerque (Ouest) service. Service started March 2000.

Under Construction

6	NEWBUILDING	13017t	00	18.6k	12P	-	122T	A	Guangzhou, CH	NL

NEWBUILDING Under construction for *Norfolkline*. Likely to enter service as the GUANGZHOU 7130011 (unofficially the CHINA II) but to be renamed shortly afterwards. To replace the MAERSK FRIESLAND on the Scheveningen – Felixstowe service.

ORCARGO

THE COMPANY *Orcargo* is a UK registered private sector company.

MANAGEMENT Managing Director: D Laidlow, **Marketing Manager:** Ken Brookman.

ADDRESS Norlantic House, Grainshore, KIRKWALL, Orkney WK15 1RE.

TELEPHONE Administration & Reservations: +44 (0)1856 873838, **Fax:** +44 (0)1856 876521.

INTERNET Website: http://www.orkneyislands.com/orcargo *(English)*

ROUTE OPERATED Invergordon *(dep: 03.30 Tue-Sat, 20.00 Sun)* – Kirkwall *(dep: 17.30 Mon-Fri, 08.00 Sun)* (9 hrs; *(1)*; 6 per week) (passengers can be carried subject to availability).

VESSEL

1	CONTENDER	2292t	73	15k	12P	-	12T	AS	Le Havre, FR	GB

CONTENDER Built as the ANTINEA for *Union Industrielle & Maritime* of France. In 1983 sold to *Euroline SpA* of Italy and renamed the FERRUCCIA. In 1986 she was sold to *White Star Enterprises*

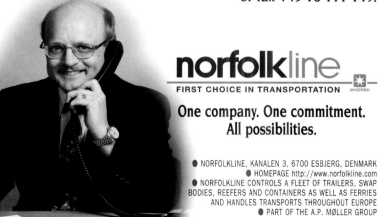
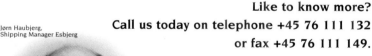
SECTION 3 – FREIGHT ONLY FERRIES

of Italy and renamed and INDIANA and in 1988 to *Quay Shipping* of the Bahamas and renamed the INDIANA I. In 1992 she was sold to *Orcargo* and renamed the CONTENDER.

P&O IRISH SEA

THE COMPANY, MANAGEMENT AND ADDRESS See Section 1.

TELEPHONE Administration: +44 (0)1253 615700, **Reservations:** *Ardrossan:* +44 (0)1292 469 211, *Cairnryan:* +44 (0)1581 200663, *Dublin:* +353(0)1 855 7001, *Fleetwood:* +44 (0)1253 615755, *Larne:* +44 (0)1574 8722001, *Liverpool:* +44 (0)151 820 1441, *Rosslare:* +353(0)1 855 7001. **Fax:** *Cairnryan:* +44 (0)1581 200282, *Larne:* +44 (0)1574 272477, *Fleetwood:* +44 (0)1253 615740.

INTERNET Website: http://www.poirishsea.com *(English)*

ROUTES OPERATED Ardrossan *(dep: 02.30 Mon-Sat, 12.00 Sun)* – Larne *(dep: 19.00 Sun-Fri, 09.00 Sat)* (4 hrs 15 mins; *(4)*; 1 per day) (the Scottish terminal will become Troon in January, 2000), Cairnryan *(dep: 02.00, 04.00*, 07.30, 09.00, 11.30*, 15.30, 17.30, 19.30*, 23.30)* – Larne *(dep: 03.30*, 05.30, 08.00*, 11.30, 13.30, 15.30*, 19.30, 21.30, 23.59)* *(*operated by passenger vessel PRIDE OF RATHIN or EUROPEAN CAUSEWAY)* (2 hrs 15 mins; *(2,10)*; up to 9 per day), Fleetwood *(dep: 03.00 Tue-Sat, 10.00 Daily, 22.00 Daily)* – Larne *(dep: 10.00 Daily, 16.00 Mon-Fri, 22.00 Daily)* (7 hrs; *(6,8,9)*; 3 per day), Liverpool *(dep: 05.00 Tue-Fri, 17.00, 10.00 Tue-Sat, 22.00 daily)* – Dublin *(dep: 05.00, 10.00 Tue-Sat, 17.00 Tue-Fri, 22.00 daily)* (8 hrs; *(1,3,5)*; 3 per day), Rosslare *(dep: 22.00 Tue, 21.30 Thu, 16.00 Sat)* – Cherbourg *(dep: 22.00 Wed, 19.00 Fri, 14.00 Sun)* (18 hrs; *(7)*; 3 per week). Vessels are sometimes moved between routes. A limited number of ordinary passengers is conveyed on the day sailings between Fleetwood and Larne, all sailings between Rosslare and Cherbourg and 10.00 (22.00 Sun) Liverpool – Dublin and Dublin – Liverpool sailings under the 'Value Route' branding. Cairnryan – Larne services are liable to change when new ro-pax vessel enters service in late summer 2000.

VESSELS

1	CELTIC STAR	11086t	91	20.8k	0P	-	64T	A	Kawajiri, JA	CY
2	EUROPEAN ENDEAVOUR	8097t	78	18.4k	107P	-	46L	BA2	Bremerhaven, GY	BD
3	EUROPEAN ENVOY	18653t	79	18.2k	107P	-	125T	A	Tamano, JA	BD
4	EUROPEAN HIGHLANDER	5897t	77	15k	12P	-	71T	A	Bremerhaven, GY	BA
5	EUROPEAN LEADER	12879t	75	17k	50P	-	110T	A	Hamburg, GY	BD
6	EUROPEAN NAVIGATOR	9085t	77	18k	42P	-	70T	A	Korneuburg, AU	BD
7	EUROPEAN PATHFINDER	8023t	75	18.5k	52P	-	72T	BA	Bremerhaven, GY	BD
8	EUROPEAN PIONEER	14387t	75	17.7k	76P	-	123T	A	Hamburg, GY	BD
9	EUROPEAN SEAFARER	10957t	75	18k	50P	-	98T	A	Hamburg, GY	BD
10	EUROPEAN TRADER	8007t	75	18k	54P	-	55L	BA2	Bremerhaven, GY	BD

CELTIC STAR Built as the KOSEI MARU for *Kanko Kisen KK Line* of Japan for domestic services. In 1998 she was sold to *Jay Management Corporation* of Cyprus and renamed the IOLAOS. In November 1998 she was chartered to *East Coast Ferries*, renamed the LOON-PLAGE and placed on their Hull – Dunkerque service. The service ceased in January 1999 and after a brief charter to *DFDS Tor Line*, she was renamed the CELTIC STAR, chartered to *P&O European Ferries (Irish Sea)* and placed on the Liverpool – Dublin route.

CELTIC SUN See Late News

EUROPEAN ENDEAVOUR Built as the EUROPEAN ENTERPRISE for *European Ferries*. In 1988 she was renamed the EUROPEAN ENDEAVOUR. She was used on freight services between Dover and Calais and Dover and Zeebrugge. If space was available, a small number of passengers was sometimes conveyed on the Zeebrugge service, although the sailings were not advertised for passengers. This ceased with the withdrawal of passenger services on this route at the end of 1991. During the summer period she provided additional freight capacity on the Dover – Calais service and has also served on other routes. In autumn 1995 she was transferred to the Cairnryan – Larne service. In 1998 accommodation was raised to provide extra freight capacity. In March 1999 began

European Envoy (John Hendy)

Northern Merchant (Mike Louagie)

also operating to Ardrossan but this ceased later in the year.

EUROPEAN ENVOY Built as the IBEX for *P&O* for *Pandoro* Irish sea services. In 1980 chartered to *North Sea Ferries*, renamed the NORSEA and used on the Ipswich – Rotterdam service. In 1986 she was renamed the NORSKY. In 1995 she returned to *Pandoro* and was re-registered in Bermuda. Later in 1995 she resumed her original name of IBEX. An additional deck was added in 1996. In late 1997 she was renamed the EUROPEAN ENVOY. She is used on the Liverpool – Dublin service.

EUROPEAN HIGHLANDER Built as the SALAHALA and chartered to *Gilnavi* of Italy for Mediterranean services. In 1990 she was purchased by *Cenargo* and chartered to *Merchant Ferries* who renamed her the MERCHANT VALIANT. She was used on the Fleetwood – Warrenpoint service until 1993 when she was chartered to *Pandoro* and placed on their Ardrossan – Larne service. Purchased by *P&O* in 1995 and renamed the LION. In early 1998 renamed the EUROPEAN HIGHLANDER.

EUROPEAN LEADER Built for *Stena Line* as the BUFFALO and due to be chartered to *P&O* for *Pandoro* Irish Sea services. Before completion she was purchased by *P&O*. In 1989 she was lengthened by 12.5m and in 1998 she was further lengthened by 15m and renamed the EUROPEAN LEADER. She is now used on the Liverpool – Dublin service.

EUROPEAN NAVIGATOR Launched as the STENA TRADER but entered service as the GOYA for *United Baltic Corporation* of Great Britain on services between Britain and Spain. In 1979 sold to *Federal Commerce* of Canada for Canadian service and renamed the FEDERAL NOVA. In 1981 briefly renamed the CARIBBEAN SKY before being sold to *Linea Manuare* of Venezuela, renamed the MANUARE VII and used on services to the USA. In 1983 she was sold to new owners who chartered her to *Navigation Central* and renamed her the OYSTER BAY. Later that year she was chartered to *European Ferries*, renamed the VIKING TRADER and used on services between Portsmouth and France. In 1989 transferred to *Pandoro* and in 1996 renamed the LEOPARD. She was renamed the EUROPEAN NAVIGATOR in 1998. Use on the Liverpool – Dublin service until March 1999 when she was transferred to the Cairnryan – Larne route. Later in 1999 she returned to the Fleetwood – Larne, to operate the third daily service which had been inaugurated by the chartered MERCHANT VENTURE.

EUROPEAN PATHFINDER Built as the EUROPEAN CLEARWAY for *European Ferries* ro-ro freight services. She was built to a standard design rather than custom built. She was used on freight services between Dover and Calais and Dover and Zeebrugge. In 1992 she was moved to the Portsmouth – Le Havre route. In 1993 she was transferred to *Pandoro* to inaugurate a new Cherbourg – Rosslare service. In 1996 she was renamed the PANTHER. In early 1998 she was renamed the EUROPEAN PATHFINDER.

EUROPEAN PIONEER Built for *Stena Line* as the BISON and due to be chartered to *P&O* for *Pandoro* Irish Sea services. Before completion she was purchased by *P&O*. Between 1989 and 1993 she was operated by *B&I Line* of Ireland on a joint service with *Pandoro* between Dublin and Liverpool. An additional deck was added in 1995. In late 1997 she was renamed the EUROPEAN PIONEER. She is now used on the Fleetwood – Larne service.

EUROPEAN SEAFARER Ordered by *Stena Line* as the UNION TRADER but completed as the UNION MELBOURNE for the *Northern Coasters Ltd* of the UK and lengthened before entering service. Chartered to the *Union Steamship Company* of New Zealand and used on services to Australia. In 1980 she was sold to another *P&O* subsidiary and renamed the PUMA. In early 1998 she was renamed the EUROPEAN SEAFARER. She is now used on the Fleetwood – Larne service.

EUROPEAN TRADER Built for *European Ferries* ro-ro freight services; built to a standard design rather than custom built. In late 1991 she was transferred to the Portsmouth – Le Havre route and in 1994 to the Felixstowe – Zeebrugge service to supplement the service provided by the two passenger vessels. In 1996 she was transferred to the Cairnryan – Larne service. In March 1999 began also operating to Ardrossan but this ceased later in the year.

European Endeavour (P&O)

Moondance (Jenny Williamson)

P&O FERRYMASTERS

THE COMPANY *P&O Ferrymasters Ltd* is a British private sector company, a subsidiary of the *Peninsular and Oriental Steam Navigation Company.*

MANAGEMENT Managing Director: J Bradshaw, **Group Tenders and Contracts Manager:** D M Brinkley.

ADDRESS *Head Office:* 11-13 Lower Brook Street, IPSWICH IP4 1AJ, *Port Office:* PO Box South Bank 12, Teesport, MIDDLESBROUGH TS6 7RZ.

TELEPHONE *Head Office:* **Administration:** +44 (0)1473 581200, **Reservations:** +44 (0)1473 58120, **Fax:** +44 (0)1473 581222, *Port Office:* **Administration:** +44 (0)1642 394600, **Reservations:** +44 (0)1642 394600, **Fax:** +44 (0)1642 394666.

INTERNET Email: *Head Office:* peter.rogers@pofm.com *Port Office:* pofmmidd@aol.com

Website: http://www.po-transeuropean.com *(English)*

ROUTE OPERATED Middlesbrough (Teesport) *(dep: Mon, Thu)* – Göteborg (Sweden) *(dep: Tue, Fri)* – Helsingborg (Sweden) *(dep: Sat)* (up to 48 hrs; *(1)*; 2 per week to Göteborg, 1 per week to Helsingborg).

VESSELS

1	ELK	14374t	78	18k	12P	-	140T	A	Ulsan, SK	GB

ELK Built for *Stena Rederi* of Sweden and chartered to *P&O Ferrymasters*. Purchased by *P&O* in 1981 and lengthened in 1986. She is managed by *P&O North Sea Ferries Ltd.*

P&O NORTH SEA FERRIES

THE COMPANY, MANAGEMENT, ADDRESS AND TELEPHONE See Section 1.

ROUTES OPERATED Hull *(dep: 21.00 Mon-Sat)* – Rotterdam (Europoort) *(dep: 21.00 Mon-Sat)* (10 hrs; *3,4)*; 6 per week), Middlesbrough (Teesport) *(dep: 20.00 Mon-Sat)* – Rotterdam (Europoort) *(dep: 21.00 Mon-Sat)* (15 hrs; *(6,7)*; 6 per week), Middlesbrough (Teesport) *(dep: 21.00 Mon-Sat)* – Zeebrugge *(dep: 21.00 Mon-Sat)* (15 hrs; *(8,9)*; 6 per week), Hull *(dep: 21.00 Mon, Wed, Fri)* – Zeebrugge *(dep: 21.00 Tue, Thu, Sat)* (13 hrs; *(5)*; 3 per week), Felixstowe *(dep: 06.00, 11.30, 18.00, 22.30)* – Rotterdam (Europoort) *(dep: 06.00, 11.30, 19.00, 23.30)* (7 hrs 30 mins; *(1,2,10,11)*; 4 per day), Felixstowe *(dep: 11.00, 23.00)* – Zeebrugge *(dep: 11.00, 23.59)* (6 hrs; *(12,13)*; 2 per day).

VESSELS

1	EUROPEAN FREEWAY	21162t	77	16.5k	166P	-	163T	A2	Ulsan, SK	GB
2	EUROPEAN TIDEWAY	21162t	77	16.5k	166P	-	163T	A2	Ulsan, SK	GB
3	NORBANK	17464t	93	22k	114P	-	156T	A	Krimpen, NL	NL
4	NORBAY	17464t	94	22k	114P	-	156T	A	Krimpen, NL	GB
5	NORCAPE	14807t	79	19.4k	12P	-	138T	A	Tamano, JA	NL
6	NORKING	17884t	80	19k	12P	-	155T	A	Rauma, FI	FI
7	NORQUEEN	17884t	80	19k	12P	-	155T	A	Rauma, FI	FI
8	NORSKY	19992t	99	20k	12P	-	210T	A	Rauma, FI	NL
9	NORSTREAM	19992t	99	20k	12P	-	210T	A	Rauma, FI	NL
10	PRIDE OF FLANDERS	16776t	78	17k	74P	-	124T	A2	Ulsan, SK	GB
11	PRIDE OF SUFFOLK	16776t	78	17k	74P	-	124T	A2	Ulsan, SK	GB
12	RODONA	6568t	80	15k	12P	-	82T	A	Karlskrona, SW	SW
13	SAPPHIRE	6568t	80	15k	12P	-	82T	A	Karlskrona, SW	SW

EUROPEAN FREEWAY Built for *Stena Rederi* as the ALPHA ENTERPRISE and chartered to *Aghiris Navigation* of Cyprus. In 1979 she was renamed the SYRIA and chartered to *Hellas Ferries* for services between Greece and Syria. In 1981 she was lengthened by 33.6m. In 1982 she was chartered to *European Ferries* and used on freight services between Felixstowe and Rotterdam. In 1983 she was renamed the STENA TRANSPORTER and in 1986 the CERDIC FERRY. In 1992 she was renamed the EUROPEAN FREEWAY and, in 1994, purchased by *P&O European Ferries*.

EUROPEAN TIDEWAY Launched as the STENA RUNNER by *Stena Rederi* of Sweden. On completion, renamed the ALPHA PROGRESS and chartered to *Aghiris Navigation* of Greece. In 1979 renamed the HELLAS and operated by *Soutos-Hellas Ferry Services* on services between Greece and Syria. In 1982 she was lengthened by 33.6m. In 1982 she was chartered to *European Ferries* and used on freight services between Felixstowe and Rotterdam. The following year she was returned to *Hellas Ferries*. In 1985 she returned to *European Ferries* and the Rotterdam service. In 1986 she was renamed the DORIC FERRY. In 1992 she was renamed the EUROPEAN TIDEWAY and, in 1994, purchased by *P&O European Ferries*.

NORBANK Built for *North Sea Ferries* for the Hull – Rotterdam service. She was owned by *Nedlloyd* and in 1996 was sold to *P&O* but retains Dutch crew and registry. Due to move to the Felixstowe – Europoort route in 2001 when replaced by new 'super ro-pax' vessels.

NORBAY Built for *North Sea Ferries* for the Hull – Rotterdam service. Owned by *P&O*. Due to move to the Felixstowe – Europoort route in 2001 when replaced by new 'super ro-pax' vessels.

NORCAPE Launched as the PUMA but, on completion chartered to *B&I Line* and renamed the TIPPERARY for their Dublin – Liverpool service. In 1989 sold to *North Sea Ferries*, renamed the NORCAPE and introduced onto the Ipswich – Rotterdam service. In 1995 that service ceased and she was moved to the Hull – Zeebrugge freight service. She retains Dutch crew and registry.

NORKING, NORQUEEN Built as the BORE KING and the BORE QUEEN for *Bore Line* of Finland for Baltic services. In 1991 chartered to *North Sea Ferries* for their Teesport – Zeebrugge service and renamed the NORKING and NORQUEEN respectively. During winter 1995/96 they were lengthened by 28.8 metres and re-engined. In 1999 transferred to the Teesport – Rotterdam service.

NORSKY, NORSTREAM Built for *Bore Line* of Finland and chartered to *P&O North Sea Ferries*. They operate on the Teesport – Zeebrugge service.

PRIDE OF FLANDERS Built as the MERZARIO ESPANIA for *Stena Rederi* of Sweden and immediately chartered to *Merzario Line* for their service between Italy and Saudi Arabia. In the same year she was renamed the MERZARIO HISPANIA. In 1979 she was chartered to *European Ferries* for their ro-ro freight service between Felixstowe and Rotterdam and renamed the NORDIC FERRY. In 1982 she served in the Falkland Islands Task Force. In 1986 she was modified to carry 688 passengers and, with sister vessel the BALTIC FERRY (now PRIDE OF SUFFOLK), took over the Felixstowe – Zeebrugge passenger service. In 1992 she was renamed the PRIDE OF FLANDERS. In 1994, purchased by *P&O European Ferries*. In 1995 the Felixstowe – Zeebrugge passenger service ceased, her additional passenger accommodation was removed, passenger capacity was reduced and she was transferred to the Felixstowe – Rotterdam freight service. In 2001 she (and sister vessel, the PRIDE OF SUFFOLK) will be replaced by the NORBANK and the NORBAY.

PRIDE OF SUFFOLK Built as the STENA TRANSPORTER, a ro-ro freight vessel for *Stena Rederi* of Sweden. In 1979 she was renamed the FINNROSE and chartered to *Finnlines*. She later served with *Atlanticargo* on their service between Europe and USA/Mexico. In 1980 she returned to *Stena Line* and resumed her original name. Later in 1980 she was chartered to *European Ferries* for their Felixstowe – Rotterdam freight-only service and renamed the BALTIC FERRY. In 1982 she served in the Falkland Islands Task Force. In 1986 she was modified in the same way as the PRIDE OF FLANDERS and moved to the Felixstowe – Zeebrugge service. In 1992 she was renamed the PRIDE OF SUFFOLK. In 1994 she was purchased by *P&O European Ferries*. In 1995 the Felixstowe – Zeebrugge passenger service ceased, her additional passenger accommodation was removed, passenger capacity was reduced and she was transferred to the Felixstowe – Rotterdam freight service.

RODONA Built as the BALDER DONA for *Dag Engström* of Sweden and undertook a number of charters in the Caribbean and Mediterranean. In 1984 she was renamed the RODONA and chartered to *Seaboard Shipping* of the USA and used on Caribbean services. In 1987 she was chartered to the *Ford Motor Company* for conveyance of privately owned trailers between Dagenham and Zeebrugge.

In 1995 *Cobelfret Ferries* took over the operation of this service and she was used on both the Purfleet – Zeebrugge and Dagenham – Zeebrugge services. In 1999 she was chartered to *P&O North Sea Ferries* to operate between Felixstowe and Zeebrugge.

SAPPHIRE Built as the BALDER VINGA for *Dag Engström* of Sweden and undertook a number of charters in the Caribbean and Mediterranean. In 1984 she was renamed the ROVINGA and chartered to *Seaboard Shipping* of the USA and used on Caribbean services. In 1985 she was renamed the AZUA. In 1987 she briefly reverted to the name ROVINGA before being renamed the SAPPHIRE and chartered to the *Ford Motor Company* for conveyance of privately owned trailers between Dagenham and Zeebrugge. Since 1995, as the RODONA.

P&O SCOTTISH FERRIES

THE COMPANY, MANAGEMENT AND ADDRESS See Section 1.

TELEPHONE Administration: +44 (0)1224 589111, **Reservations:** +44 (0)1224 589111, **Fax:** +44 (0)1224 574411.

INTERNET Email: passenger@poscottishferries.co.uk **Website:** http://www.poscottishferries.co.uk *(English)*

ROUTES OPERATED Aberdeen – Lerwick (14 hrs; *(1)*; up to 3 per week). There are no fixed sailing times. One southbound trip returns via Stromness or Kirkwall taking approx. 20 hours.

VESSEL

1	ST ROGNVALD	5297t	70	16 k	12P	-	41L	A	Lübeck, GY	GB

ST ROGNVALD Launched as the RHONETAL but renamed the NORCAPE on delivery and chartered to *North Sea Ferries* for their Hull – Rotterdam service; in 1972 she inaugurated their Hull – Zeebrugge service. In 1974 she returned to her owners and resumed the name RHONETAL. In 1975 sold to *Meridional D'Armements* of France for services to Corsica and renamed the RHONE. In 1987 sold to *Conatir* of Italy for Mediterranean services and renamed the MARINO TORRE. In 1989 taken on six months charter to *P&O Scottish Ferries*. In 1990 she was purchased by them and renamed the ST ROGNVALD. She initially operated alongside and then replaced the ST MAGNUS (1206t, 1970). Earlier calls at Leith, Hanstholm (Denmark) and Stavanger (Norway) have now been discontinued.

P&O STENA LINE

THE COMPANY AND ADDRESS See Section 1.

MANAGEMENT Freight Director: Brian Cork.

TELEPHONE Administration: See Section 1, **Reservations:** +44 (0)1304 863344, **Fax:** +44 (0)1304 863399, **Telex:** 96316.

ROUTES OPERATED Dover *(dep: 00.30, 04.30, 08.30, 12.30, 16.30, 20.30)* – Zeebrugge *(dep: 03.30, 07.30, 11.30, 15.30, 19.30, 23.30)* (4 hrs 30 mins; *(1,2,3)*; 6 per day). Services are sometimes diverted to Calais according to traffic conditions.

VESSELS

1	EUROPEAN HIGHWAY	22986t	92	21k	200P	-	120L	BA2	Bremerhaven, GY	GB
2	EUROPEAN PATHWAY	22986t	92	21k	200P	-	120L	BA2	Bremerhaven, GY	GB
3	EUROPEAN SEAWAY	22986t	91	21k	200P	-	120L	BA2	Bremerhaven, GY	GB

EUROPEAN HIGHWAY, EUROPEAN PATHWAY, EUROPEAN SEAWAY Built for *P&O European Ferries* for the Dover – Zeebrugge freight service. In 1998 they were transferred to *P&O Stena Line*. In summer 1999 the EUROPEAN HIGHWAY operated full time between Dover and Calais. She returned to the Dover – Zeebrugge route in the autumn when the P&OSL AQUITAINE was transferred to the Dover – Calais service.

SCA TRANSFOREST

THE COMPANY *SCA Transforest* is a Swedish company.

MANAGEMENT Managing Director (UK): Bo Frölander,

ADDRESS Interforest Terminal London Ltd, 44 Berth, TILBURY DOCK Essex RM18 7HR.

TELEPHONE Administration & Reservations: +44 (0)1375 48 85 00, **Fax:** +44 (0)1375 48 85 03

INTERNET Email: bo.frolander@transforest.sca.se **Website:** http://www.transforest.sca.se

ROUTE OPERATED Umeå *(dep: Mon, Thu)* – Husum *(dep: Mon, Thu)* – Sundsvall *(dep: Tue, Fri)* – Iggesund *(dep: Tue, Fri)* – Oskarshamn *(dep: Sat)* – Tilbury *(arr/dep: Sat, Tue)* – Rotterdam (Europoort) *(arr/dep: Sun, Wed)* – Umeå *(arr: Mon, Thu)* (8/9 day round trip; *(1,2,3)*; 2 per week).

VESSELS

1	OBBOLA	18265t	96	16k	OP	-	-	A	Sevilla, SP	SW
2	ORTVIKEN	18265t	97	16k	OP	-	-	A	Sevilla, SP	SW
3	ÖSTRAND	8265t	96	16k	OP	-	-	A	Sevilla, SP	SW

OBBOLA, ORTVIKEN, ÖSTRAND Built for *Gorthon Lines* and chartered to *SCA Transforest*. They are designed for the handling of forest products in non-wheeled 'casettes'

SEA CONTAINERS

THE COMPANY, MANAGEMENT, ADDRESS AND TELEPHONE See Section 1.

ROUTE OPERATED No dedicated freight services are currently operated.

VESSELS

1•	PEVERIL	5254t	71	16k	12P	-	40T	A	Kristiansand, NO	IM
2•	PICASSO	5689t	77	16k	12P	-	64T	A	Hamburg, GY	CI

PEVERIL Built as the HOLMIA for *Rederi AB Silja* of Finland. She was used on *Silja Line* cargo and ro-ro services between Norrtälje (Sweden) and Turku (Finland). In 1973 she was sold and renamed the A S D METEOR. Later that year she was sold to *P&O Ferries* for their joint Heysham – Belfast service with *Sealink* and renamed the PENDA. In 1980 she was renamed the N F JAGUAR and transferred to freight services between Southampton and Le Havre. In 1981 she was chartered to *IOMSP Co* for a Douglas – Liverpool freight service and in 1983 she was demise chartered by *James Fisher* of Barrow and chartered to *IOMSP Co*; she was renamed the PEVERIL. The freight service was switched to Heysham in 1985. The charter ended in December 1992 and she was purchased by the *IOMSP Co.* She was replaced by the BELARD in 1997 and was laid up but was chartered to *Irish Ferries* in November 1997 to operate between Rosslare and Pembroke. In 1998 the BELARD was sold and she returned to service. She was replaced by the ro-pax ferry BEN-MY-CHREE in August 1998 and laid up at Birkenhead. She is, however, liable to be used when the BEN-MY-CHREE is being overhauled – although this did not happen during winter 2000.

PICASSO Built as the WUPPERTAL for *J A Reinecke* of Germany and chartered out. In 1978 she was renamed the CANAIMA but the following year she resumed her original name. Charters included *North Sea Ferries*, with spells on both the Ipswich – Rotterdam and Hull – Zeebrugge services, *Tor Lloyd* and *DFDS*. In 1987 she was renamed the BEAVERDALE. She had a number of further charters, including *North Sea Ferries* where she operated from 1989 to 1991 between Teesport and Zeebrugge. In 1991 she was purchased by *Sea Containers*, renamed the POKER and chartered out. In 1995 she was briefly chartered to *Mannin Line* (an *IOMSP* subsidiary) to operate between Great Yarmouth and IJmuiden (Netherlands). Later that year she was renamed the PICASSO and chartered to *DFDS*. In 1996 she was transferred to *Hoverspeed Falcon Sea Freight* (a joint venture between *Hoverspeed* and *Falcon Distribution*) and introduced onto the Folkestone – Boulogne route. In early 1998, *Hoverspeed* ceased to have commercial involvement in the service but continued to crew the vessel, which remains owned by *Sea Containers*. She was chartered to *Falcon Seafreight*. In summer 1998 the charter was terminated and she was laid up. Later in 1998, she was chartered again, in

Elk (Philippe Holthof)

Norbay (Mile Louagie)

order to operate a two ship service. She began operating in 1999 but ceased after a few months and was again laid up at Birkenhead.

SEAFRANCE

THE COMPANY, MANAGEMENT, ADDRESS, TELEPHONE AND INTERNET See Section 1.

ROUTE OPERATED Calais *(dep: 02.30, 06.30, 14.30, 18.30, 22.30)* – Dover *(dep: 03.30, 07.30, 15.30, 19.30, 23.30)* (1 hr 30 mins; *(1)*; up to 5 per day). Service operates according to market demand; otherwise all traffic is conveyed on the multi-purpose ferries.

VESSEL

1	SEAFRANCE NORD									
	PAS-DE-CALAIS	13727t	87	21.5k	80P	-	114T	BA2	Dunkerque, FR	FR

SEAFRANCE NORD PAS-DE-CALAIS Built for *SNCF* for the Dunkerque (Ouest) – Dover train ferry service. Before being used on this service (which required the construction of a new berth at Dover (Western Docks)) in May 1988, she operated road freight services from Calais to Dover Eastern Docks. The train ferry service continued to operate following the opening of the Channel Tunnel in 1994, to convey road vehicles and dangerous loads which were banned from the tunnel. However, it ceased in December 1995 and, after a refit, in February 1996 she was renamed the SEAFRANCE NORD PAS-DE-CALAIS and switched to the Calais – Dover service, primarily for road freight vehicles and drivers but also advertised as carrying up to 50 car passengers. Now freight-only.

SEATRUCK FERRIES

THE COMPANY *Seatruck Ferries Ltd* is a British private sector company, owned by *Crescent plc.*

MANAGEMENT Managing Director: Kevin Hobbs, **Sales Director:** Alastair Eagles.

ADDRESS *Warrenpoint (HQ):* Seatruck House, The Ferry Terminal, WARRENPOINT, County Down BT34 3JR. *Heysham:* North Quay, Heysham Port, Heysham, MORECAMBE, Lancs LA3 2UL.

TELEPHONE Administration: +44 (0)16937 54411, **Reservations:** *Warrenpoint:* +44 (0)28 3075 4400, *Heysham:* +44 (0)1524 853512. **Fax:** *Admin:* +44 (0)16937 54545, *Reservations – Warrenpoint:* +44 (0)28 3077 3737, *Reservations – Heysham:* +44 (0)1524 853549.

INTERNET Email: alistair@seatruck-ferries.co.uk

ROUTES OPERATED Heysham *(dep: 08.00 Tue-Sat, 20.00 Mon, 21.00 Tue-Sun)* – Warrenpoint *(dep: 09.00 Tue-Sat, 19.00 Mon, 20.00 Tue-Sat, 17.00 Sun)* (8 hrs; *(1,2)*; 2 per day).

VESSELS

1	MOONDANCE	5881t	78	15k	12P	-	70T	A	Bremerhaven, GY	BA
2	RIVERDANCE	6041t	77	15k	12P	-	70T	A	Bremerhaven, GY	BA

MOONDANCE Built as the EMADALA for *Emadala Shipping* and chartered to *Gilnavi* of Italy for Mediterranean service. In 1987 she was purchased by *Gilnavi*. In 1990 sold to *Cenargo* of Great Britain and chartered to *Merchant Ferries* for their Heysham – Warrenpoint service and renamed the MERCHANT VICTOR. She was withdrawn from that service in 1993 and was chartered out to a number of operators. In 1997 she was chartered to *Seatruck Ferries* and renamed the MOONDANCE. In 1998 she was purchased by *Seatruck Ferries.*

RIVERDANCE Built as the MASHALA for *Mashala Shipping* and chartered to *Gilnavi* of Italy for Mediterranean services. After a long period out of service in the mid-nineteen eighties, in 1987 she was sold, renamed the HALLA and chartered for Caribbean service. In 1988 she was renamed the TIKAL. In 1989 she was sold to *Schiaffino Line* of France, renamed the SCHIAFFINO and put into service between Ramsgate and Oostende. In 1990 the company was taken over by *Sally Ferries* and in 1991 she was chartered to *Belfast Freight Ferries*. In 1993 she was renamed the SALLY EUROBRIDGE. In January 1994, she was chartered to *North Sea Ferries* to operate between Hull and Zeebrugge and renamed the EUROBRIDGE. In summer 1994 she returned to *Sally Ferries,* resumed the name SALLY EUROBRIDGE and became the second vessel on the Ramsgate – Vlissingen service; in the autumn the British terminal was switched to Dartford. In 1995 she was chartered to *Norfolk Line*, renamed the EUROBRIDGE and also sold by *Sally Ferries*. In 1996 she was chartered to *Seatruck Ferries* and renamed the RIVERDANCE. In 1997 she was purchased by *Seatruck Ferries*.

STENA LINE

THE COMPANY, MANAGEMENT, ADDRESS, TELEPHONE & INTERNET See Section 1.

ROUTE OPERATED Hoek van Holland *(dep: 12.30, 20.15, 23.15)* – Harwich *(dep: 07.45, 11.15, 23.00)* (7 hrs 30 mins; *(1,2,3)*; 3 per day).

VESSELS

1	ROSEBAY	13700t	76	17k	63P	-	135T	A	Hamburg, GY	CY
2	STENA SEARIDER	21019t	69	17k	120P	-	198T	AS2	Helsinki, FI	IM
3	STENA SEATRADER	17991t	73	17.5k	221P	-	174T	AS2	Nakskov, DK	NL

ROSEBAY Built as the TRANSGERMANIA for *Poseidon Schiffahrt AG* of Germany interests for *Finncarriers- Poseidon* services between Finland and West Germany. In 1991 chartered to *Norse Irish Ferries* and used on their freight service between Liverpool and Belfast. In 1992 she was returned to *Finncarriers* and in 1993 sold to Cypriot interests for use in the Mediterranean and renamed the ROSEBAY. In 1994 chartered to *Stena Line* to inaugurate a new service between Harwich and Rotterdam (Frisohaven). In 1995 the service was switched to Hoek van Holland following the construction of a new linkspan. She also, during the summer, carried cars towing caravans, motor caravans and their passengers. In 1997 she was chartered to *Sally Freight* and renamed the EUROSTAR. Later in 1997 she was renamed the EUROCRUISER. In 1998 she returned on charter to *Stena Line* and resumed the name ROSEBAY. In 1999 she was temporarily transferred to the Irish Sea. To be withdrawn in autumn 2000 when the STENA BRITANNICA (see Section 1) is delivered.

STENA SEARIDER Built as the FINNCARRIER for *Finnlines* of Finland for service between Finland, Denmark and Germany. In 1975 renamed the POLARIS. In 1984 sold to *Rederi AB Nordö* of Sweden to operate between Malmö (Sweden) and Travemünde (Germany) and renamed the SCANDINAVIA. In 1987 she was rebuilt to increase capacity from 122 trailers to 200. In 1989 the name of the company was changed to *Nordö Link* and she was renamed the SCANDINAVIA LINK. In 1990 she was sold to *Stena Line*, renamed the STENA SEARIDER and used on their Göteborg (Sweden) – Travemünde service. In 1991 she was chartered out for service in the Caribbean and renamed the SEARIDER. In 1992 she was chartered to *Norse Irish Ferries* and renamed the NORSE MERSEY. In 1995 she was replaced by a new vessel of the same name and returned to *Stena Line*, resumed the name STENA SEARIDER and resumed operating between Göteborg and Travemünde and Göteborg and Kiel. In May 1997, she was transferred to the Hoek van Holland – Harwich service. To be withdrawn in autumn 2000 when the STENA BRITANNICA (see Section 1) is delivered.

STENA SEATRADER Built as the SVEALAND for *Lion Ferry AB* of Sweden and chartered to *Statens Järnvägar (Swedish State Railways)* for the train ferry service between Trelleborg (Sweden) and Sassnitz (Germany (DDR)). The charter ceased in 1980 and in 1982 she was sold to *Rederi AB Nordö* of Sweden. She was lengthened by 33.7 metres, renamed the SVEALAND AV MALMÖ and used on their lorry/rail wagon service between Malmö and Travemünde. In 1986 she was rebuilt with a higher superstructure and in 1987 she was renamed the SVEA LINK, the service being renamed *Nordö Link*. In 1990 she was sold to *Stena Line*, renamed the STENA SEATRADER and introduced onto the Hoek van Holland – Harwich service. To be withdrawn in autumn 2000 when the STENA HOLLANDICA (see Section 1) is delivered.

Countances (Kevin Mitchell)

TRANSEUROPA SHIPPING LINES

THE COMPANY *TransEuropa Shipping Lines* is a Slovenian private sector company, owned by *Denval Ltd* of the UK. They operate the Ramsgate – Oostende service in a joint venture with *HR Services (Hogg Robinson Group), Diaz Haulage* and the *Port of Oostende*. Agents in both Ramsgate and Oostende are *Ostend Cargo Handling Services Ltd (OCHS)* (also part of the *Hogg Robinson Group*). Operations started in November 1998, replacing those of *Sally Ferries*.

MANAGEMENT *Denval:* **Managing Director:** Mr J D Dias, *OCHS:* **Managing Director:** G Bartlett, **Operations Director:** G Fordham.

ADDRESS *TSL:* Vojkovo nabrezje 38, 6000 KOPER, Slovenia, *Denval:* 156 High Street, SEVENOAKS, Kent TN13 1XE, *OCHS: Belgium:* Slijkensesleenweg 18, 8400 OOSTENDE, Belgium, *UK:* Ferry Terminal, Ramsgate New Port, RAMSGATE, Kent CT11 8RP.

TELEPHONE *Denval:* +44 (0)1732 458288, **Fax:** +44 (0)1732 458277, *OCHS:* **Admin & Reservations (Belgium):** +32 (0)59 32 10 10, **Reservations (UK):** +44 (0)1843 585151, **Fax: Admin (Belgium):** +32 (0)59 32 24 96, **Reservations (UK):** +44 (0)1843 580894.

INTERNET Website: http://www.portofoostende.be/tsl/

ROUTE OPERATED Ramsgate *(dep: 01.00 Mon-Sat, 05.30 Tue-Sat, 13.30 Sun-Fri, 17.30 Mon-Fri, 18.00 Sun, 22.30 Mon-Thu*)* – Oostende *(dep: 01.00 Tue-Sat, 07.30 Mon-Fri, 13.00 Sun-Fri, 17.30 Mon-Fri*, 18.00 Sat, 20.30 Sun-Fri)* (4 hrs; (1,3,4(*=operated by 4)); 5 per day). Note: Timetable subject to change if and when the LARKSPUR enters service. It is possible that a passenger service will be offered from spring 2000 but, at the time of going to press, no details were available.

VESSELS

1	EUROVOYAGER	12110t	78	22k	1500P	54C	68T	BA2	Hoboken, BE	CY
2	LARKSPUR	14458t	76	17.5k	1040P	-	58L	BA2	Bremerhaven, GY	BA

| 3 | PRIMROSE | 12046t | 76 | 22k | 1200P | 354C | 68T | BA2 | Hoboken, BE | CY |
| 4 | ROSEANNE | 7744t | 82 | 17k | 12P | - | 73T | AS | Vigo, SP | CY |

EUROVOYAGER Built as the PRINS ALBERT for *RMT* of Belgium for the Oostende – Dover service. During 1986 she had an additional vehicle deck added. In 1994 the British port became Ramsgate. Withdrawn after 28th February 1997 and laid up. In 1998 she was sold to *Denval Marine Consultants*, renamed the EUROVOYAGER and chartered to *Sally Line*. In July, she entered service with *Sally Freight*. In November the *Sally Freight* service ended and she immediately began operating for *TESL*.

LARKSPUR Built as the GEDSER for *Gedser-Travemünde Ruten* of Denmark for their service between Gedser (Denmark) and Travemünde (Germany). In 1986 she was purchased by *Thorsviks Rederi A/S* of Norway and chartered to *Sally Ferries*, re-registered in the Bahamas, renamed the VIKING 2 and entered service on the Ramsgate – Dunkerque service. In early 1989 she was renamed the SALLY SKY and during winter 1989/90 she was 'stretched' to increase vehicle capacity. At the end of 1996 she was withdrawn from the Dunkerque service. In 1997 she was renamed the EUROTRAVELLER, transferred to *Holyman-Sally Ferries* and, in March, was introduced onto the Ramsgate – Oostende route. In 1998, when *Holyman-Sally Ferries* came to an end, she operated in a freight-only role for *Sally Line* under the *Sally Freight* name. Passenger services were resumed in May, under the name of *Sally Direct*. All *Sally Line* operations ended in November 1998 and she was withdrawn for sale and laid up. In 1999 sold to *Denval* and renamed the LARKSPUR. She was given a major refit at Dunkerque. She is expected to enter service in spring 2000 when a passenger service is launched.

PRIMROSE Built as the PRINCESSE MARIE-CHRISTINE for *Regie voor Maritiem Transport* of Belgium for the Oostende – Dover service. During 1985 she had an extra vehicle deck added, increasing vehicle capacity. Passenger capacity was increased by 200 by the conversion of an upper deck 'garage' into passenger accommodation. In January 1994 the British port became Ramsgate. In 1994 chartered briefly to *Sally Ferries* and operated between Ramsgate and Dunkerque. Since then a spare vessel and withdrawn in early 1997. In 1998 sold to *Denval Marine Consultants* of the UK and renamed the PRIMROSE. In 1999 she began operating for *TESL* between Ramsgate and Oostende.

ROSEANNE Built as the REINA DEL CANTABRICO for *Labiad Andalusia* of Spain and chartered to *Matina Line* for services between Europe and West Africa. In 1983 renamed the SALAH LABIAD but resumed her original name in 1985. In 1987 she was sold, renamed the FAROY and chartered to *Elbe-Humber Roline* for their service between Immingham and Cuxhaven. In 1989 sold to *Denval* and renamed the ROSEANNE; she was chartered to *P&O European Ferries* and used on their Felixstowe – Zeebrugge service. In 1991 chartered to *Norfolk Line*. In 1996 this charter ended and she was chartered to *Lineas Suardiaz* of Spain. In 2000 chartered to *TESL* and placed on the Oostende – Ramsgate service. As she is slower than the other vessels and a stern loader, she is only able to do one round trip per day. She may be withdrawn if and when the LARKSPUR enters traffic.

TRANSFENNICA

THE COMPANY *Transfennica Ltd* is a Finnish private sector company.

MANAGEMENT President: Rolf G W Eriksson, **Marketing Manager (UK):** Kim Hilton, **Operations Manager (UK):** Andrew Prior.

ADDRESS *Finland:* Eteläranta 12, FIN-00130 HELSINKI, Finland, *UK:* Finland House, 47 Berth, Tilbury Freeport, TILBURY, Essex RM18 7EH.

TELEPHONE Administration & Reservations: *Finland:* +358 (0)9 13262, *UK:* +44 (0)1375 363 900, **Fax:** *Finland:* +358 (0)9 652377, *UK:* +44 (0)1375 840 888.

INTERNET Email: *Finland:* info@transfennica.com *UK:* info.uk@transfennica.com

Website: http://www.transfennica.com

ROUTES OPERATED *Finland – Tilbury service (three ships, each on weekly cycle):* Hamina *(arr/dep: Mon)* – Hanko *(arr/dep: Tue)* – Tilbury *(arr/dep: Fri)*, *((1)*; 1 per week), Rauma *(arr/dep: Thu)* – Tilbury *(arr/dep: Mon)* *((2)*; 1 per week), Hamina *(arr/dep: Fri)* – Tilbury *(arr/dep: Tue)* *((3)*; 1 per week), **Finland –**

Felixstowe service (three ships on three weekly cycle): Kemi *(dep: Mon)* – Oulu *(dep: Tue)* – Felixstowe *(arr/dep: Sun)* – Kemi *(arr/dep: Thu)* – Oulu *(arr/dep: Fri)* – Antwerpen *(arr/dep: Wed)* – Felixstowe *(arr/dep: Thu)* – Kemi *(arr: Mon)* – Oulu *(arr: Tue)* ((5,6,7); 2 per week), *Finland – Warrenpoint service:* Rauma *(dep: Wed)* – Warrenpoint *(arr: Tue)* ((4); alternate weeks (vessel returns empty)).

Ships are run primarily for the carriage of forest products from Finland to UK and other North European countries.

VESSELS

1	CAROLINE RUSS	10471t	99	21k	12P	-	134T	A2	Hamburg, GY	GY
2	PAULINE RUSS	10488t	99	21k	12P	-	134T	A2	Hamburg, GY	GY
3	SEAGARD	10471t	99	21k	12P	-	134T	A2	Hamburg, GY	GY
4	TRANS FENNIA	7307t	82	-	0P	-	-	A	Leirvik I Sogn, NO	NO
5	UNITED CARRIER	12251t	98	20k	12P	-	140T	A2	Rissa, NO	FI
6	UNITED EXPRESS	12251t	97	20k	12P	-	140T	A2	Rissa, NO	FI
7	UNITED TRADER	12251t	98	20k	12P	-	140T	A2	Rissa, NO	FI

CAROLINE RUSS, PAULINE RUSS, SEAGARD Built for *Ernst Russ* of Germany and chartered to *Transfennica*. They operate on the Tilbury services.

TRANS FENNIA Built for *Euro Trans Skip AS* of Norway. Chartered to *Transfennica* and used on the Warrenpoint service. She is classified as a pallet carrier rather than a ro-ro.

UNITED CARRIER, UNITED TRADER Built for *Birka Line* of Finland and chartered to *Transfennica*. They are currently used on the Felixstowe services.

UNITED EXPRESS Built for *United Shipping* of Finland and chartered to *Transfennica*. They are currently used on the Felixstowe services.

TRUCKLINE FERRIES

THE COMPANY *Truckline Ferries* is *Brittany Ferries'* freight division.

MANAGEMENT Managing Director: Ian Carruthers, **Freight Director:** John Clarke.

ADDRESS New Harbour Road, POOLE, Dorset BH15 4AJ.

INTERNET Website: http://www.truckline.co.uk *(English)* **Email:** truckline@truckline.co.uk

TELEPHONE Administration & Reservations: +44 (0)1202 675048, **Fax:** +44 (0)1202 679828, **Telex:** 41744, 41745.

ROUTES OPERATED Cherbourg (*Winter*: dep: 09.30 Wed, Fri, Sun, 18.30 Tue, Thu, Sat, 23.45 Mon, Wed, Fri, Sun, *Summer*: 02.00 Mon, Sat, Sun, 09.30 Tue, Thu, 14.30 Fri, Sat, Sun, 18.30 Mon, Wed, 23.45 Tue, Thu) – Poole (*Winter*: dep: 16.00 Mon, Wed, Fri, Sun, 08.30, 23.45 Tue, Thu, Sat, *Summer*: dep: 16.00 Tue, Thu, 08.30, 23.45 Mon, Wed, 07.30, 23.45 Fri, Sat, Sun) (4 hrs 30 mins; *(1)*; 1/2 per day). Note: Operates with *Brittany Ferries* passenger vessel BARFLEUR to provide three or four sailings every 24 hrs. Caen-Portsmouth (6hrs; *(Purbeck - se Late News)*; 1 per day)

VESSEL

1	COUTANCES	6507t	78	17k	58P	-	64T	BA	Le Havre, FR	FR

COUTANCES Built for *Truckline Ferries* for their Cherbourg – Poole service. In 1986 lengthened to increase vehicle capacity by 34%.

Section 4 – CHAIN, CABLE ETC FERRIES

In addition to the ferries listed above, there are a number of short chain ferries, cable ferries and ferries operated by unpowered floats:

BOURNEMOUTH-SWANAGE MOTOR ROAD AND FERRY COMPANY

Address Company: Shell Bay, Studland, SWANAGE, Dorset. **Tel:** +44 (0)1929 450203 (**Fax:** +44 (0)1929 450498), **Ferry:** Floating Bridge, Ferry Way, Sandbanks, POOLE, Dorset BH13 7QN. **Tel:** +44 (0)1929 450203.

Route: Sandbanks – Studland (Dorset).

1	BRAMBLE BUSH BAY	93	400P	48C	BA	Hessle, GB

BRAMBLE BUSH BAY chain ferry, built for the *Bournemouth-Swanage Motor Road and Ferry Company.*

CUMBRIA COUNTY COUNCIL

Address: Community, Economy & Environment Department, Citadel Chambers, CARLISLE CA3 8SG. **Tel:** +44 (0)1228 606744, **Fax:** +44 (0)1228 606755.

INTERNET Email: john.robinson@cumbriacc.gov.uk **Website:** http://www.cumbria.gov.uk *(English (County Council web site – little about ferry))*

Route: Bowness-on-Windermere – Far Sawrey.

1	MALLARD	90	140P	18C	BA	Borth, Dyfed, GB

MALLARD Chain Ferry built for *Cumbria County Council.*

ISLE OF WIGHT COUNCIL (COWES FLOATING BRIDGE)

Address: Ferry Office, Medina Road, COWES, Isle of Wight PO31 7BX. **Tel:** +44 (0)1983 293041

Route: Cowes – East Cowes.

1	NO 5	76	-	15C	BA	East Cowes, GB

NO 5 Chain ferry built for *Isle of Wight County Council,* now *Isle of Wight Council.*

KING HARRY STEAM FERRY COMPANY

Address: Feock, TRURO, Cornwall TR3 6QJ. **Tel:** +44 (0)1872 862312, **Fax:** +44 (0)1872 863355.

INTERNET Email: kingharryferry@feock.fsbusiness.co.uk

Route: Across River Fal, King Harry Ferry (Cornwall).

1	KING HARRY FERRY	74	100P	28C	BA	Falmouth, GB

KING HARRY FERRY Chain ferry built for *King Harry Steam Ferry Company.*

PHILIP LTD

Address: Dart Marina, Sandquay Road, DARTMOUTH, Devon TQ6 9PH. **Tel:** +44 (0)1803 833351.

Route: Dartmouth – Kingswear (Devon) across River Dart (higher route) (forms part of A379).

1	HIGHER FERRY	60	200P	18C	BA	Dartmouth, GB

HIGHER FERRY Diesel electric paddle propelled vessel guided by cross-river cables. Built by *Philip Ltd.*

REEDHAM FERRY

Address: Reedham Ferry, Ferry Inn, Reedham, NORWICH NR13 3HA. **Tel:** +44 (0)1493 700429, **Fax:** +44 (0)1493 700999.

Route: Acle – Reedham – Norton (across River Yare, Norfolk).

1	REEDHAM FERRY	84	12P	3C		BA	Oulton Broad, GB

REEDHAM FERRY Chain ferry built for *Reedham Ferry*. Maximum weight, 12 tons.

SOUTH HAMS DISTRICT COUNCIL

Address: Lower Ferry Office, The Square, Kingswear, DARTMOUTH, Devon TQ6 0AA. **Tel:** +44 (0)1803 752342, **Fax:** +44 (0)1803 752227.

Route: Dartmouth – Kingswear (Devon) across River Dart (lower route).

1	THE TOM AVIS	94	50P	8C		BA	Fowey, GB
2	THE TOM CASEY	89	50P	8C		BA	Portland, GB

THE TOM AVIS, THE TOM CASEY Floats propelled by tugs built for *South Hams District Council*.

TORPOINT FERRY

Address: 2 Ferry Street, TORPOINT, Cornwall PL11 2AX. **Tel:** +44 (0)1752 812233, **Fax:** +44 (0)1752 816873.

INTERNET Website: http://www.tamarbridge.co.uk

Route: Devonport (Plymouth) – Torpoint (Cornwall) across the Tamar. Pre-booking is not possible and the above number cannot be used for that purpose.

1	LYNHER	61	350P	48C		BA	Southampton, GB
2	PLYM	68	350P	54C		BA	Bristol, GB
3	TAMAR	60	350P	48C		BA	Southampton, GB

LYNHER, PLYM, TAMAR Chain ferries built for the *Torpoint Ferry*. The three ferries operate in parallel on their own 'track'.

WATERFORD CASTLE HOTEL

Address: The Island, WATERFORD, Irish Republic. **Tel:** +353 (0)51 78203.

INTERNET Email: info@waterfordcastle.com **Website:** http://www.waterfordcastle.com *(English (mainly about hotel; little about ferry))*

Route: Grantstown – Little Island (in River Suir, County Waterford).

1	LITTLE ISLAND FERRY	68	24P	6C		BA	Cork, IR

LITTLE ISLAND FERRY Chain ferry built for *Waterford Castle Hotel*.

SECTION 5 – MAJOR PASSENGER FERRIES

There are a surprisingly large number of passenger only ferries operating in the British Isles, mainly operated by launches and small motor boats. There are, however, a few 'major' operators who operate only passenger vessels (of rather larger dimensions) and have not therefore been mentioned previously.

Channel Hoppers VARANGERFJORD (417t, 1990, 167 passengers) (Fjellstrand 38m catamaran). **Route operated (summer only:** Portsmouth – St Helier (Jersey) – St Anne (Alderney). *Note:* The original *Channel Hoppers* company went into liquidation in 1999. It is believed that the service may resume under the auspices of *Finnmark Fylkesrederi og Ruteselskap,* owners of the VARANGERFJORD. No information is available at time of going to press.

Clyde Marine Motoring FENCER (18t, 1976, 33 passengers), KENILWORTH (44t, 1936, 97 passengers (ex HOTSPUR II (Southampton – Hythe ferry) 1979)), ROVER (48t, 1964, 120 passengers), THE SECOND SNARK (45t, 1938, 120 passengers), POOLE SCENE (119t, 1974, 249 passengers). **Route operated:** Gourock – Kilcreggan – Helensburgh (generally the KENILWORTH is used on the ferry services and other vessels on excursions). **Tel:** +44 (0)1475 721281, **Fax:** +44 (0)1475 888023.

Dart Pleasure Craft EDGCUMBE BELLE (357, 1957, 150 passengers), KINGSWEAR BELLE (43t, 1972, 257 passengers). **Route operated:** Dartmouth – Kingswear. Note: Pleasure craft owned by this operator are also used for the ferry service on some occasions. **Tel:** +44 (0)1803 834488, **Fax:** +44 (0)1803 835248, **Email:** sales@riverlink.co.uk **Website:** http://www.riverlink.co.uk *(English)*

Doolin Ferry Company/O'Brien Shipping DONEMARK (70t, 1978, 65 pass), HAPPY HOOKER (77t, 1989, 96 passengers), ROSE OF ARAN (113t, 1976, 66 passengers), TRANQUILITY (43t, 1988, 48 passengers). **Route operated:** Doolin – Inishere, Doolin – Inishmaan, Doolin – Inishmore. OILEAN ARANN (416t, 1992, 190 passengers). **Route operated:** Galway – Inishere, Galway – Inishmaan, Galway – Inishmore. **Tel:** +353 (0)65 7074455, **Fax:** +353 (0)65 7074417, **Email:** doolinferries@eircom.net **Web Site:** http://homepage.eircom.net/~doolinferries/ *(English)*

Gosport Ferry GOSPORT QUEEN (159t, 1966, 250 passengers), PORTSMOUTH QUEEN (159t, 1966, 250 passengers), SOLENT ENTERPRISE (274t, 1971, 250 passengers (ex GAY ENTERPRISE 1979) (mainly used on excursion work)). **Route operated:** Gosport – Portsmouth. **Tel:** +44 (0)23 9252 4551, **Email:** info@gosportferry.co.uk **Web Site:** http://www.gosportferry.co.uk *(English)*

Hovertravel COURIER (1986, 84 passengers) (BHC AP1-88/100 hovercraft (to be converted to AP1-88/100s in 2000)) (ex BENIDORM 1993, ex COURIER 1990), DOUBLE O SEVEN (1989, 98 passengers) (BHC AP1-88/100 hovercraft), FREEDOM 90 (1990, 98 passengers) (BHC AP1-88/100s hovercraft (converted from AP1-88/100 in 1999)), IDUN VIKING (1983, 98 passengers) (BHC AP1-88/100 hovercraft), LIV VIKING (1985, 82 passengers) (BHC AP1-88/100 hovercraft), FREJA VIKING (1985, 82 passengers) (BHC AP1-88/100 hovercraft). **Route operated:** Southsea – Ryde. **Tel:** +44 (0)1983 811000, **Fax:** +44 (0)1983 562216, **Email:** info@hovertravel.co.uk, **Website:** http://www.hovertravel.co.uk *(English)*

Island Ferries ARAN EXPRESS (117t, 1984, 180 passengers), ARAN FLYER (170t, 1988, 208 passengers), ARAN SEABIRD (164t, 1976, 181 passengers), GALWAY BAY (107t, 150 passengers), DRAÍOCHT NA FARRAIGE (200t, 2000, 272 passengers (catamaran)), SEA SPRINTER (16t, 1993, 36 passengers). **Routes operated:** Rossaveal (Co Galway) – Aran Islands. **Tel:** +353 (0)91, 561767/568903 (572273 after 19.00), **Fax:** +353 (0)91 568538, **Email:** island@iol.ie, **Website:**

http://www.aranislandferries.com *(English)*.

Lundy Company OLDENBURG (288t, 1958, 267 passengers). **Routes operated:** Bideford – Lundy Island, Ilfracombe – Lundy Island, Clovelly – Lundy Island, Watchet – Lundy Island, Porthcawl – Lundy Island, Porthcawl – Ilfracombe. **Tel:** +44 (0)1237 470422, **Fax:** +44 (0)1237 477779, **Email:** LundySO@aol.com **Web Site:** http://www.lundyisland.co.uk *(English)*

Mersey Ferries MOUNTWOOD (464t, 1960, 750 passengers), ROYAL DAFODIL (ex OVERCHURCH 1999) (468t, 1962, 860 passengers), WOODCHURCH (464t, 1960, 750 passengers). **Routes operated:** Liverpool – Birkenhead (Woodside), Liverpool – Wallasey (Seacombe). **Tel:** +44 (0)151 630 1030, **Fax:** +44 (0)151 639 0609, **Website:** http://www.merseyworld.com/ferries *(English)*

Nexus (trading name of Tyne & Wear PTE) PRIDE OF THE TYNE (222t, 1993, 350 passengers), SHIELDSMAN (93t, 1976, 350 passengers). **Route operated:** North Shields – South Shields. Also cruises South Shields – Newcastle. **Tel:** +44 (0)191 454 8183, **Fax:** +44 (0)191 427 9510, **Web Site:** www.nexus.org.uk

Strathclyde Passenger Transport RENFREW ROSE (65t, 1984, 50 passengers), YOKER SWAN (65t, 1984, 50 passengers). **Route operated:** Renfrew – Yoker. Note: although this a passenger only service, the vessels are built as small front loading car ferries and are able to convey one vehicle if necessary. This facility is sometimes used for the conveyance of ambulances. **Tel:** +44 (0)141 333 3159, **Fax:** +44 (0)141 432 1025, **Email:** liz.parkes@spt.co.uk

Waverley Excursions BALMORAL (735t, 1949, 800 passengers), WAVERLEY (693t, 1947, 950 passengers). **Routes operated:** Excursions all round British Isles. However, regular cruises in the Clyde and Bristol Channel provide a service which can be used for transport purposes and therefore both vessels are, in a sense, ferries. **Tel:** +44 (0)141 221 8152, **Fax:** +44 (0)141 248 2150, **Email:** ellie@waverley99.freeserve.co.uk

White Horse Fast Ferries MARTIN CHUZZLEWIT (25.6t, 1995, 60 passengers (tri-maran)), **Route operated:** Gravesend (Kent) – Tilbury (Essex), ABEL MAGWITCH (25.6t, 1999, 60 passengers (tri-maran)), EBENEZER SCROOGE (4.3t, 1992, 12 passengers), URIAH HEEP (25.6t, 1999, 60 passengers (tri-maran)), PHILIP PIRRIP (25.6t, 1999, 60 passengers (tri-maran)), WILKINS MICAWBER (25.6t, 1996, 60 passengers), DANIEL QUILP (25.6t, 2000, 60 passengers (tri-maran)), **Routes operated:** Embankment (London) – Canary Wharf, Greenwich – Greenwich Millennium Dome. *Head Office:* **Tel:**. +44 (0)1793 618566, **Fax:** +44 (0)1793 488428, **Email:** post@whitehorse.co.uk, *Local Office:* **Tel:** +44 (0)1474 566220, **Fax:** +44 (0)1474 362390, **Email:** fastferries@whitehorse.co.uk **Website:** http://www.whitehorse.co.uk/fastferries *(English)*

White Horse Ferries GREAT EXPECTATIONS (66t, 1992, 162 passengers) (catamaran), HOTSPUR IV (50t, 1946, 125 passengers). **Route operated:** Southampton – Hythe (Hants). *Head Office:* **Tel:**. +44 (0)1793 618566, **Fax:** +44 (0)1793 488428, *Local Office:* **Tel:** +44 (0)23 8084 0722, **Fax:** +44 (0)23 8084 6611, **Email:** post@hytheferry.co.uk **Website:** http://www.hytheferry.co.uk *(English)*

Silja Serenade (Miles Cowsill)

Section 6 – NORTHERN EUROPE

ÅNEDIN LINE

THE COMPANY *Ånedin Line* is the trading name of *Rederi AB Alandia*, a Swedish company.

MANAGEMENT Managing Director: Björn Ericson, **Marketing Manager:** Torsten Sundberg.

ADDRESS PO Box 1151, S-11181 STOCKHOLM, Sweden.

TELEPHONE Administration: +46 (0)8-456 2200, **Reservations:** +46 (0)8-456 2200, **Fax:** +46 (0)8-10 07 41.

ROUTE OPERATED Cruises from Stockholm to Mariehamn (Åland) (22 hrs; *(1)*; 1 per day).

CONVENTIONAL FERRY

1	BALTIC STAR	3564t	53	15k	400P	0C	0L	-	Stockholm, SW	PA

BALTIC STAR Built as the BIRGER JARL for *Stockholms Rederi AB Svea* of Sweden to operate between Stockholm and Turku and Stockholm and Helsinki. She was a crane loading car ferry with capacity for 25 cars, since removed. In 1973 she was sold to *Jacob Line*, to operate between Pietarsaari (Finland) and Skellefteå (Sweden); she was renamed the BORE NORD. In 1974 she started a service from Turku to Visby (Gotland) but this was short lived and, for a time, she served as an accommodation vessel at Stavanger. In 1977 she was sold to *Mini Carriers* of Finland who renamed her the MINISEA and announced plans for a new Finland – Sweden service. These plans did not materialise and in 1978 she was acquired by the *Caribbean Shipping Company* of Panama, chartered to *Rederi AB Alandia*, renamed the BALTIC STAR and started operating 24 hour cruises. In 1997, following changes to Swedish customs regulations, these became 22 hour cruises, allowing a regular departure time each day.

BALTIC FERRY LINE

THE COMPANY *Baltic Ferry Line* is a Swedish company who act as agents for Baltic service provided by Russian owned companies.

ADDRESS Box 45069, SE-10430 STOCKHOM, Sweden.

TELEPHONE Reservations: *Sweden:* +46 (0)8-456 2250.

Website: http://www.scansov.se (not yet live)

ROUTE OPERATED Stockholm – Riga (Latvia) (18 hrs; *(2)*; 3 per week), Stockholm – St Petersburg (Russia) (*(1)*; 1 per week).

CONVENTIONAL PASSENGER FERRY

1	MIKHAIL SHOLOKHOV	12798t	86	20k	412P	344C	45T	A	Szczecin, PO	RU
2	RUSS	12798t	86	20k	409P	344C	45T	A	Szczecin, PO	RU

RUSS Built as the KONSTANTIN CHERNENKO for *Far Eastern Shipping* of the Soviet Union and later of Russia. She was engaged in cruising. In 1988 renamed the RUSS. In 1996 chartered to *LS Redereja* of Latvia to start a service from Riga to Stockholm (trading as *LS Line*). Permission to convey passengers from Sweden was obtained in April 1997. In 1998 the company changed its name to *Ferry Serviss*. In 1999 the service was taken over by Russian interests.

MIKHAIL SHOLOKHOV Built for *Far Eastern Shipping* of the Soviet Union and later of Russia. In 1999 started a service from Stockholm to St Petersburg.

Hamlet (Mike Louagie)

Christian IV (Miles Cowsill)

BASTØ FOSEN

THE COMPANY *Bastø Fosen* is a Norwegian private sector company, a subsidiary of *Fosen Trafikklag* of Trondheim.

MANAGEMENT Managing Director: Olav Brein, **Operations Manager:** Jan F Jonas.

ADDRESS PO Box 94, 3191 HORTEN, Norway.

TELEPHONE Administration: +47 33 03 17 40, **Reservations:** not applicable, **Fax:** +47 33 03 17 49.

INTERNET Email: basto@fosen.no **Website:** http://www.basto-fosen.no *(Norwegian)*

ROUTE OPERATED Moss – Horten (across Oslofjord, Norway) (30 mins; *(1,2,3)*; up to every 45 mins).

CONVENTIONAL FERRIES

1	BASTØ I	5505t	97	14k	550P	220C	18L	BA	Fevaag, NO	NO
2	BASTØ II	5505t	97	14k	550P	220C	18L	BA	Fevaag, NO	NO

BASTØ I, BASTØ II Built for *Bastø Fosen*.

BIRKA CRUISES

THE COMPANY *Birka Cruises* is an Åland Islands company.

MANAGEMENT Managing Director: Michael Larkner.

ADDRESS Box 15131, Södermalmstorg 2, S-104 65 STOCKHOLM, Sweden.

TELEPHONE Administration: +46 (0)8-702 7200, **Reservations:** +46 (0)8-702 7230, **Fax:** +46 (0)8-714 9830.

INTERNET Email: info@ birkacruises.com **Website:** http://www.birkacruises.com

ROUTES OPERATED Stockholm – Mariehamn (Åland) – Stockholm (cruise) (22 hrs 30 mins; *(1)*; 1 per day (except when Gdynia cruise operates), Stockholm – Visby (Gotland) – Gdynia (Poland) – Stockholm (cruise); 70 hrs 30 mins; *(1)*; weekly, June to mid-August). Note: although primarily a cruise service, conventional passengers can be conveyed.

CRUISE SHIP

1p	BIRKA PRINCESS	22412t	86	21k	1500P	0C	0L	-	Helsinki, FI	FI

BIRKA PRINCESS Built for *Birka Cruises*. As built, she had capacity for 10 cars, loaded via a side door. During winter 1998/99 she was the subject of a major refit to modernise her and increase passenger capacity; the vehicle facility was removed.

BORNHOLMSTRAFIKKEN

THE COMPANY *BornholmsTrafikken* is a Danish state owned company.

MANAGEMENT Managing Director: Vacant, **Sales and Marketing Manager:** Eddie Ørpe.

ADDRESS Havnen, DK-3700 RØNNE, Denmark.

TELEPHONE Administration: +45 56 95 18 66, **Reservations:** +45 56 95 18 66, **Fax:** +45 56 91 07 66.

INTERNET Email: info@bornholmferries.dk **Website:** http://www.bornholmferries.dk *(Danish, German)*

ROUTES OPERATED Conventional Ferry: Rønne (Bornholm, Denmark) – København (7 hrs; *(1,2)*; 1 or 2 per day), Rønne – Ystad (Sweden) (2 hrs 30 mins; *(1,2)*; 1 per day), Rønne – Fährhafen Sassnitz (Germany) (3 hrs 30 mins; *(1,2)*; up to 6 per week), **Fast Ferry:** Ystad (Sweden) – Rønne (1 hr 20 mins; *(3)*; up to 5 per day).

CONVENTIONAL FERRIES

| 1 | JENS KOFOED | 12131t | 79 | 19.5k | 1500P | 262C | 44T | BA | Aalborg, DK | DK |
| 2 | POVL ANKER | 12131t | 78 | 19.5k | 1500P | 262C | 44T | BA | Aalborg, DK | DK |

JENS KOFOED, POVL ANKER Built for *BornholmsTrafikken*. Used on the Rønne – København, Rønne – Ystad and Rønne – Fährhafen Sassnitz services.

FAST FERRY

| 3 | VILLUM CLAUSEN | 5989t | 99 | 42k | 1000P | 186C | - | BA | Fremantle, AL | DK |

VILLUM CLAUSEN Austal Auto-Express 86 catamaran built for *BornholmsTrafikken*.

COLOR LINE

THE COMPANY *Color Line ASA* is a Norwegian private sector stock-listed limited company. The company merged with *Larvik Line* of Norway (which owned *Scandi Line*) in 1996. *Larvik Line's* operations were incorporated into *Color Line* in 1997; *Scandi Line* continued as a separate subsidiary until 1999, when it was also incorporated into *Color Line*.

MANAGEMENT Managing Director: Trygve Sigerset, **Marketing Manager:** Elisabeth Anspach.

ADDRESS *Commercial:* Postboks 1422 Vika, 0115 OSLO, Norway. *Technical Management:* Color Line Marine AS, PO Box 2090, N-3210 SANDEFJORD, Norway.

TELEPHONE Administration: +47 22 94 44 00, **Reservations:** +47 22 94 44 44. **Fax:** +47 22 83 07 76.

INTERNET Website: http://www.colorline.com *(Norwegian, English)* http://www.colorscandiline.com *(English)*

ROUTES OPERATED Conventional Ferries: Oslo – Kiel (Germany) (19 hrs 30 mins; *(5,7)*; 1 per day), Oslo – Hirtshals (Denmark) (8 hrs 30 mins; *(3)*; 1 per day), Moss (Norway) – Hirtshals (Denmark) (7 hrs; *(9)*; 1 per day (3 per week in winter)), Kristiansand (Norway) – Hirtshals (4 hrs 30 mins; *(2,9)*; 2 per day), Larvik (Norway) – Moss (Norway) – Frederikshavn (Denmark) (6 hrs 15 mins; *(6)*; 1 or 2 per day), Sandefjord (Norway) – Strömstad (Sweden) (2 hrs 30 mins; *(1,3,8)*; 6 per day) (under the name *Color Scandi Line*). **Fast Ferry (under the name 'Color Line Express')** **Summer only:** Kristiansand – Hirtshals (2 hrs 25 mins; *(10)*; 3 per day).

CONVENTIONAL FERRIES

1	BOHUS	8772t	71	19.5k	1480P	280C	40T	BA	Aalborg, DK	NO
2	CHRISTIAN IV	21699t	82	21k	2000P	530C	64T	BA2	Bremerhaven, GY	NO
3	COLOR FESTIVAL	34417t	85	22k	2000P	440C	88T	BA2	Helsinki, FI	NO
4	COLOR VIKING	19763t	85	17.5k	1750P	320C	42T	BA2	Nakskov, DK	NO
5	KRONPRINS HARALD	31914t	87	21.5k	1432P	700C	100T	BA	Turku, FI	NO
6	PETER WESSEL	29706t	81	21k	2200P	650C	80T	BA2	Landskrona, SW	NO
7	PRINSESSE RAGNHILD	35438t	81	19.5k	1875P	770C	78T	BA	Kiel, GY	NO
8	SANDEFJORD	5678t	65	17.8k	1100P	145C	30T	BA	Lübeck, GY	NO
9	SKAGEN	12333t	75	19.5k	1238P	400C	22T	BA	Aalborg, DK	NO

BOHUS Built as the PRINSESSAN DESIREE for *Rederi AB Göteborg-Frederikshavn Linjen* of Sweden (trading as *Sessan Linjen*) for their first service between Göteborg and Frederikshavn. In 1981 the company was taken over by *Stena Line* and she became surplus to requirements. During 1981 she had a number of charters including *B&I Line* of Ireland and *Sealink* UK. In 1982 she was chartered to *Sally Line* to operate as second vessel on the Ramsgate – Dunkerque service between June and September. She bore the name VIKING 2 in large letters on her hull although she was never officially renamed and continued to bear the name PRINSESSAN DESIREE on her bow and stern. In September 1982 she returned to *Stena Line* and in 1983 she was transferred to subsidiary company *Varberg-Grenaa Line* for their service between Varberg (Sweden) and Grenaa (Denmark) and renamed the EUROPAFÄRJAN. In 1985 she was renamed the EUROPAFÄRJAN II. In 1986, following

Color Festival (William Mayes)

Gitte 3 (Speckus Ferry Information)

a reorganisation within the *Stena Line* Group, ownership was transferred to subsidiary company *Lion Ferry AB* and she was named the LION PRINCESS. In 1993 she was sold to *Scandi Line* and renamed the BOHUS. In 1999 *Scandi Line* operations were integrated into *Color Line*.

CHRISTIAN IV Built as the OLAU BRITANNIA for *Olau Line* of Germany for their service between Vlissingen (Netherlands) and Sheerness (England). In 1989 sold to *Nordström & Thulin* of Sweden for delivery in spring 1990. She was subsequently resold to *Fred. Olsen Lines* of Norway and, on delivery, renamed the BAYARD and used on their service between Kristiansand and Hirtshals. In December 1990 she was acquired by *Color Line* and in 1991 renamed the CHRISTIAN IV.

COLOR FESTIVAL Built as the SVEA for *Johnson Line* for the *Silja Line* Stockholm – Mariehamn – Turku service. During winter 1991/92 she was extensively rebuilt and in 1991 renamed the SILJA KARNEVAL; ownership was transferred to *Silja Line*. In 1993 she was sold to *Color Line* and renamed the COLOR FESTIVAL. She is used on the Oslo – Hirtshals service.

COLOR VIKING Built as the PEDER PAARS for *DSB (Danish State Railways)* for their service between Kalundborg (Sjælland) and Århus (Jylland). In 1990 purchased by *Stena Line* of Sweden for delivery in 1991. In 1991 renamed the STENA INVICTA and entered service on the *Sealink Stena Line* Dover – Calais service. She was withdrawn from the route in February 1998, before the formation of *P&O Stena Line* but ownership was transferred to that company. In summer 1998, she was chartered to *Silja Line* to operate between Vaasa and Umeå under the marketing name 'WASA JUBILEE'. In autumn 1998 she was laid up at Zeebrugge. She remained there until autumn 199 when she was chartered to *Stena Line* to operate between Holyhead and Dublin. In 2000 she was chartered to *Color Line* and renamed the COLOR VIKING and in April entered service on the Sandefjord – Strömstad service.

KRONPRINS HARALD Built for *Jahre Line* of Norway for the Oslo – Kiel service. In 1991 ownership was transferred to *Color Line*.

PETER WESSEL Built for *Rederi AB Gotland* of Sweden. A sister vessel of the VISBY (see *Destination Gotland*), it was intended that she should be named the GOTLAND. However, she was delivered as the WASA STAR and chartered to *Vaasanlaivat* of Finland and used on their Vaasa – Sundsvall service. In 1982 she was chartered to *Karageorgis Line* of Greece for service between Patras (Greece) and Ancona (Italy). This charter was abruptly terminated in 1983 following a dispute over payment of charter dues. She returned the Baltic and was laid up until February 1984 when she was sold to *Larvik Line*. She was renamed the PETER WESSEL. In 1988 she was lengthened. In 1996 acquired by *Color Line*. She remains on the Larvik – Moss – Frederikshavn route.

PRINSESSE RAGNHILD Built for *Jahre Line* of Norway for the Oslo – Kiel service. In 1991 ownership transferred to *Color Line*. In 1992 rebuilt in Spain with an additional midships section and additional decks.

SANDEFJORD Built as the VIKING III for *Otto Thoresen* of Norway for the *Thoresen Car Ferries* Southampton (England) – Cherbourg and Southampton – Le Havre services. During the winter, until 1970/71, she was chartered to *Lion Ferry* of Sweden for their Harwich – Bremerhaven service. In 1967 the service was acquired by *European Ferries* of Great Britain, trading as *Townsend Thoresen*. She was chartered to this organisation and retained Norwegian registry. During winter 1971/72 and 1972/73 she was chartered to *Larvik Line*. She became surplus to requirements following the delivery of the 'Super Vikings' in 1975 and was the subject of a number of short term charters until 1982 when she was sold to *Da-No Linjen* of Norway, renamed the TERJE VIGEN and used on their Fredrikstad (Norway) – Frederikshavn (Denmark) service. In 1986 she was sold to *KG Line* to operate between Kaskinen (Finland) and Gävle (Sweden) and renamed the SCANDINAVIA. In 1990 she was sold *Johnson Line* and used on *Jakob Line* service, being renamed the FENNO STAR. In 1991 she was sold to *Scandi Line* and renamed the SANDEFJORD but served briefly as the FENNO STAR on the *Corona Line* service between Karlskrona and Gdynia before being introduced onto the Sandefjord – Strömstad service in 1992. In 1999 *Scandi Line* operations were integrated into *Color Line*.

SKAGEN Built as the BORGEN for *Fred. Olsen Lines* of Norway for Norway – Denmark services. In December 1990 acquired by *Color Line* and in 1991 renamed the SKAGEN. Until 1997 she operated mainly between Hirtshals and Kristiansand. She now also operates between Hirtshals and Moss.

Although built with rail freight capacity, this is no longer used.

FAST FERRY

10	SILVIA ANA L	7895t	96	38k	1250P	238C	4L	A	San Fernando, SP	BA

SILVIA ANA L Bazan Alhambra monohull vessel built for *Buquebus* of Argentina. Initially operated between Buenos Aires (Argentina) and Piriapolis (Uruguay). In 1997 chartered to *Color Line* to operate between Kristiansand and Hirtshals. During winter 1997/98 she again operated in South America but returned to *Color Line* in spring 1998. This has been repeated during following winters.

DESTINATION GOTLAND

THE COMPANY *Destination Gotland AB* is a Swedish private sector company owned by *Rederi AB Gotland*. It took over the operations of services to Gotland from 1st January 1998 on a six year concession. Originally jointly owned by *Rederi AB Gotland* and *Silja Line*, *Silja Line* involvement in the company ceased at the end of 1998.

MANAGEMENT Managing Director: Jan-Eric Nilsson, **Marketing Manager:** Per-Erling Evensen.

ADDRESS PO Box 1234, 621 23 VISBY, Gotland, Sweden.

TELEPHONE Administration: +46 (0)498-20 18 00, **Reservations:** +46 (0)498-20 10 20, **Fax:** +46 (0)498-20 18 90.

INTERNET Email: per-erling.evensen@destinationgotland.se

Website: http://www.destinationgotland.se *(Swedish, English)*

ROUTES OPERATED Conventional Ferries all year: Visby (Gotland) – Nynäshamn (Swedish mainland) (5 hrs 30 mins; *(1,2)*; 1/2 per day), Visby – Oskarshamn (Swedish mainland) (4 hrs 30 mins; *(1,2)*; 1/2 per day), **Fast Ferry summer only:** Visby (Gotland) – Nynäshamn (2 hrs 50 mins; *(3)*; up to 2 per day), Visby – Oskarshamn (Swedish mainland) (2 hrs 25 mins; *3*); up to 1 per day).

CONVENTIONAL FERRIES

1	THJELVAR	16829t	81	19k	1500P	440C	76L	BA2	Helsinki, FI	SW
2	VISBY	23775t	80	20k	1800P	510C	45L	BA2	Landskrona, SW	SW

THJELVAR Built as the TRAVEMÜNDE for *Gedser-Travemünde Ruten* of Denmark for their service between Gedser (Denmark) and Travemünde (Germany). In 1986 the company's trading name was changed to *GT Linien* and in 1987, following the take-over by *Sea-Link AB* of Sweden, it was further changed to *GT Link*. The vessel's name was changed to the TRAVEMÜNDE LINK. In 1988 she was purchased by *Rederi AB Gotland* of Sweden, although remaining in service with *GT Link*. Later in 1988 she was chartered to *Sally Ferries* and entered service in December on the Ramsgate – Dunkerque service. She was renamed the SALLY STAR. In 1997 she was transferred to *Silja Line*, to operate between Vaasa and Umeå during the summer period and operated under the marketing name WASA EXPRESS (although not renamed). She returned to *Rederi AB Gotland* in autumn 1997, renamed the THJELVAR and entered service with *Destination Gotland* in January 1998.

VISBY Built as the VISBY for *Rederi AB Gotland* of Sweden for their services between the island of Gotland and the Swedish mainland. In 1987, the franchise to operate these services was lost by the company and awarded to *Nordström & Thulin* of Sweden. A subsidiary called *N&T Gotlandslinjen AB* was formed to operate the service. The VISBY was chartered to this company and managed by *Johnson Line*, remaining owned by *Rederi AB Gotland*. In early 1990 she was chartered to *Sealink* and renamed the FELICITY. After modifications at Tilbury, she was, in March 1990, introduced onto the Fishguard – Rosslare route. Later in 1990 she was renamed the STENA FELICITY. In summer 1997 she was returned to *Rederi AB Gotland* for rebuilding, prior to her entering service with *Destination Gotland* in January 1998. She was renamed the VISBY.

FAST FERRY

3	GOTLAND	5632t	99	35k	700P	140C	-	A	Nantes, FR	SW

GOTLAND Alstom Leroux Corsair 11500 monohull vessel built for *Rederi AB Gotland* and chartered to *Destination Gotland*.

Under Construction

4	NEWBUILDING 1	29000t	01	28.5k	1500P	500C	106L	BA	Goangzhou, CH	SW
5	NEWBUILDING 2	29000t	01	28.5k	1500P	500C	106L	BA	Goangzhou, CH	SW

NEWBUILDING 1, NEWBUILDING 2 Under construction for *Rederi AB Gotland*. One at least is likely to be used on *Destination Gotland* service.

DFDS SEAWAYS

THE COMPANY *DFDS Seaways A/S* is the passenger division of *DFDS Group*, a Danish private sector company.

MANAGEMENT Managing Director DFDS A/S: Thorleif Blok, **Managing Director DFDS Seaways A/S:** Bo-Lennart Thorbjörnsson.

ADDRESS Sankt Annæ Plads 30, DK-1295 KØBENHAVN K, Denmark.

TELEPHONE Administration: +45 33 42 33 42, **Reservations:** +45 33 42 30 00, **Fax:** +45 33 42 33 41.

INTERNET Website: http://www.dfdsseaways.com *(Danish, Dutch, English, German, Norwegian, Swedish)*

ROUTE OPERATED København – Helsingborg (Sweden) – Oslo (Norway) (16 hrs; *(1,2)*; 1 per day). See Section 1 for services operating to Britain.

CONVENTIONAL FERRIES

1	CROWN OF SCANDINAVIA	35498t	94	19.5k	2136P	450C	80T	BA2	Split, CR	DK
2	QUEEN OF SCANDINAVIA	33730t	81	21k	1624P	430C	86T	BA	Turku, FI	DK

CROWN OF SCANDINAVIA Launched for *Euroway* for their Lübeck – Travemünde – Malmö service. However, political problems led to serious delays and, before delivery, the service had ceased. She was purchased by *DFDS*, renamed the CROWN OF SCANDINAVIA and introduced onto the København – Oslo service.

QUEEN OF SCANDINAVIA Built as the FINLANDIA for *EFFOA* of Sweden for *Silja Line* services between Helsinki and Stockholm. In 1990 she was sold to *DFDS*, renamed the QUEEN OF SCANDINAVIA and introduced onto the København – Helsingborg – Oslo service.

REDERIJ DOEKSEN

THE COMPANY *Rederij G Doeksen & Zonen bv* is a Dutch public sector company. Ferries are operated by subsidiary *Terschellinger Stoomboot Maatschappij*, trading as *Rederij Doeksen*.

MANAGEMENT Managing Director: H Oosterbeek, **Marketing Manager:** C Dekker.

ADDRESS Willem Barentskade 21, Postbus 40, 8880 AA WEST TERSCHELLING, Netherlands.

TELEPHONE Administration: +31 (0)562 44 21 41, **Reservations:** +31 (0)562 44 61 11, **Fax:** +31 (0)562 44 32 41.

ROUTES OPERATED Harlingen (Netherlands) – Terschelling (Frisian Islands) (2 hrs; *(1,2)*; up to 4 per day), Harlingen (Netherlands) – Vlieland (Frisian Islands) (1 hrs 45 mins; *(3)*; 3 per day).

CONVENTIONAL FERRIES

1	FRIESLAND	3583t	89	14k	1750P	122C	12L	BA	Krimpen, NL	NL
2	MIDSLAND	1812t	74	15.5k	1200P	55C	6L	BA	Emden, GY	NL
3	OOST-VLIELAND	1350t	70	15k	1100P	45C	4L	BA	Emden, GY	NL

FRIESLAND Built for *Rederij Doeksen*. Used on the Harlingen – Terschelling route.

MIDSLAND Built as the RHEINLAND for *AG Ems* of Germany. In 1993 purchased by *Rederij Doeksen* and renamed the MIDSLAND. Used mainly on the Harlingen – Terschelling route but also used on the Harlingen – Vlieland service. She is now a reserve vessel.

OOST-VLIELAND Built as the OSTFRIESLAND for *AG Ems* of Germany. In 1981 purchased by *Rederij Doeksen* and renamed the SCHELLINGERLAND. In 1994 renamed the OOST VLIELAND. Now mainly used on the Harlingen – Vlieland service.

Rederij Doeksen also operate the Harding 35m passenger only catamaran KOEGELWIECK (439t, 1992, 317 passengers) and the SBF Shipbuilders 31m monohull NAJADE (164t, 1999, 184 passengers) between Harlingen and Terschelling, Harlingen and Vlieland and Terschelling and Vlieland.

EASY LINE

THE COMPANY *Easy Line A/S* is a Danish company, jointly owned by *Eidsiva Rederi ASA* of Norway and *Fosen Trafikklag ASA* of Norway.

MANAGEMENT Managing Director: Tom Bringsværd.

ADDRESS Gedser Landevej 58, DK-4874 GEDSER, Denmark.

TELEPHONE Administration & Reservations: +45 54 16 04 00, **Fax:** +45 54 16 05 57.

INTERNET Email: info@easy-line.dk **Website:** http://www.easy-line.dk *(Danish)*

ROUTE OPERATED Gedser (Denmark) – Rostock (Germany) (2 hrs 10 mins; *(1,2)*; 6 per day).

CONVENTIONAL FERRIES

1	ANJA 11	4101t	88	13k	253P	170C	24T	BA	Sunderland, GB	DK
2	GITTE 3	4296t	87	12.7k	300P	170C	24T	BA	Sunderland, GB	DK

ANJA 11 Built as the SUPERFLEX KILO for *Vognmandsruten* of Denmark. In 1989 sold to *Mercandia* and renamed the MERCANDIA I. In 1990 she began operating on the *Kattegatbroen* Juelsminde – Kalundborg service. In 1996 this service ceased but it has not proved possible to use her on the *Sundbroen* Helsingør – Helsingborg service. In 1997 chartered to *Litorina Line* to inaugurate a new service between Öland and Gotland. In 1998, sold to *Eidsiva Rederi* and renamed the ANJA 11. She inaugurated a new service between Gedser and Rostock. Note: she initially carried the name 'ANJA #11' but the '#' character did not form part of her registered name. This character was subsequently removed.

GITTE 3 Built as the SUPERFLEX DELTA for *Vognmandsruten* to establish a new service between Korsør (Sjælland) and Nyborg (Fyn). In 1990 this company was taken over by *DIFKO* and she was renamed the DIFKO STOREBÆLT. In 1998, following the opening of the Great Belt fixed link, the service ceased and she was laid up. In 1999 she was chartered to *Easy Line* and renamed the GITTE 3. Laid up after August 1999.

ECKERÖ LINE

THE COMPANY *Eckerö Line Ab Oy* is a Finnish company, 100% owned by *Eckerö Linjen* of Åland, Finland. Until January 1998, the company was called *Eestin-Linjat*.

MANAGEMENT Managing Director: Jarl Danielsson, **Marketing Director:** Håkan Nordström.

ADDRESS Hietalahdenranta 13, FIN-00180 HELSINKI, Finland.

TELEPHONE Administration: +358 (0)9 22885421, **Reservations:** +358 (0)9 2288544, **Fax:** +358 (0)9 22885222.

INTERNET Email: info@eckeroline.fi **Website:** http://www.eckeroline.fi *(Swedish, Finnish, English, German)*

ROUTE OPERATED Helsinki – Tallinn (Estonia) (3 hrs 30 mins; *(1)*; 1 per day).

CONVENTIONAL FERRY

1	NORDLANDIA	21473t	81	21k	2048P	530C	64T	BA	Bremerhaven, GY	FI

NORDLANDIA Built as the OLAU HOLLANDIA for *Olau Line* of Germany for the service between Vlissingen (Netherlands) and Sheerness (England). In 1989 she was replaced by a new vessel of the same name and she was sold to *Nordström & Thulin*. She was renamed the NORD GOTLANDIA and introduced onto *Gotlandslinjen* services between Gotland and the Swedish mainland. In 1997 she was purchased by *Eckerö Linjen* of Åland for delivery in early 1998, following the ending of *Nordström & Thulin's* concession to operate the Gotland services. She was renamed the NORDLANDIA and placed on the *Eckerö Line* Helsinki – Tallinn service, operating day trips.

Eckerö Line also utilise the ALANDIA of associated company *Eckerö Linjen*.

ECKERÖ LINJEN

THE COMPANY *Eckerö Linjen* is an Åland Islands company.

MANAGEMENT Managing Director: Jarl Danielsson, **Marketing Director:** Christer Lindman.

ADDRESS Torggatan 2, Box 158, FIN-22100 MARIEHAMN, Åland.

TELEPHONE Administration: +358 (0)18 28000, **Reservations:** +358 (0)18 28300, **Fax:** +358 (0)18 28380.

INTERNET Website: http://www.eckerolinjen.fi *(Finnish)*

ROUTE OPERATED Eckerö (Åland) – Grisslehamn (Sweden) (2 hrs; *(1,2)*; 5 per day).

CONVENTIONAL FERRIES

1	ALANDIA	6754t	72	17k	1320P	225C	34T	BA	Papenburg, GY	FI
2	ROSLAGEN	6652t	72	18.7k	1200P	225C	34T	BA	Papenburg, GY	FI

ALANDIA Built as the DIANA for *Rederi AB Slite* of Sweden for *Viking Line* services. In 1979 she was sold to *Wasa Line* of Finland and renamed the BOTNIA EXPRESS. In 1982 she was sold to *Sally Line* of Finland; later that year she was sold to *Suomen Yritysraheitis Oy* and chartered back. In 1992 she was sold to *Eckerö Linjen* and renamed the ALANDIA. She is also used by subsidiary company *Eckerö Line*.

ROSLAGEN Built as the VIKING 3 for *Rederi AB Sally* and used on *Viking Line* Baltic services. In 1976 she was sold to *Vaasanlaivat* of Finland for their service between Vaasa (Finland) and Umeå/Sundsvall (Sweden) and renamed the WASA EXPRESS. In 1982 *Vaasanlaivat* was taken over by *Rederi AB Sally* and in April 1983 she resumed her original name, was transferred to *Sally Line* and used on the Ramsgate – Dunkerque service. She remained in the Channel during winter 1983/4 on freight-only services. However, in early 1984 she returned to *Vaasanlaivat* and resumed the name WASA EXPRESS. In 1988 she was sold to *Eckerö Linjen* and renamed the ROSLAGEN. During winter 1992/3 she operated between Helsinki and Tallinn for *Estonia New Line* and returned to *Eckerö Linjen* in the spring.

ELBE-FERRY

THE COMPANY *Elbe-Ferry GmbH & Co KG* is a subsidiary of *E H Harms GmbH*, a German private sector company.

MANAGEMENT Managing Director: F P Harms.

ADDRESS Am Fährhafen, 27472 CUXHAVEN, Germany.

TELEPHONE Administration & Reservations: +49 (0)4721 79 790, **Fax:** +49 (0)4721 79 79 20.

INTERNET Email: info@elbe-ferry.de **Website:** http://www.elbe-ferry.de *(German)*

ROUTE OPERATED Cuxhaven – Brunsbüttel (across mouth of River Elbe) (1 hr 30 mins; *(1,2,3)*; 2 hourly).

CONVENTIONAL FERRIES

1	HINRICH-WILHELM KOPF	5148t	64	16k	450P	124C	23T	BA	Aalborg, DK	GY
2	JOCHEN STEFFEN	5293t	60	17k	450P	157C	23T	BA	Aalborg, DK	GY
3	WILHELM KAISEN	1553t	67	12k	250P	55C	15L	BA	Århus, DK	GY

HINRICH-WILHELM KOPF Built as the PRINSESSE ELISABETH for *DSB* for the Århus – Kalundborg service. In 1986 transferred to the Helsingør – Helsingborg service. In 1998, sold to *E H Harms GmbH* of Bremen. In 1999 she was renamed the HINRICH-WILHELM KOPF and inaugurated a new service between Cuxhaven and Brunsbüttel.

JOCHEN STEFFEN Built as the PRINSESSE ANNE-MARIE for *DSB* for the Århus – Kalundborg service. In 1986 transferred to the Helsingør – Helsingborg service, generally as a relief vessel. Following the withdrawal of the REGULA and URSULA she became a regular vessel with a Swedish crew. Withdrawn in 1997. In 1998, sold to *E H Harms GmbH* of Bremen. In 1999 she was renamed the JOCHEN STEFFEN and inaugurated a new service between Cuxhaven and Brunsbüttel.

WILHELM KAISEN Built as the NAJADEN, a vehicle/train ferry for *DSB* for the Helsingør – Helsingborg service. In 1987 converted to a vehicle ferry and transferred to the Fynshav – Bøjden service. In 1997, transferred to subsidiary SFDS A/S. In 1998 she was sold to *E H Harms GmbH* of Bremen. In 1999 she was renamed the WILHELM KAISEN and inaugurated a new service between Cuxhaven and Brunsbüttel.

AG EMS

THE COMPANY *AG Ems* is a German public sector company.

MANAGEMENT Managing Director & Chief Executive: B W Brons, **Marine Superintendent:** J Alberts, **Marketing Manager & Assistant Manager:** P Eesmann, **Operating Manager:** Konrad Huismann.

ADDRESS Am Aussenhafen, Postfach 1154, 26691 EMDEN, Germany.

TELEPHONE Administration & Reservations: +49 (0)4921 89 070 or +49 (0)4921 89 07 22, **Fax:** +49 (0)4921 89 07 42.

INTERNET Email: info@ag-ems.de **Website:** http://www.ag-ems.de *(German)*

ROUTES OPERATED Emden (Germany) – Borkum (German Frisian Islands) (2 hrs; *(1,2,3)*; up to 4 per day), Eemshaven (Netherlands) – Borkum (55 mins; *(1,2,3)*; up to 4 per day).

CONVENTIONAL FERRIES

1	MÜNSTERLAND	1859t	86	15.5k	1200P	70C	10L	BA	Leer, GY	GY
2	OSTFRIESLAND	1859t	85	15.5k	1200P	70C	10L	BA	Leer, GY	GY
3	WESTFALEN	1812t	72	15.5k	1200P	65C	10L	BA	Emden, GY	GY

MÜNSTERLAND, OSTFRIESLAND, WESTFALEN Built for *AG Ems*. The WESTFALEN was rebuilt in 1994.

Services also operated by 33k Fjellstrand 38m passenger only catamaran NORDLICHT (435t, 1989) and the 11.5k 358 passenger only ferry WAPPEN VON BORKUM (287t, 1976, rebuilt 1995) (previously PRINCESS ISABELLA).

Nordlandia (John Hendy)

Jochen Steffen (Mike Louagie)

ESTLINE

THE COMPANY *EstLine AB* is a Swedish private sector company owned by the *Estonian Shipping Company (ESCO Ltd)* of Estonia.

MANAGEMENT Managing Director: Ulf Hagen, **Marketing Manager:** Anna Ingeman.

ADDRESS Frihamnen, Magasin 2, Box 27304, S-10254 STOCKHOLM, Sweden.

TELEPHONE Administration: +46 (0)8-666 6000, **Reservations:** +46 (0)8-667 0001, **Fax: *Admin:*** +46 (0)8-666 6025, ***Reservations:*** +46 (0)8-666 6052.

INTERNET Email: passenger@estline.se **Website:** http://www.estline.com *(Estonian, Finnish, Swedish, English)*

ROUTE OPERATED Stockholm – Tallinn (Estonia) (14 hrs; *(1,2)*; 1 per day).

CONVENTIONAL FERRIES

1	BALTIC KRISTINA	12281t	73	19k	578P	344C	44T	BA	Turku, FI	ES
2	REGINA BALTICA	18345t	80	21.3k	1450P	500C	78T	BA	Helsinki, FI	ES

BALTIC KRISTINA Built as the BORE 1 for *Ångfartygs AB Bore* of Finland for *Silja Line* services between Turku and Stockholm. In 1980, *Bore Line* left the *Silja Line* consortium and disposed of its passenger ships. She was acquired by *EFFOA* of Finland and continued to operate on *Silja Line* service, being renamed the SKANDIA. In 1983 she was sold to *Stena Line* and renamed the STENA BALTICA. She was then resold to *Latvia Shipping* of the USSR, substantially rebuilt, renamed the ILLICH and introduced onto a Stockholm – Leningrad (now Sankt-Peterburg) service trading as *ScanSov Line*. In 1986 operations were transferred to *Baltic Shipping Company*. In 1992 she inaugurated a new service between Stockholm and Riga but continued to also serve Sankt-Peterburg. In 1995 the Swedish terminal was changed to Nynäshamn. In late 1995 arrested and laid up in Stockholm. In 1997, services were planned to restart between Kiel and Sankt-Peterburg under the auspices of a German company called *Baltic Line*, with the vessel renamed the ANASTASIA V. However, this did not materialise and she was sold to *Windward Line* of Barbados and renamed the WINDWARD PRIDE. In 1997, she was chartered to *ESCO*, and renamed the BALTIC KRISTINA. In late 1997 she sailed for *EstLine* between Stockholm and Tallinn in a freight-only role. Following a major refurbishment, she entered service with *EstLine* in May 1998, allowing a daily full passenger service to be operated.

REGINA BALTICA Built as the VIKING SONG for *Rederi AB Sally* of Finland and used on the *Viking Line* service between Stockholm and Helsinki. In 1985 replaced by the MARIELLA of *SF Line* and sold to *Fred. Olsen Lines*. She was named BRAEMAR and used on services between Norway and Britain as well as Norway and Denmark. Services to Britain ceased in June 1990 and she continued to operate between Norway and Denmark. She was withdrawn in 1991 and sold to *Rigorous Shipping* of Cyprus (a subsidiary of *Fred. Olsen Lines*). She was chartered to the *Baltic Shipping Company* of Russia, renamed the ANNA KARENINA and inaugurated a service between Kiel and Sankt-Peterburg (St Petersburg). In 1992 a Nynäshamn call was introduced. In 1996 the service ceased and she was returned to her owners and renamed the ANNA K. Later in 1996 she was sold to *Empremare Shipping Co Ltd* of Cyprus (a company jointly owned by *Nordström & Thulin* and *Estonian Shipping Company*), chartered to *EstLine* and renamed the REGINA BALTICA.

FINNLINES (FINNCARRIERS)

THE COMPANIES *Finnlines Ltd* is a Finnish private sector company. *Finncarriers Oy Ab* is a subsidiary operating ro-ro and ro-pax services.

MANAGEMENT Managing Director: Asser Ahleskog, **Marketing Director:** Simo Airas.

ADDRESS *Finncarriers*: PO Box 197, Porkkalankatu 7, FIN-00181 HELSINKI, Finland.

TELEPHONE Administration & Reservations: +358 (0)10 34350, **Fax:** +358 (0)10 3435200.

INTERNET Email: info@finncarriers.fi **Websites:** http://www.finncarriers.fi http://www.finnlines.fi

ROUTES OPERATED All year: Helsinki – Lübeck (36 hrs; *(2,3,4,5)*; 1 per day), Helsinki – Travemünde (32 hrs; *(1,6)*; 4 per week). **Note:** frequencies refer to services which convey passengers.

CONVENTIONAL FERRIES

1	FINNCLIPPER	30500t	99	22k	440P	-	206T	BA	Puerto Real, SP	SW
2	FINNHANSA	32531t	94	21.3k	112P	-	250T	A2	Gdansk, PO	FI
3	FINNPARTNER	32534t	94	21.3k	112P	-	250T	A2	Gdansk, PO	FI
4	FINNTRADER	32534t	95	21.3k	112P	-	250T	A2	Gdansk, PO	FI
5	TRANSEUROPA	32534t	95	21.3k	90P	-	250T	A2	Gdansk, PO	GY
6	TRANSLUBECA	24727t	90	20k	84P	-	175T	A	Gdansk, PO	GY

FINNCLIPPER, 'Ro-pax' vessels ordered by *Stena Ro-Ro* of Sweden. In 1998 they were sold, before delivery, to *Finnlines*. Entered service on the Helsinki – Travemünde route in 1999.

FINNHANSA, FINNPARTNER, FINNTRADER 'Ro-pax' vessels built for *Finnlines Oy* of Finland to provide a daily service conveying both freight and a limited number of cars and passengers on a previously freight-only route.

TRANSEUROPA 'Ro-pax' vessel build for *Poseidon Schiffahrt* of Germany to operate on a joint service between Lübeck and Helsinki. In 1997 *Poseidon Schiffahrt* was acquired by *Finnlines*.

TRANSLUBECA 'Ro-pax' vessel build for *Poseidon Schiffahrt* of Germany to operate between Lübeck and Helsinki. In 1995 she inaugurated a new Lübeck – Turku service. In 1997 *Poseidon Schiffahrt* was acquired by *Finnlines*. In 1998 she operated between Helsinki and Travemünde. In 1999 she was chartered to *DFDS Tor Line* and operated between Göteborg and Harwich. In 2000 she returned to the Helsinki and Travemünde route.

FINNLINK

Finnlines also operate a freight only service between Kapellskär (Sweden) and Naantali (Finland) under the name *FinnLink*. Although this is strictly outside the scope of this book, the service is operated by ro-pax vessels which could be brought back into full passenger service:

THE COMPANY *FinnLink Oy* is a subsidiary of *Finnlines*.

ADDRESS Satamatic 11, FIN-21100, Naantali, Finland.

TELEPHONE Administration & Reservations: +358 (0)10 436 7620, **Fax:** 358 (0)10 436 7660.

INTERNET Website: http://www.finnlink.fi

ROUTE OPERATED Kapellskär (Sweden) – Naantali (Finland) (6 hrs; *(7,8,9)*; 3 per day)

VESSELS

7	FINNARROW	25996t	96	21k	200P	800C	200T	BA2	Kodja, IN	FI
8	FINNEAGLE	30500t	99	22k	440P	-	206T	BA2	Puerto Real, SP	SW
9	FINNFELLOW	14297t	73	18k	48P	170C	94T	AS	Turku, FI	FI

FINNARROW Built as the GOTLAND for *Rederi AB Gotland* for charter. In 1997 briefly chartered *Tor Line* and then to *Nordic Trucker Line*, to operate between Oxelösund and St Petersburg (a ro-ro service). In June 1997 she was chartered to *SeaWind Line*, enabling a twice daily passenger service to be operated. In late 1997 she was sold to *Finnlines* and renamed the FINNARROW. She started operating twice weekly between Helsinki and Travemünde. During summer 1998 she was transferred to *FinnLink*; a bow door was fitted.

FINNEAGLE As the FINNCLIPPER of *Finnlines*. On delivery in late 1999 she entered service with *FinnLink*. During winter 2000 she was converted to double-deck loading. She may operate on the Helsinki -Travemünde route at a later date.

FINNFELLOW Built for *Finncarriers*. In 1989 transferred to *FinnLink*.

FJORD LINE

THE COMPANY *Fjord Line* is 100% owned by *Bergen-Nordhordland Rutelag AS (BNR)*, a Norwegian company.

MANAGEMENT Managing Director: Ove Solem, **Marketing Manager:** Svein Vidar Ersvær.

ADDRESS Skoltegrunnskaien, PO Box 6020, N-5020 BERGEN, Norway.

TELEPHONE Administration: +47 55 54 87 00, **Reservations:** +47 55 54 88 00, **Fax:** +47 55 54 86 01.

INTERNET Email: fjordline@fjordline.com **Website:** http://www.fjordline.com *(Norwegian, Danish, English)*

ROUTE OPERATED Bergen – Egersund (Norway) – Hanstholm (Denmark) (15 hrs 30 mins; *(1)*; 3 per week), Egersund – Hanstholm (6 hrs 45 mins; *(1)*; 7 per week in summer). Also UK route – see Section 1.

CONVENTIONAL FERRY

1	BERGEN	16794t	93	20k	882P	160C	40L	BA	Rissa, NO	NO

BERGEN Built for *Rutelaget Askøy-Bergen* and used on *Fjord Line* service.

HH-FERRIES

THE COMPANY *HH-Ferries* is a Danish/Swedish private sector company.

MANAGEMENT Managing Director: Lars Meijer, **Marketing Manager:** Jon Cavalli-Björkman.

ADDRESS Atlantgatan 2, S-252 25 HELSINGBORG, Sweden.

TELEPHONE Administration: +46 (0)42-26 80 00, **Reservations:** *Denmark:* +45 49 26 01 55, *Sweden:* +46 (0)42-19 8000, **Fax:** *Denmark:* +45 49 26 01 56, *Sweden:* +46 (0)42-28 10 70.

INTERNET Email: admin@hhferries.se **Website:** http://www.hhferries.se *(Swedish, Danish, English)*

ROUTE OPERATED Helsingør – Helsingborg (20 mins; *(1,2)*; every 30 minutes).

CONVENTIONAL FERRIES

1	MERCANDIA IV	4296t	89	13k	420P	170C	24T	BA	Sunderland, GB	DK
2	MERCANDIA VIII	4296t	87	13k	420P	170C	24T	BA	Sunderland, GB	DK

MERCANDIA IV Built as the SUPERFLEX NOVEMBER for *Vognmandsruten* of Denmark. In 1989 sold to *Mercandia* and renamed the MERCANDIA IV. In 1990 she began operating on their *Kattegatbroen* Juelsminde – Kalundborg service. In 1996 she was transferred to their *Sundbroen* Helsingør – Helsingborg service. In 1997 the service and vessel were leased to *HH-Ferries*. She has been equipped to carry dangerous cargo.

MERCANDIA VIII Built as the SUPERFLEX BRAVO for *Vognmandsruten* of Denmark and used on their services between Nyborg and Korsør and København (Tuborg Havn) and Landskrona (Sweden). In 1991 she was chartered to *Scarlett Line* to operate on the København and Landskrona route. In 1993 she was renamed the SVEA SCARLETT but later in the year the service ceased and she was laid up. In 1996 she was purchased by *Mercandia*, renamed the MERCANDIA VIII and placed on their *Sundbroen* Helsingør – Helsingborg service. In 1997 the service and vessel was leased to *HH-Ferries*.

Finneagle (Speckus Ferry Information)

Kronprins Frederik (William Mayes)

HURTIGRUTEN

SERVICE The *'Hurtigruten'* is the *'Norwegian Coastal Express Service'*. It is part cruise, part passenger ferry, part cargo line and part car ferry (although this is a fairly minor part of the operation). The service operated by a consortium of two operators – *Ofotens og Vesteraalen Dampskipsselskab* and *Troms Fylkes Dampskipsselskab.*

ADDRESS *Ofotens og Vesteraalen Dampskipsselskab*: Postboks 43, 8501 NARVIK, Norway, *Troms Fylkes Dampskipsselskab*: 9005 TROMSØ, Norway.

TELEPHONE Administration: *Ofotens og Vesteraalen D/S:* +47 76 96 76 96, *Troms Fylkes D/S:* +47 77 64 82 00, **Reservations:** *Norway:* 810 30 000, *UK:* +44 (0)20 7371 4011, **Fax:** *Ofotens og Vesteraalen D/S:* +47 76 96 76 11, *Troms Fylkes D/S:* +47 77 64 82 40, *Reservations (UK):* +44 (0)20 7371 4070.

INTERNET Email: booking@ovds.no booking@tfds.no **Website:** http://www.hurtigruten.no *(English, Norwegian, German, Dutch, Spanish, Finnish, French, Italian and Swedish)*

ROUTE OPERATED Bergen – Kirkenes with many intermediate calls. Daily departures throughout the year. The round trip takes just under 11 days.

CONVENTIONAL FERRIES

1	HARALD JARL	2621t	60	16k	410P	4C	-	C	Trondheim, NO	NO
2	KONG HARALD	11204t	93	18k	691P	50C	-	SC	Stralsund, GY	NO
3	LOFOTEN	2621t	64	16k	410P	4C	-	C	Oslo, NO	NO
4	MIDNATSOL	6167t	82	18k	550P	40C	-	SC	Ulsteinvik, NO	NO
5	NARVIK	6257t	82	18k	550P	40C	-	SC	Trondheim, NO	NO
6	NORDKAPP	11386t	96	18k	691P	50C	-	SC	Ulsteinvik, NO	NO
7	NORDLYS	11204t	94	18k	691P	50C	-	SC	Stralsund, GY	NO
8	NORDNORGE	11384t	97	18k	691P	50C	-	SC	Ulsteinvik, NO	NO
9	POLARLYS	11341t	96	18k	691P	50C	-	SC	Ulsteinvik, NO	NO
10	RICHARD WITH	11205t	93	18k	691P	50C	-	SC	Stralsund, GY	NO
11	VESTERÅLEN	6261t	83	18k	550P	40C	-	SC	Harstad, NO	NO

HARALD JARL Built for *Nordenfjeldske D/S*. In 1988 she was sold to *Troms Fylkes Dampskibsselskap.*

KONG HARALD Built for *Troms Fylkes D/S.*

LOFOTEN Built for *Vesteraalens D/S*. In 1984 she was sold to *Finnmark Fylkesrederi og Ruteselskap.* In 1996 she was sold to *Ofotens og Vesteraalen D/S.*

MIDNATSOL Built for *Troms Fylkes D/S.*

NARVIK Built for Built for *Ofoten D/S*. Since 1984 owned by *Ofotens og Vesteraalen D/S.*

NORDKAPP Built for *Ofotens og Vesteraalen D/S.*

NORDLYS Built for *Troms Fylkes D/S.*

NORDNORGE Built for *Ofotens og Vesteraalen D/S.*

POLARLYS Built for *Troms Fylkes D/S.*

RICHARD WITH Built for *Ofotens og Vesteraalen D/S.*

VESTERÅLEN Built for *Vesteraalens D/S*. Since 1984 owned by *Ofotens og Vesteraalen D/S.*

LISCO

THE COMPANY *Lisco* is the trading name of the *Lithuanian Shipping Company*, a Lithuanian state owned company. Passenger and cargo services are marketed by *Krantas Shipping*.

ADDRESS 24 J. Janonio Str, KLAÌPEDA LT-5813, Lithuania.

TELEPHONE *Lisco* **(Klaìpeda):** **Administration:** +370 (0)6 393101, **Fax:** +370 (0)6 393121, **Telex:** 278126 lisco lt, *Krantas* **(Klaìpeda):** **Reservations:** +370 (0)6 365444, **Fax:** +370 (0)6 365443, **Telex:** 278350 KRANT LT, *Krantas: (Stockholm):* **Reservations:** +46 (0)8-673 3200, **Fax:** +46 (0)8-673 6303.

INTERNET Email: *Lisco:* lisco@klaìpeda.omnitel.net *Krantas:* krantaspass@klaìpeda.omnitel.net

Website: *Lisco:* http://www.lisco.lt *(English, German)* *Krantas:* http://www.krantas.lt *(English)*

ROUTES OPERATED Klaìpeda (Lithuania) – Stockholm (18 hrs; *(3)*; 2 per week), Klaìpeda – Kiel (25-30 hrs; *(1,2)*; up to 6 per week (joint with *Scandlines Euroseabridge* under the *Kiel-Klaìpeda-Express* name)), Klaìpeda – Fährhafen Sassnitz (Germany) (18 hrs; *(2)*; 6 per week) (Joint service with *Scandlines Euroseabridge*).

CONVENTIONAL FERRIES

1	KAUNAS	25606t	89	16k	202P	460C	90T	A2	Wismar, GE	LT
2	KLAÌPEDA	21980t	87	16k	12P	-	90T	A	Wismar, GE	LT
3	PALANGA	11630t	79	20k	102P	-	80T	A	Le Havre, FR	LT
4	VILNIUS	21800t	87	19k	120P	460C	90T	A2	Wismar, GE	LT

KAUNUS, VILNIUS Train ferries built for *Lisco* of the former Soviet Union and used by to operate between Klaìpeda and Mukran in Germany (DDR). This was part of a series of vessels built to link the USSR and Germany (DDR), avoiding Poland. In 1994 they were modified to increase passenger capacity in order to offer a limited passenger facilities and placed on a Klaìpeda – Kiel service.

KLAÌPEDA Train ferry as KAUNUS, VILNIUS – but not converted to ro-pax format. Operates on the Klaìpeda – Fährhafen Sassnitz route (Fährhafen Sassnitz is the new name for Mukran).

PALANGA Built as the MONTE STELLO for *SNCM* of France for Mediterranean service; rebuilt in 1992 to increase passenger capacity. In 1996 sold to *Lisco*, renamed the PALANGA; she was placed on the Klaìpeda – Kiel service. In 1997 she was placed on the Klaìpeda – Stockholm service.

MOLS-LINIEN

THE COMPANY *Mols-Linien A/S* is a Danish private sector company; previously a subsidiary of *J Lauritzen A/S*, it was, in 1988 sold to *DIFKO No LXII (Dansk Investeringsfond)*. Since 1994 shares in the company have been traded on the stock exchange. In January 1999 a 40% share in the company was acquired by *Scandlines Danmark A/S*. Their *Scandlines Cat-Link* Århus – Kalundborg service became part of *Mols-Linien* in February 1999 and the service was switched from Kalundborg to Odden in April 1999. The Ebeltoft – Odden ro-pax service was transferred to the Århus – Kalundborg route in January 2000.

MANAGEMENT Managing Director: Preben Wolff, **Marketing Manager:** Christian Hingelberg.

ADDRESS Færgehavnen, DK-8400 EBELTOFT, Denmark.

TELEPHONE Administration: +45 89 52 52 00, **Reservations:** +45 70 10 14 18, **Fax:** *Admin:* +45 89 52 52 90, *Reservations:* +45 89 52 52 92.

INTERNET Email: Mols-Linien@Mols-Linien.dk **Website:** http://www.Mols-Linien.dk *(Danish)*

ROUTES OPERATED Ro-pax Ferries: Århus (Jylland) – Kalundborg (Sjælland) (2hr 40 mins; *(1,2)*; 7 per day), **Fast Ferries:** Århus – Odden (Sjælland) (1 hr 5 mins; *(4)*; every 3 hrs), Ebeltoft (Jylland) – Odden (45 mins; *(3,5)*; hourly).

RO-PAX FERRIES

| 1 | MAREN MOLS | 14221t | 96 | 19k | 600P | 344C | 100T | BA2 | Frederikshavn, DK | DK |
| 2 | METTE MOLS | 14221t | 96 | 19k | 600P | 344C | 100T | BA2 | Frederikshavn, DK | DK |

MAREN MOLS, METTE MOLS 'Ro-pax' vessels built for *Mols-Linien*. Initially operated on the Ebeltoft – Odden route. In January 2000 switched to the Århus – Kalundborg route.

FAST FERRIES

3	MAI MOLS	3971t	96	43.4k	450P	120C	-	BB	Aalborg, DK	DK
4	MAX MOLS	5617t	98	43k	800P	220C	-	A	Hobart, AL	BA
5	MIE MOLS	3971t	96	43.4k	450P	120C	-	BB	Aalborg, DK	DK

MAI MOLS Danyard SeaJet 250 catamaran built for *Mols-Linien*.

MAX MOLS InCat 91 metre catamaran, built speculatively. In spring 1998, following *InCat's* acquisition of a 50% share in *Scandlines Cat-Link A/S*, she was sold to that company and named the CAT-LINK IV. In 1999 purchased by *Mols-Linien* and renamed the MAX MOLS.

MIE MOLS Danyard SeaJet 250 catamaran built for *Mols-Linien*.

REEDEREI NORDEN-FRISIA

THE COMPANY *Aktiengesellschaft Reederei Norden-Frisia* is a German public sector company.

MANAGEMENT President/CEO: Dr Stegmann, **Managing Director/CFO:** Prok. Graw.

ADDRESS Postfach 1262, 26534 NORDERNEY, Germany.

TELEPHONE Administration: +49 (0)4932 91 30, **Fax:** +49 (0)4932 91 310.

INTERNET Email: info@reederei-frisia.de **Website:** http://www.reederei-frisia.de *(German)*

ROUTES OPERATED *Car Ferries:* Norddeich (Germany) – Norderney (German Frisian Islands) (1 hr; *(1,3,5)*; up to 15 per day), Norddeich – Juist (German Frisian Islands) (1 hr 20 mins; *(2,4,6)*; up to 15 per day), *Passenger only fast ferry:* Norderney – Helgoland (1hr 15 mins; *(CAT NO 1)*), Cuxhaven – Helgoland (1 hr; *(CAT NO 1)*).

CONVENTIONAL FERRIES

1	FRISIA I	1020t	70	12.3k	1500P	55C	-	-	Papenburg, GY	GY
2	FRISIA II	1125t	78	12k	1340P	55C	-	-	Papenburg, GY	GY
3	FRISIA V	1007t	65	11k	1442P	55C	-	-	Papenburg, GY	GY
4	FRISIA VI	768t	68	12k	1096P	35C	-	-	Papenburg, GY	GY
5	FRISIA VIII	1058t	62	12.5k	1340P	55C	-	-	Papenburg, GY	GY
6	FRISIA IX	571t	80	10k	785P	9C	-	-	Oldersum, GY	GY

FRISIA I, FRISIA II, FRISIA V, FRISIA VI, FRISIA VIII, FRISIA IX Built for *Reederei Norden-Frisia*. Passenger figures relate to the summer seasons. Capacity is reduced during the winter.

Reederei Norden-Frisia also operate three passenger only vessels – the CAT NO 1 (963t, 1999) (high-speed catamaran), FRISIA III (710t, 1960) and the FRISIA X (187t, 1972).

Mai Mols (William Mayes)

Stena Germanica (N.Meads)

NORDIC JET LINE

THE COMPANY *Nordic Jet Line* an cvx international company, registered in Estonia. Main shareholders are *Förde Reederei Seetouristik* of Germany, *Finnmark Fylkesrederi og Ruteselskap* of Norway and *Kværner Fjellstrand* (shipbuilders) of Norway.

MANAGEMENT Managing Director: Mikael Granrot, **Deputy Managing Director:** Götz Becker.

ADDRESS *Estonia:* Virv Valaik 4, TALLINN, Estonia, *Finland:* Kanavaterminaali K5, 00160 HELSINKI, Finland.

TELEPHONE *Estonia:* **Administration:** +372 (0)6 137200, **Reservations:** +372 (0)6 137000, **Fax:** +372 (0)6 137222, *Finland:* **Administration:** +358 (0)9 68177150, **Reservations:** +358 (0)9 681770, **Fax:** +358 (0)9 6817111.

INTERNET Email: info@njl.fi **Website:** http://www.njl.fi *(English, Finnish, Swedish, Estonian, German)*

ROUTE OPERATED Helsinki (Finland) – Tallinn (Estonia) (1 hrs 30 mins; *(1,2)*; up to 6 per day (all year except during winter ice period)).

FAST FERRIES

1	BALTIC JET	2273t	99	36k	430P	52C	-	A	Omastrand, NO	NO
2	NORDIC JET	2273t	98	36k	430P	52C	-	A	Omastrand, NO	NO

BALTIC JET, NORDIC JET Kværner Fjellstrand JumboCat 60m catamarans built for *Nordic Jet Line*. Alternative traffic mix is 38 cars and 2 buses.

POLFERRIES

THE COMPANY *Polferries* is the trading name of *Polska Zegluga Baltycka (Polish Baltic Shipping Company)*, a Polish state owned company.

MANAGEMENT General Director & President of the Board: Jacek Henryk Dorski, **Marketing & Sales Director:** Rafal Jablonski.

ADDRESS ul. Portowa 41, PL 78-100 KOLOBRZEG, Poland.

TELEPHONE Administration: +48 (0)94 35 25 211, **Reservations:** *Swinoujscie:* +48 (0)91 32 16 140, *Gdansk:* +48 (0)58 34 36 978, **Fax:** *Admin:* +48 (0)94 35 26 612, *Reservations (Swinoujscie):* +48 (0)91 32 16 168, *Reservations (Gdansk):* +48 (0)58 34 30 975.

INTERNET Email: info@polferries.com.pl **Website:** http://www.polferries.com.pl *(Polish, English)*

ROUTES OPERATED Swinoujscie – Ystad (7 hrs; *(4)*; 1 per day), Swinoujscie – Malmö (9 hrs; *(1)*; 1 per day), Swinoujscie – København (9 hrs 45 mins; *(2)*; 5 per week), Swinoujscie – Rønne (6 hrs; *(2)*; 1 per week), Gdansk – Nynäshamn (Sweden) (19 hrs; *(3)*; 3 per week). Note: services subject to change from May 2000.

CONVENTIONAL FERRIES

1	NIEBOROW	8697t	73	22k	920P	225C	36T	BA	Rendsburg, GY	PO
2	POMERANIA	12087t	78	18.2k	1000P	146C	38T	BA	Szczecin, PO	PO
3	ROGALIN	10241t	72	21k	920P	225C	22T	BA	Nantes, FR	PO
4	SILESIA	10553t	79	19k	984P	277C	38T	BA	Szczecin, PO	PO

NIEBOROW Built for *Prinzenlinien* of Germany as PRINZ HAMLET for the Harwich – Hamburg service. In 1981 *Prinzenlinien* was acquired by *DFDS*. In 1987 she was renamed the PRINS HAMLET, re-registered in Denmark and transferred to the seasonal Newcastle – Esbjerg and Newcastle – Göteborg summer services. During winter 1987/88 she operated for *B&I Line* of Ireland between Rosslare and Pembroke Dock. At the end of the 1988 summer season she was acquired by a *Stena Line* subsidiary, chartered to *Polferries* and renamed the NIEBOROW. Currently used on the Swinoujscie – Malmö route.

POMERANIA Built for *Polferries*. In 1978 and 1979 she briefly operated between Felixstowe and Swinoujscie via København. In recent years she was the regular vessel on the Gdansk – Helsinki service before that service was withdrawn. She was rebuilt in 1997. Used on the Swinoujscie – København and Swinoujscie – Rønne routes.

ROGALIN Built as the AALLOTAR for the *EFFOA* of Finland. Used on overnight *Silja Line* services (joint with *Svea Line* of Sweden and *Bore Line* of Finland) between Stockholm and Helsinki. Later used on the Stockholm – Mariehamn – Turku service. In 1978 she was sold to *Polferries*. She was renamed the ROGALIN and operated on various services between Poland, West Germany and Scandinavia. In 1983 she was chartered to *Farskip* of Iceland from the end of May until September, renamed the EDDA and inaugurated a service between Reykjavik (Iceland), Newcastle and Bremerhaven (Germany). In September of that year she returned to *Polferries* and resumed the name ROGALIN. This service was not repeated in 1984 and she continued to operate for *Polferries* until chartered (with crew) by *Swansea Cork Ferries* in 1987. She was renamed the CELTIC PRIDE and inaugurated a new Swansea – Cork service. This service also operated during summer 1988 but during winter 1987/88 and after the 1988 summer season she was returned to *Polferries* and resumed the name ROGALIN, operating on Baltic services. She did not serve with *Swansea Cork Ferries* in 1989 or 1990 but in 1991 she was taken on charter (again with crew) and was again renamed the CELTIC PRIDE. This charter terminated at the end of 1992 and she returned to the Baltic and resumed the name ROGALIN. Used on the Gdansk – Nynäshamn route.

SILESIA Built for *Polferries*. Rebuilt during winter 1997/98, although not as extensively as the POMERANIA. Used on the Swinoujscie – Ystad route.

PROVINCIALE STOOMBOOTDIENSTEN IN ZEELAND

THE COMPANY *Provinciale Stoombootdiensten in Zeeland* is a Dutch public sector company.

MANAGEMENT Managing Directors: D F Vos & H E C M Thomaes.

ADDRESS Prins Hendrikweg 10, 4382 NS VLISSINGEN, Netherlands (*Correspondence:* Postbus 171, 4380 AD VLISSINGEN, Netherlands).

TELEPHONE Administration: +31 (0)118 46 09 00, **Reservations:** not applicable, **Fax:** +31 (0)118 46 80 96.

INTERNET Email: psdiz@world.access **Website:** http://www.zeeland.nl

ROUTES OPERATED Vlissingen – Breskens (20 mins; *(1,2)*; half hourly), Perkpolder – Kruiningen (20 mins; *(3,5)*; half hourly).

CONVENTIONAL FERRIES

1	KONINGIN BEATRIX	7910t	93	17k	1000P	210C	22L	BA2	Vlissingen, NL	NL
2	PRINS JOHAN FRISO	7865t	97	16.5k	1000P	210C	22L	BA2	Vlissingen, NL	NL
3	PRINS WILLEM-ALEXANDER	7038t	70	16.5k	1000P	234C	22L	BA2	Hardinxveld, NL	NL
4	PRINSES CHRISTINA	6831t	68	16.5k	1000P	234C	22L	BA2	Hardinxveld, NL	NL
5	PRINSES JULIANA	8166t	86	14.5k	1000P	210C	22L	BA2	Hardinxveld, NL	NL

KONINGIN BEATRIX Built for *bv Veerboot Westerschelde* (a subsidiary of *De Schelde Shipyards*) and chartered to *PSD*. Purchased by *PSD* in 1997. Used on the Vlissingen – Breskens service.

PRINS JOHAN FRISO Built for *PSD*. Used on the Vlissingen – Breskens service.

PRINS WILLEM-ALEXANDER Built for *PSD*. Used on the Perkpolder – Kruiningen service.

PRINSES CHRISTINA Built for *PSD*. Used on the Perkpolder – Kruiningen service until autumn 1997 when she became a spare vessel.

PRINSES JULIANA Built for *PSD*. Initially used on the Vlissingen – Breskens service. In 1997 she was replaced by the PRINS JOHAN FRISO and, in the autumn, transferred to the Perkpolder – Kruiningen service.

Sassnitz (William Mayes)

Pomerania and Felix (Dominic McCall)

RÖMÖ-SYLT LINIE

THE COMPANY *Römö-Sylt Linie GmbH* is a German company, a subsidiary of *FRS (Förde Reederei Seetouristik)* of Flensburg.

MANAGEMENT Managing Director: P Rathke.

ADDRESS *Germany:* Am Fahrahleger, D-25992 LIST, Germany. *Denmark:* Kilebryggen, DK-6792 RØMØ, Denmark.

TELEPHONE Administration (Germany): +49 (0)4651 87 04 75, **Reservations (Denmark):** +45 73 75 53 03, **Fax:** *Admin:* +49 (0)4651 87 14 46, *Reservations:* +45 73 75 53 05.

INTERNET Email: romo-sylt@post12.tele.dk **Website:** http://www.romo-sylt.dk *(Danish, German)*

ROUTE OPERATED List (Sylt, Germany) – Havneby (Rømø, Denmark) (45 mins; *(1,2)*; variable – half hourly at peaks). Note: the island of Rømø is linked to the Danish mainland by a road causeway; the island of Sylt is linked to the German mainland by a rail-only causeway on which cars are conveyed on shuttle wagons.

CONVENTIONAL FERRIES

1	VIKINGLAND	1963t	74	11k	420P	60C	8L	BA	Husum, GY		GY
2	WESTERLAND	1509t	71	11k	400P	40C	5L	BA	Husum, GY		GY

VIKINGLAND, WESTERLAND Built for *Römö-Sylt Linie.*

SCANDLINES (DENMARK & GERMANY)

THE COMPANY *Scandlines AG* is a German company, 50% owned by *Deutsche Bahn AG (German Railway)* (which is owned by the Federal Government) and 50% owned by the Kingdom of Denmark. In 1998 it took over *DFO (Deutsche Fährgesellschaft Ostsee mbH)* of Germany (renamed *Scandlines Deutschland GmbH)* and *Scandlines A/S* of Denmark (renamed *Scandlines Danmark A/S).* A 50% share in *Euroseabridge GmbH* was acquired in 1998 (by *Scandlines A/S* of Denmark before the merger with *DFO)* and the remaining 50% in 1999; the name has been changed to *Scandlines Euroseabridge GmbH.*

Scandlines A/S was formerly *DSB Rederi A/S* and before that the Ferries Division of *DSB (Danish State Railways).* DFO was formed in 1993 by the merging of the Ferries Divisions of *Deutsche Bundesbahn (German Federal Railways)* (which operated in the Federal Republic of Germany) and *Deutsche Reichsbahn (German State Railways)* (which operated in the former DDR).

Swedish state operator *Scandlines AB* also trades under this name but remains a separate company. Danish domestic routes are operated by subsidiary company *Scandlines Sydfynske A/S,* and are marketed as part of the *Scandlines* network.

MANAGEMENT Chairman: Dr Eberhard Sinnecker, **Managing Director:** Ole Rendbæk, **Head of Passenger Services:** Geir Jansen.

ADDRESS *Denmark:* Dampfærgevej 10, DK-2100 KØBENHAVN Ø, Denmark. *Germany:* Hochhaus am Fährhafen, D-18119 ROSTOCK-WARNEMÜNDE, Germany.

TELEPHONE *Denmark:* **Administration:** +45 35 29 02 00, **Reservations:** +45 33 15 15 15, **Fax:** +45 35 29 02 01. *Germany:* **Administration:** +49 (0)381 54 35 680, **Reservations:** +49 (0)180 53 43 441, +49 (0)180 53 43 443, **Fax:** +49 (0)180 53 43 442, +49 (0)180 53 43 444.

INTERNET Email: info@scandlines.de info@scandlines.dk **Websites:** http://www.scandlines.dk *(Danish)* http://www.scandlines.de *(German)*

ROUTES OPERATED Conventional Ferries: Helsingør (Sjælland, Denmark) – Helsingborg (Sweden) (25 mins; *(7,24)*; every 20 mins) (joint with *Scandlines AB* of Sweden), Rødby (Lolland, Denmark) – Puttgarden (Germany) (45 mins; *(2,8,17,18,21 (8 road freight only))*; half hourly train/vehicle ferry + additional road freight only sailings), Gedser (Falster, Denmark) – Rostock (Germany) (2 hrs; *(3,11)*; 4-7 per day), Rostock (Germany) – Trelleborg (Sweden) (5 hrs 30 mins (7 hrs night); *(12)*; 3 per day) (joint with *Scandlines AB* of Sweden), Fährhafen Sassnitz (Germany) – Trelleborg (3 hrs 30 mins; *(20)*; 5 per day) (joint with *Scandlines AB* of Sweden), Fährhafen Sassnitz – Rønne (Bornholm, Denmark) (3 hrs 45 mins; *(19)*; 1 or 2 per day (summer), 1 per day, weekends only (winter).

Danish domestic services operated by subsidiary *Scandlines Sydfynske A/S (formerly Sydfynske Dampskibsselskab (SFDS))* and forming part of *Scandlines* network: Fynshav (Als) – Bøjden (Fyn) (50 mins; *(23)*; two hourly), Esbjerg (Jylland) – Nordby (Fanø) (20 mins; *(4,13)*; half hourly), Spodsbjerg (Langeland) – Tårs (Lolland) (45 mins; *(5,14,22)*; hourly).

Germany – Latvia & Lithuania routes operated by subsidiary *Scandlines Euroseabridge GmbH*: Kiel – Klaìpeda (Lithuania) (25 hrs; *(6)*; 6 per week (joint with *Lisco* of Lithuania under the *Kiel-Klaìpeda-Express* name)), Fährhafen Sassnitz (Germany) – Klaìpeda (18 hrs; *(15)*; 6 per week (joint with *Lisco – Scandlines Euroseabridge* ro-pax vessel 3 times per week, *Lisco* ro-ro KLAÌPEDA 3 times per week)), Rostock (Germany) – Liepaja (Latvia) (24 hrs; *(1)*; 2 per week).

Denmark – Lithuania route operated by *Scandlines Balticum Seaways* division: Århus (Denmark) – Aabenraa (Denmark) – Klaìpeda (Lithuania) (from 30 hrs; *(25)*; 2 per week from Aabenraa (1 westbound via Århus), 1 per week from Århus).

Sweden – Latvia route operated by *Amber Line* division: Karlshamn (Sweden) – Liepaja (Latvia) (16 hrs 30 mins; *(9)*; 3 per week). Note: this route is not joint with *Scandlines AB* and the name *Scandlines* cannot therefore be used.

CONVENTIONAL FERRIES

1	ASK	11160t	82	18k	64P	291C	76T	AS	Venezia, IT	DK
2	DEUTSCHLAND	15187t	97	18.5k	900P	305C	480r	BA	Krimpen, NL	GY
3	DRONNING MARGRETHE II	10850t	73	16.5k	1500P	211C	30T	BA	Nakskov, DK	DK
4	FENJA	751t	98	11k	400P	38C	4L	BA	Svendborg, DK	DK
5	FRIGG SYDFYEN	1676t	84	12k	338P	50C	8L	BA	Svendborg, DK	DK
6	GREIFSWALD	24084t	88	15.5k	120P	100C	100L	A2	Wismar, GE	LB
7	HAMLET	10067t	97	13k	1000P	240C	36L	BA2	Rauma, FI	DK
8	HOLGER DANSKE	2779t	76	14.5k	600P	55C	14T	BA	Aalborg, DK	DK
9	KAHLEBERG	10271t	83	15.5k	74P	-	50T	AS	Wismar, GE	LB
10•	KARL CARSTENS	12829t	86	18.1k	1500P	333C	44T	BA2	Kiel, GY	GY
11	KRONPRINS FREDERIK	16071t	81	19.5k	2280P	-	494r	BA	Nakskov, DK	DK
12	MECKLENBURG-VORPOMMERN									
		36185t	96	18k	887P	440C	945r	A2	Bremerhaven, GY	GY
13	MENJA	751t	98	11k	400P	38C	4L	BA	Svendborg, DK	DK
14	ODIN SYDFYEN	1698t	82	12k	338P	50C	8L	BA	Svendborg, DK	DK
15	PETERSBURG	25353t	86	15k	140P	100C	100L	A2	Wismar, GE	LB
16•	PRINS JOACHIM	16071t	80	18k	2280P	-	494r	BA	Nakskov, DK	DK
17	PRINS RICHARD	14621t	97	16.5k	900P	286C	118r	BA	Frederikshavn, DK	DK
18	PRINSESSE BENEDIKTE	14621t	97	16.5k	900P	286C	118r	BA	Frederikshavn, DK	DK
19	RÜGEN	12289t	72	20.5k	1468P	220C	480r	A2	Rostock, GE	GY
20	SASSNITZ	21154t	89	17k	800P	100C	711r	A2	Frederikshavn, DK	GY
21	SCHLESWIG-HOLSTEIN	15550t	97	18.5k	900P	294C	480r	BA	Krimpen, NL	GY
22	SPODSBJERG	1478t	72	12k	300P	48C	9L	BA	Nakskov, DK	DK
23	THOR SYDFYEN	1479t	78	12k	300P	50C	9L	BA	Århus, DK	DK
24	TYCHO BRAHE	10845t	91	13.5k	1250P	240C	259r	BA	Tomrefjord, NO	DK
25	URD	11030t	81	17k	64P	291C	76T	AS	Venezia, IT	DK

ASK Built as the LUCKY RIDER, a ro-ro freight ferry, for *Delpa Maritime* of Greece. In 1985 she was acquired by *Stena Line* and renamed the STENA DRIVER. Later that year she was acquired by *Sealink British Ferries* and renamed the SEAFREIGHT FREEWAY to operate freight-only services between Dover and Dunkerque. In 1988 she was sold to *SOMAT* of Bulgaria for use on *Medlink* services in the Mediterranean and renamed the SERDICA. In 1990 she was sold and renamed the NORTHERN

HUNTER. In 1991 she was sold to *Blæsbjerg* of Denmark, renamed the ARKA MARINE and chartered to *DSB*. She was the converted into a ro-pax vessel, renamed the ASK and introduced onto the Århus – Kalundborg service. Purchased by *Scandlines* in 1997. Withdrawn at the end of 1998. In 1999 she was, after some modification, transferred to *Scandlines Euroseabridge* and placed on the Travemünde – Klaipeda route. In 2000 she was transferred to the Rostock – Liepaja route.

DEUTSCHLAND Train/vehicle ferry built for *DFO* for the Puttgarden – Rødby service.

DRONNING MARGRETHE II Train/vehicle ferry built for *DSB* for the Nyborg – Korsør service. In 1981 transferred to the Rødby – Puttgarden service. An additional vehicle deck was added in 1982. Withdrawn in 1997. In 1998 became a back-up freight-only vessel on the Rødby – Puttgarden and Gedser – Rostock routes. In 1999 she replaced the fast ferry BERLIN EXPRESS (4675t, 1995) as regular vessel on the Gedser – Rostock route.

FENJA Built for *SFDS A/S* for the Esbjerg – Nordby service.

FRIGG SYDFYEN Vehicle ferry built for *Sydfyenske Dampskibsselskab (SFDS)* of Denmark for the service between Spodsbjerg and Tårs. In 1996, this company was taken over by *DSB Rederi*.

GREIFSWALD Built as a train ferry for *DSR* of Germany (DDR) to operate on the service between Mukran and Klaipeda (Lithuania). In 1994 she was rebuilt to introduce road vehicle and additional passenger capacity. In 1996 she was transferred to the new *Euroseabridge* Travemünde – Klaipeda service. During winter 1998/99 she was chartered to *Stena Line* to operate between Göteborg and Kiel. She was then chartered to the British *Ministry of Defence* for use in the Balkans. In November 1999 she was transferred to the Kiel – Klaipeda route.

HAMLET Vehicle ferry built for *Scandlines* for the Helsingør – Helsingborg service.

HOLGER DANSKE Built as a train/vehicle ferry for *DSB* for the Helsingør – Helsingborg service. In 1991 transferred to the Kalundborg – Samsø route (no rail facilities). In 1997, transferred to subsidiary *SFDS A/S*. Withdrawn by the end of November 1998 when the service passed *Samsø Linien*. In 1999 began operating between Rødby and Puttgarden as a road freight only vessel, carrying, among others, loads which cannot be conveyed on passenger vessels.

KAHLEBERG Built for *DSR* of Germany (DDR). In 1991 chartered to *TT Line* for *TR Line* service between Rostock and Trelleborg. In 1997 she returned to *DSR* to operate for *Euroseabridge*. She initially operated on the Travemünde – Klaipeda service. In 1999 she was transferred to the formerly freight only Rostock – Liepaja service. In 2000 replaced by the ASK and transferred to the *Amber Line* Karlshamn – Liepaja route.

KARL CARSTENS Train/vehicle ferry built for *DB* and used on the Puttgarden – Rødby service. Withdrawn at the end of 1997. Initially used as a reserve vessel but now laid up.

KRONPRINS FREDERIK Train/vehicle ferry built for *DSB* for the Nyborg – Korsør service. Withdrawn in 1997. After modification, she was transferred to the Gedser – Rostock route (no rail facilities).

MECKLENBURG-VORPOMMERN Train/vehicle ferry built for *DFO* for the Rostock – Trelleborg service.

MENJA Built for *SFDS A/S* for the Esbjerg – Nordby service.

ODIN SYDFYEN Vehicle ferry built for *Sydfyenske Dampskibsselskab (SFDS)* of Denmark for the service between Spodsbjerg and Tårs. In 1996, this company was taken over by *DSB Rederi*.

PETERSBURG Built as the MUKRAN for *DSR* of Germany (DDR) . In 1995 she was rebuilt to introduce road vehicle and additional passenger capacity and was renamed the PETERSBURG. She inaugurated the Travemünde service in 1995 but is now used on the Fährhafen Sassnitz – Klaipeda service. This service is operated jointly with the *Lisco* vessel KLAIPEDA, a sister vessel which has not been converted to ro-pax format.

PRINS JOACHIM Train/vehicle ferry, built for *DSB* for the Nyborg – Korsør service. Withdrawn in 1997. Laid up.

PRINS RICHARD, PRINSESSE BENEDIKTE Train/vehicle ferries, built for *DSB Rederi* for the Rødby

– Puttgarden service.

RÜGEN Train/vehicle ferry built for *Deutsche Reichsbahn* of Germany (DDR) for services between Trelleborg and Sassnitz. In 1993 ownership was transferred to *DFO*. Since 1989 she has been used on the Fährhafen Sassnitz – Rønne service. In 1998 and 1999 she also operated between Ystad and Rønne but this will not be repeated in 2000.

SASSNITZ Train/vehicle ferry built for *Deutsche Reichsbahn*. In 1993 ownership transferred to *DFO*. Used on the Fährhafen Sassnitz – Trelleborg service.

SCHLESWIG-HOLSTEIN Train/vehicle ferry built for *DFO* for the Puttgarden – Rødby service.

SPODSBJERG Vehicle ferries built for *Sydfyenske Dampskibsselskab (SFDS)* of Denmark for the service between Spodsbjerg and Tårs. In 1996, this company was taken over by *DSB Rederi*.

THOR SYDFYEN Vehicle ferries built for *Sydfyenske Dampskibsselskab (SFDS)* of Denmark for the service between Spodsbjerg and Tårs. In 1996, this company was taken over by *DSB Rederi*. In 1998 she was transferred to the Fynshav – Bøjden route.

TYCHO BRAHE Train/vehicle ferry, built for *DSB* for the Helsingør – Helsingborg service.

URD Built as the EASY RIDER, a ro-ro freight ferry, for *Delpa Maritime* of Greece and used on Mediterranean services. In 1985 she was acquired by *Sealink British Ferries* and renamed the SEAFREIGHT HIGHWAY to operate freight-only service between Dover and Dunkerque. In 1988 she was sold to *SOMAT* of Bulgaria for use on *Medlink* services in the Mediterranean and renamed the BOYANA. In 1990 she was sold to *Blæsbjerg* of Denmark, renamed the AKTIV MARINE and chartered to *DSB*. In 1991 she was converted into ro-pax vessel, renamed the URD and introduced onto the Århus – Kalundborg service. Purchased by *Scandlines* in 1997. Withdrawn at the end of May 1999 and, after modification, transferred to the *Balticum Seaways* (later *Scandlines Balticum Seaways*) Århus – Aabenraa – Klaìpeda route.

SCANDLINES (SWEDEN)

THE COMPANY *Scandlines AB* (formerly *SweFerry*) is a Swedish company, a subsidiary of *Statens Järnvägar (Swedish State Railways)*. In autumn 1999 it was announced that the company had been sold to *Stena Line AB* of Sweden. However, this sale was opposed by *Scandlines AG*, who claimed a prior right to purchase the company, based on a 1990 agreement between *SJ* and *DSB (Danish State Railways)*. *Scandlines AG* were granted an interim injunction which has prevented the sale. The matter has been referred to an arbitration tribunal in Oslo and a ruling is expected in July.

MANAGEMENT Managing Director: Åke Svensson.

ADDRESS Knutpunkten 43, S-252 78 HELSINGBORG, Sweden.

TELEPHONE Administration: +46 (0)42-18 62 00, Reservations: *Helsingborg:* +46 (0)42-18 61 00, *Trelleborg:* +46 (0)410-621 00, Fax: *Admin:* +46 (0)42-18 60 49, *Reservations – Helsingborg:* +46 (0)42-18 74 10, *Reservations – Trelleborg:* +46 (0)410-620 29.

INTERNET Email: man@mbox303.swipnet.se Website: http://www.scandlines.se *(Swedish)*

ROUTES OPERATED Conventional Ferries: Helsingborg (Sweden) – Helsingør (Denmark) (25 mins; *(1)*; every 20 mins), Trelleborg (Sweden) – Rostock (Germany) (6 hrs; *(3)*; 4 per day), Trelleborg – Fährhafen Sassnitz (Germany) (3 hrs 30 mins; *(4)*; 3 per day), Trelleborg (Sweden) – Travemünde (Germany) (8 hrs; *(2)*; 1 per day – freight-only). All routes are joint with *Scandlines AG* except Trelleborg – Travemünde.

CONVENTIONAL FERRIES

1	AURORA AF HELSINGBORG	10918t	92	14.9k	1250P	240C	260r	BA	Tomrefjord, NO	SW
2	GÖTALAND	18060t	73	18.5k	400P	118C	811r	AS2	Nakskov, DK	SW
3	SKÅNE	42558t	98	21k	600P	-	1120r	AS2	Puerto Real, SP	SW
4	TRELLEBORG	20028t	82	21k	900P	108C	755r	A2	Landskrona, SW	SW

AURORA AF HELSINGBORG Train/vehicle ferry built for *SweFerry* for *ScandLines* joint service.

Owned by *Aurora 93 Trust* of the USA and chartered to *Scandlines*.

GÖTALAND Train/vehicle ferry built for *Statens Järnvägar (Swedish State Railways)* for freight services between Trelleborg and Sassnitz. In 1990 transferred to *SweFerry*. In 1992 modified to increase passenger capacity in order to run in passenger service. She is was on the Trelleborg – Rostock service until autumn 1998 when she was replaced by the SKÅNE. She then inaugurated a new freight-only Trelleborg – Travemünde service.

SKÅNE Train/vehicle ferry built for an American trust and chartered to *Scandlines*. She is used on the Trelleborg – Rostock service.

TRELLEBORG Train/vehicle ferry built for *Svelast* of Sweden (an *SJ* subsidiary). In 1990 ownership transferred to *SweFerry*. She is used on the Trelleborg – Fährhafen Sassnitz service.

FAST FERRY

5•	FELIX	5307t	96	36k	616P	150C	-	BA	Hamilton, AL	SW

FELIX Austal Ships Auto Express 82 catamaran built for the Limhamn – Dragør service (jointly owned with *Scandlines AG*). Built as the FELIX; shortly after delivery she was renamed the FELIX I. In 1997 she was renamed the FELIX. Laid up in autumn 1999.

SEAWIND LINE

THE COMPANY *SeaWind Line* is a Swedish private sector company owned by *Silja Service Oy*.

MANAGEMENT Managing Director: Sören Lindman, **Marketing Manager:** Ole Engblom.

ADDRESS Linnankatu 84, FIN-20100 TURKU, Finland.

TELEPHONE Administration & Reservations: +358 (0)2 2102 800, **Fax:** +358 (0)2 2102 810.

INTERNET Email: Website: http://www.seawind.fi *(English, Swedish, Finnish)*

ROUTE OPERATED Stockholm (Sweden) – Långnäs (Åland) – Turku (Finland) (10 hrs 45 mins; *(1)*; 1 per day conveys passengers, *(2)*; 1 per day freight only;).

CONVENTIONAL FERRIES

1	SEA WIND	15879t	71	18k	260P	60C	600r	BAS	Helsingør, DK	SW
2	STAR WIND	13788t	77	18k	119P	100C	598r	A	Bergen, NO	SW

SEA WIND Train/vehicle ferry built as the SVEALAND for *Stockholms Rederi AB Svea* and used on the *Trave Line* Helsingborg (Sweden) – København (Tuborg Havn) – Travemünde freight service. Later she operated between Travemünde and Malmö, first for *Saga Line* and then for *TT-Saga Line*. In 1984 she was rebuilt to increase capacity and renamed the SAGA WIND. In 1989 she was acquired by *SeaWind Line*, renamed the SEA WIND and inaugurated a combined rail freight, trailer and lower priced passenger service between Stockholm and Turku.

STAR WIND Train/vehicle ferry built as the ROSTOCK for *Deutsche Reichsbahn* of Germany (DDR) . Used on freight services between Trelleborg and Sassnitz. In 1992 modified to increase passenger capacity in order to run in passenger service. In 1993 ownership transferred to *DFO* and in 1994 she opened a new service from Rostock to Trelleborg. In 1997 she was used when winds preclude the use of the new MECKLENBURG-VORPOMMERN. Following modifications to this vessel in late 1997, the ROSTOCK continued to operate to provide additional capacity until the delivery of the SKÅNE of *Scandlines AB*, after which she was laid up. In 1999 she was sold to *SeaWind Line* and is initially operating in freight-only mode. It is planned to lengthen her and make her suitable for Baltic overnight service; however, she is unlikely to operate in passenger mode in 2000.

SILJA LINE

THE COMPANY *Silja Line* is a subsidiary of *Silja Oyj Abp* (formerly *Neptun Maritime Oyj*), a company based in Finland. In 1993 the services of *Jakob Line* and *Vaasanlaivat* were integrated into *Silja Line*. In 1998 the headquarter functions were concentrated in Finland, with marketing organisations in Sweden, Estonian and Germany. In 1999 a 51% holding in *Neptun Maritime Oyj* was acquired by *Sea Containers Ltd* of Great Britain; 1% was then disposed of to *Rederi AB Gotland* of Sweden. In 2000, that company's *SeaCat Sweden* operation, operated by *SeaCat AB* (wholly owned by *Sea Containers*), is now marketed as *Silja Line SeaCat*, along with a new Helsinki – Tallinn SeaCat service, operated by an Estonian subsidiary of *Sea Containers*.

MANAGEMENT President: Jukka Suominen, **Managing Director Passenger Services:** Riitta Vermas, **Managing Director Cargo:** Sören Lindman.

ADDRESS POB 880, Mannerheimintie 2, FIN-00101 HELSINKI, Finland.

TELEPHONE Administration: *Finland:* +358 (0)9 18041, **Reservations:** *Finland:* +358 (0)9 1804 422, *Sweden:* +46 (0)8-222 140, **Fax:** *Finland*: +358 (0)9 1804 279, *Sweden:* +46 (0)8-667 8681.

INTERNET Email: info@silja.com **Website:** http://www.silja.com *(English, Finnish and Swedish)*

ROUTES OPERATED Conventional Ferries: *All year:* Helsinki (Finland) – Mariehamn (Åland) – Stockholm (Sweden) (16 hrs; *(5,6)*; 1 per day), Turku (Finland) – Mariehamn (Åland) (day)/Långnäs (Åland) (night) – Stockholm (Sweden) (11 hrs; *(3,4)*; 2 per day), Vaasa (Finland) – Umeå (Sweden) (4 hrs; *(7)*; 1/2 per day) (operated by subsidiary *Vaasanlaivat*), **Winter only:** Helsinki – Tallinn (Estonia) (3 hrs 30 mins (4 hrs 30 mins in ice period); *(2)*; 1 per day), **Summer only:** Helsinki – Tallinn – Rostock (Germany) (24 hrs (Helsinki – Tallinn, 2 hr 30 min, Tallinn – Rostock, 19 hrs)); *(2)*; 3 per week), **Fast Ferries (Under *Silja Line* SeaCat name):** Helsinki – Tallinn (1 hrs 30 mins; *(9)*; up to 4 per day, Göteborg (Sweden) – Frederikshavn (Denmark) (1 hr 45 mins; *(8)*; up to 3 per day), Göteborg – Langesund (Norway) *(8)*; up to 3 per week).

CONVENTIONAL FERRIES

1•	FENNIA	10542t	66	18k	1200P	265C	36T	BA	Landskrona, SW	FI
2	FINNJET	32940t	77	31k	1790P	374C	50T	BA	Helsinki, FI	FI
3	SILJA EUROPA	59912t	93	21.5k	3000P	400C	78T	BA	Papenburg, GY	FI
4	SILJA FESTIVAL	34414t	85	22k	2000P	400C	88T	BA2	Helsinki, FI	SW
5	SILJA SERENADE	58376t	90	21k	2641P	450C	78T	BA	Turku, FI	FI
6	SILJA SYMPHONY	58377t	91	21k	2641P	450C	78T	BA	Turku, FI	SW
7	WASA QUEEN	16546t	75	22k	1200P	240C	38T	BA	Nantes, FR	FI

FENNIA Built for *Rederi AB Silja* of Finland to operate services between Sweden and Finland. In 1970 she was transferred to *Stockholms Rederi AB Svea*, when *Silja Line* became a marketing organisation. In 1983 she was withdrawn and operated for a short period with *B&I Line* of Ireland between Rosslare and Pembroke Dock. In 1984 she was sold to *Jakob Line*. In 1985 she was sold to *Vaasanlaivat*. In 1992 she was returned to *Jakob Line*. During winter 1992/3 she operated for *Baltic Link* between Norrköping (Sweden) and Riga (Latvia), but returned to *Silja Line* in summer 1993 and was used on the Vaasa – Umeå and Pietarsaari – Skellefteå services. The latter service will not operate in 1999 and, on 1st July, she was transferred to the new *Vaasanlaivat*, a subsidiary formed to operate the Vaasa – Umeå link. In September 1999 she was replaced by the WASA QUEEN and withdrawn. Laid up.

FINNJET Built for *Finnlines* to operate between Helsinki and Travemünde, replacing several more conventional ferries with intermediate calls. Her exceptionally fast speed was achieved by the use of jet turbine engines. During winter 1981/82 she was equipped with diesel engines for use during periods when traffic did not justify so many crossings per week. Later the trading name was changed to *Finnjet Line*. In 1986 the company was acquired by *EFFOA* and the trading name changed to *Finnjet Silja Line*. In winter 1997/98 she operated between Helsinki and Tallinn (Muuga Harbour). In summer 1998 operated a weekly Travemünde – Tallinn – Helsinki – Travemünde triangular service in addition to two weekly Travemünde – Helsinki round trips. In autumn 1998 she resumed operating between Helsinki and Tallinn and in summer 1999 she operated Helsinki – Tallinn – Rostock.

Vana Tallinn and Finnjet (John Hendy)

Stena Saga (Mike Louagie)

SILJA EUROPA Ordered by *Rederi AB Slite* of Sweden for *Viking Line* service between Stockholm and Helsinki and due to be called EUROPA. In 1993, shortly before delivery was due, the order was cancelled. A charter agreement with her builders was then signed by *Silja Line* and she was introduced onto the Stockholm – Helsinki route as SILJA EUROPA. In early 1995 she was transferred to the Stockholm – Turku service.

SILJA FESTIVAL Built as the WELLAMO for *EFFOA* for the *Silja Line* Stockholm – Mariehamn – Turku service. In 1990, following the sale of the FINLANDIA to *DFDS*, she was transferred to the Stockholm – Helsinki service until the SILJA SERENADE was delivered later in the year. During winter 1991/92 she was extensively rebuilt and in 1991 renamed the SILJA FESTIVAL; ownership was transferred to *Silja Line*. In 1993 she was transferred to the Malmö – Travemünde service of *Euroway*, which was at this time managed by *Silja Line*. This service ceased in 1994 and she was transferred to the Vaasa – Sundsvall service. In 1994 and 1995 she operated on this route during the peak summer period and on the Helsinki – Tallinn route during the rest of the year. The Vaasa – Sundsvall service did not operate in summer 1996 and she continued to operate between Helsinki and Tallinn. In 1997 she was transferred to the Stockholm – Turku route replacing the SILJA SCANDINAVIA (see the GABRIELLA, *Viking Line*).

SILJA SERENADE, SILJA SYMPHONY Built for *Silja Line* for the Stockholm – Helsinki service. In 1993, SILJA SERENADE was transferred to the Stockholm – Turku service but in early 1995 she was transferred back to the Helsinki route.

WASA QUEEN Built as the BORE STAR for *Bore Line* of Finland for *Silja Line* services between Finland and Sweden (Helsinki – Stockholm, Turku – Stockholm). She also performed a number of cruises. In 1981 *Bore Line* left the *Silja Line* consortium and she was sold to the *Finland Steamship Company* (*EFFOA*) and renamed the SILJA STAR. In January 1986 she was sold to *Sea Containers* to inaugurate, in May 1986, a new service between Venice and Istanbul connecting with the Orient Express rail service, also operated by a subsidiary of *Sea Containers*. She was re-named the ORIENT EXPRESS. During winter 1986/7 she was chartered to *Club Sea Inc* of the USA to operate Caribbean cruises and renamed the CLUB SEA but this charter was terminated prematurely and she was laid up for a time. In 1989 she was renamed the EUROSUN and chartered to *Europe Cruise Lines* for Mediterranean and Canary Island Cruises. In 1991 she was chartered to *Damens Service Far East*, renamed the ORIENT SUN and operated cruises from Singapore. In 1992 she 'returned home' as WASA QUEEN for *EffJohn* subsidiary *Wasa Line* and received Finnish registration. She was used on the Vaasa – Umeå service during the summer period when the FENNIA moved to the Pietarsaari – Skellefteå route but at other times she operated mainly on the Helsinki – Tallinn service. From 1997-1999 she remained permanently on the Helsinki – Tallinn service, operating either day trips or two return trips per day. In autumn 1999 she was transferred full time to the Vaasa – Umeå route.

FAST FERRIES

| 8 | SEACAT DANMARK | 3003t | 91 | 37k | 432P | 80C | - | BA | Hobart, AL | GB |
| 9 | SUPERSEACAT FOUR | 4697t | 99 | 38k | 752P | 164C | - | A | Riva Trigoso, IT | IT |

SEACAT DANMARK InCat 74m catamaran. Christened in 1991 as the HOVERSPEED BELGIUM and renamed HOVERSPEED BOULOGNE before leaving the builders yard. She was the third SeaCat, introduced in 1992 to enable a three vessel service to be operated by *Hoverspeed* across the Channel, including a new SeaCat route between Folkestone and Boulogne (replacing the *Sealink Stena Line* ferry service which ceased at the end of 1991). With the HOVERSPEED FRANCE (now SEACAT ISLE OF MAN) and the HOVERSPEED GREAT BRITAIN she operated on all three Channel routes (Dover – Calais, Dover – Boulogne and Folkestone – Boulogne). In 1993 she was transferred to *SeaCat AB* and renamed the SEACATAMARAN DANMARK and inaugurated a new high-speed service between Göteborg and Frederikshavn. For legal reasons it was not possible to call her the SEACAT DANMARK as intended but in 1995 these problems were resolved and she was renamed the SEACAT DANMARK. From January 1996 transferred to the new joint venture company *ColorSeaCat KS*, jointly with *Color Line* of Norway. During winter 1996/97 she operated on the Dover – Calais route. *ColorSeaCat* did not operate in 1997 and she again operated for *SeaCat AB*. In autumn 1997 she replaced the SEACAT SCOTLAND on the Stranraer – Belfast route. During summer 1998, she operated for the *IOMSP Co*. In 1999 operated for *Sea Containers Ferries Scotland* between Belfast and Heysham and Belfast and Douglas. In 2000 she was transferred to *SeaCat AB* to operate between Göteborg, Frederikshavn and Langesund under the *Silja Line SeaCat* branding.

SUPERSEACAT FOUR Fincantieri MDV1200 monohull vessel. Laid-up following delivery. In 2000 transferred to an Estonian subsidiary of *Sea Containers* to operate between Helsinki and Tallinn under the *Silja Line SeaCat* branding. The service is marketed by *Silja Line*.

STENA LINE

THE COMPANY *Stena Line AB* is a Swedish private sector company.

MANAGEMENT Managing Director: Bo Severed. **Marketing Manager:** Fredrik Lantz, **Ship Management Director:** Håkan Sieners, **Communication Director:** Åsa Lindell Byström.

ADDRESS S-405 19 GÖTEBORG, Sweden (*Visitors' address:* Danmark Terminal, Masthuggskajen).

TELEPHONE Administration: +46 (0)31-85 80 00, **Reservations:** +46 (0)31-704 00 00, **Fax:** +46 (0)31-24 10 38.

INTERNET Email: info@stenaline.com **Website:** http://www.stenaline.com *(English, Swedish)*

ROUTES OPERATED Conventional Ferries: Göteborg (Sweden) – Frederikshavn (Denmark) (3 hrs 15 mins; *(1,3,4,7)*; 7 per day), Göteborg – Kiel (Germany) (14 hrs; *(3,7)*; 1 per day), Frederikshavn – Oslo (Norway) (8 hrs 45 mins; *(6)*; 1 per day), Varberg (Sweden) – Grenaa (Denmark) (4 hrs; *(5)*; 2 per day), Karlskrona (Sweden) – Gdynia (Poland) (10 hrs 30 mins; *(2)*; 1 per day), **Fast Ferry:** Göteborg – Frederikshavn (2 hrs; *(8)*; 4 per day).

CONVENTIONAL FERRIES

1	STENA DANICA	28727t	83	19.5k	2274P	555C	136T	BA2	Dunkerque, FR	SW
2	STENA EUROPE	24828t	81	19k	2076P	456C	140T	BA2	Göteborg, SW	PO
3	STENA GERMANICA	38772t	87	20k	2400P	550C	140T	BA2	Gdynia, PO	SW
4	STENA JUTLANDICA	29691t	96	21.5k	1500P	550C	175T	BA	Krimpen, NL	SW
5	STENA NAUTICA	19763t	86	19.4k	2000P	330C	48T	BA	Nakskov, DK	BD
6	STENA SAGA	33750t	81	22k	2000P	510C	86T	BA	Turku, FI	SW
7	STENA SCANDINAVICA	38756t	88	20k	2400P	5500C	140T	BA2	Gdynia, PO	SW

STENA DANICA Built for *Stena Line* for the Göteborg – Frederikshavn service. Sister vessel STENA JUTLANDICA was transferred to the Dover – Calais service in July 1996 and renamed the STENA EMPEREUR (now P&OSL PROVENCE). This vessel is listed in Section 1.

STENA EUROPE Built as the KRONPRINSESSAN VICTORIA for *Göteborg – Frederikshavn-Linjen* of Sweden (trading as *Sessan Linjen*) for their Göteborg – Frederikshavn service. Shortly after delivery, the company was taken over by *Stena Line* and services were marketed as *Stena-Sessan Line* for a period. In 1982 she was converted to an overnight ferry by the conversion of one vehicle deck to two additional decks of cabins and she was switched to the Göteborg – Kiel route (with, during the summer, daytime runs from Göteborg to Frederikshavn and Kiel to Korsør (Denmark)). In 1989 she was transferred to the Oslo – Frederikshavn route and renamed the STENA SAGA. In 1994, transferred to *Stena Line bv*, renamed the STENA EUROPE and operated between Hoek van Holland and Harwich. She was withdrawn in June 1997, transferred to the *Lion Ferry* Karlskrona – Gdynia service and renamed the LION EUROPE. In 1998 she was transferred back to *Stena Line* (remaining on the same service) and renamed the STENA EUROPE.

STENA GERMANICA, STENA SCANDINAVICA Built for *Stena Line* for the Göteborg – Kiel service. Names were swapped during construction in order that the STENA GERMANICA should enter service first. There were originally intended to be four vessels. Only two were delivered to *Stena Line*. The third (due to be called the STENA BALTICA) was sold by the builders as an unfinished hull to *Fred. Olsen Lines* of Norway and then resold to *ANEK* of Greece who had her completed at Perama and delivered as EL VENIZELOS for service between Greece and Italy. The fourth hull (due to be called the STENA POLONICA) was never completed. During the summer period, the vessel arriving in Göteborg overnight from Kiel operates a round trip to Frederikshavn before departing for Kiel the following evening. During winter 1998/99 they were modified to increase freight capacity and reduce the number of cabins.

STENA JUTLANDICA Train/vehicle 'ro-pax' vessel built for *Stena Line* to operate between Göteborg and Frederikshavn. She was launched as the STENA JUTLANDICA III and renamed on entry into service. During winter she operates in 'freight-only' mode.

STENA NAUTICA Built as the NIELS KLIM for *DSB (Danish State Railways)* for their service between Århus (Jylland) and Kalundborg (Sjælland). In 1990 she was purchased by *Stena Rederi* of Sweden and renamed the STENA NAUTICA. In 1992 she was chartered to *B&I Line*, renamed the ISLE OF INNISFREE and introduced onto the Rosslare – Pembroke Dock service, replacing the MUNSTER (8093t, 1970). In 1993 she was transferred to the Dublin – Holyhead service. In early 1995 she was chartered to *Lion Ferry*. She was renamed the LION KING. In 1996 she was replaced by a new LION KING and renamed the STENA NAUTICA. During summer 1996 she was chartered to *Trasmediterranea* of Spain but returned to *Stena Rederi* in the autumn and remained laid up during 1997. In December 1997 she was chartered to *Stena Line* and placed on the Halmstad – Grenaa route. This route ended on 31 January 1999 and she was transferred to the Varberg – Grenaa route.

STENA PRINCE Built as the PRINSESSAN CHRISTINA for *Göteborg – Frederikshavn-Linjen* of Sweden (trading as *Sessan Linjen*) for their service between Göteborg and Frederikshavn. In 1979 she was purchased by *JCE Safe Rederi* (a subsidiary of *Consafe Offshore* (an oil industry supply company)) and chartered back to *Sessan Linjen*. In 1981 she was delivered to *JCE Safe Rederi* and renamed the SAFE CHRISTINA. She was intended to be used as an accommodation vessel but in August 1981 she was chartered to *Sally Line* for service between Ramsgate (England) and Dunkerque (France) and continued to operate until October when the service was suspended for the winter. In 1982 *JCS Safe Rederi* formed *Vinga Line* and operated the vessel on the Göteborg – Frederikshavn route in competition with *Stena Line*. However, after ten days they agreed to sell the vessel back to *Stena Line* and the service ended. She was re-introduced onto *Stena Line*'s Göteborg – Frederikshavn service and reverted to the name PRINSESSAN CHRISTINA. In 1983 she inaugurated a new service between Frederikshavn and Moss (Norway) and was renamed the STENA NORDICA. In 1985 she was transferred to the Grenaa – Helsingborg (Sweden) service, following *Stena Line*'s acquisition of the service, replacing EUROPAFÄRJAN IV (4391t, 1967) and renamed the EUROPAFÄRJAN I. In 1986, following a reorganisation within the *Stena Group*, ownership was transferred to subsidiary company *Lion Ferry AB* and she was renamed the LION PRINCE. In 1998 she was transferred back to *Stena Line* and renamed the STENA PRINCE. She operated between Varberg and Grenaa until February 1999 when she was replaced by the STENA NAUTICA and withdrawn.

STENA SAGA Built as the SILVIA REGINA for *Stockholms Rederi AB Svea* of Sweden. She was registered with subsidiary company *Svea Line* of Turku, Finland and was used on *Silja Line* services between Stockholm and Helsinki. In 1981 she was sold to *Johnson Line* and in 1984 sold to a Finnish Bank and chartered back. In 1990 she was purchased by *Stena Line* of Sweden for delivery in 1991. In 1991 she was renamed the STENA BRITANNICA and took up service on the Hoek van Holland – Harwich service for Dutch subsidiary *Stena Line bv*, operating with a British crew. In 1994 she was transferred to the Oslo – Frederikshavn route and renamed the STENA SAGA.

FAST FERRY

8	STENA CARISMA	8631t	97	40k	900P	210C	-	A	Kristiansand, NO	SW

STENA CARISMA Westamarin HSS 900 craft built for *Stena Line* for the Göteborg – Frederikshavn service. Work on a sister vessel, approximately 30% completed, was ceased.

SUPERFAST FERRIES

THE COMPANY *SuperFast Ferries* is a Greek company, owned by *Attica Enterprises*.

MANAGEMENT Managing Director: Alexander P Panagopulos, **Corporate Marketing Director:** Yannis B Criticos.

ADDRESS *Greece:* 157 Alkyonidon Avenue, Voula, GR-16673 ATHENS, Greece, *Northern Europe:* Not yet established.

TELEPHONE Administration: +30 (0)1 9691100, **Reservations:** not yet established, **Fax:** +30 (0)1 9691190.

INTERNET Email: criticos@superfast.com **Website:** http://www.superfast.com

ROUTES TO BE OPERATED Rostock (Germany) – Södertälje (Sweden) (17 hrs; *(1,2,3,4)*; 1 per day) and Rostock (Germany)– Hanko (Finland), (17 hrs; *(1,2,3,4)*; 1 per day). Services are subject to confirmation and are expected to start in early 2001.

Under Construction

1	SUPERFAST VII	29800t	01	29.2k	604P	1000C	125L	BA2	Kiel, GY	GR
2	SUPERFAST VIII	29800t	01	29.2k	604P	1000C	125L	BA2	Kiel, GY	GR
3	SUPERFAST IX	29800t	01	29.2k	604P	1000C	125L	BA2	Kiel, GY	GR
4	SUPERFAST X	29800t	01	29.2k	604P	1000C	125L	BA2	Kiel, GY	GR

SUPERFAST VII, SUPERFAST VIII, SUPERFAST IX and SUPERFAST X Under construction for *Attica Enterprise* for use by *SuperFast Ferries*. It is currently planned that they will operate in the Baltic as shown above.

TALLINK

THE COMPANY *Tallink* is the trading name of *AS Hansatee Grupp*, an Estonian company owned by the *AS Infortar (50.38%)*, *Union Bank of Estonia* (24.88%), *Tallink Grupp AS* (5.7%) and others. Services are marketed outside Estonia by *Tallink Finland Oy*, owned by *Hansatee Grupp*.

MANAGEMENT Director, Tallink Finland Oy: Keijo Mehtonen.

ADDRESS PO Box 195, 00181 HELSINKI, Finland.

TELEPHONE Administration: +358 (0)9 228211, **Reservations:** +358 (0)9 22821211, **Fax:** +358 (0)9 228 21242.

INTERNET Email: keijo.mehtonen@www.tallink.fi **Websites:** http://www.tallink.ee *(Finnish, Estonian, English)*

ROUTE OPERATED Conventional Ferries: Helsinki – Tallinn (Estonia) (3 hrs 30 mins; *(1,2,3,4)*; up to 4 per day), **Fast Ferry:** Helsinki – Tallinn (1 hrs 30 mins; *(5)*; up to 3 per day).

CONVENTIONAL FERRIES

1	FANTAASIA	16630t	79	21.3k	1700P	549C	60T	BA2	Turku, FI	ES
2	GEORG OTS	12549t	80	20k	1200P	110C	26T	BA	Gdansk, PO	ES
3	MELOODIA	17955t	79	21k	1500P	480C	58T	BA2	Papenburg, GY	ES
4	VANA TALLINN	10002t	74	18k	1500P	300C	48L	BAS	Helsingør, DK	ES

FANTAASIA Built as the TURELLA for *SF Line* of Finland for the *Viking Line* Stockholm – Mariehamn – Turku service and later moved to the Kapellskär – Mariehamn – Naantali service. In 1988 she was sold to *Stena Line*, renamed the STENA NORDICA and placed onto the Frederikshavn – Moss (night) and Frederikshavn – Göteborg (day) service. In 1996 the Frederikshavn – Moss service ceased and she was transferred to subsidiary *Lion Ferry* and renamed the LION KING. She operated between Halmstad and Grenaa. In December 1997 she was sold to *Tallink Line Ltd* of Cyprus and renamed the FANTAASIA. In February 1998, after substantial modification, she was placed on the *Tallink* service.

GEORG OTS Built for *Estonian Shipping Company*. Chartered to *Tallink*.

MELOODIA Built as DIANA II for *Rederi AB Slite* for *Viking Line* services between Stockholm and Turku, Mariehamn, Kapellskär and Naantali. In 1992 sold to a *Nordbanken* and chartered to *TT-Line* of Germany (trading as *TR-Line*) for service between Trelleborg and Rostock. In 1994 sold and chartered to *EstLine* and renamed the MARE BALTICUM. During winter 1994/95 she was completely renovated. In 1996, following the delivery of the REGINA BALTICA, she was chartered to *Tallink* and renamed the MELOODIA.

VANA TALLINN Built as the DANA REGINA for *DFDS* and used on their Esbjerg – Harwich service until 1983 when she was moved to the København – Oslo route. In 1990 she was sold to *Nordström*

& Thulin of Sweden, renamed the NORD ESTONIA and used on the *EstLine* Stockholm – Tallinn service. In 1992 she was chartered to *Larvik Line* to operate as a second vessel between Larvik and Frederikshavn and renamed the THOR HEYERDAHL. In 1994 she was sold to *Inreko Ships Ltd*, chartered to *Tallink* and renamed the VANA TALLINN. In November 1996 she was withdrawn and in December 1996 she was chartered to a new company called *TH Ferries* and resumed sailings between Helsinki and Tallinn. In January 1998 she was sold to *Hansatee* subsidiary *Vana Tallinn Line Ltd* of Cyprus and placed on *Tallink* service. *TH Ferries* then ceased operations.

FAST FERRY

5	TALLINK AUTOEXPRESS	4859t	95	32k	586P	150C	-	BA	Fremantle, AL	ES

TALLINK AUTOEXPRESS Austal Ships Auto Express 79 catamaran ordered by *Sea Containers* and launched as the AUTO EXPRESS 96. On completion she was renamed the SUPERSEACAT FRANCE. However, due to a dispute between *Sea Containers* and the builders, delivery was not taken and it was announced that she was to be sold to *Stena Rederi* of Sweden, renamed the STENA LYNX IV and chartered to *Stena Line* (*UK*), inaugurating a Newhaven – Dieppe service in February 1996. This did not happen and she was instead sold to *DSB Rederi* (now *Scandlines Danmark A/S*) and, in summer 1996, she was chartered to *Cat-Link* and renamed the CAT-LINK III. In 1999 she was sold to *Tallink* and renamed the TALLINK AUTOEXPRESS.

Tallink also operate the TALLINK EXPRESS I (432t, 1989, 271 passengers (ex SLEIPNER, 1997)), a Fjellstrand 38m passenger-only catamaran.

TESO

THE COMPANY *TESO* is a Dutch public sector company. Its full name is *Texels Eigen Stoomboot Onderneming*.

MANAGEMENT Managing Director: R Wortel.

ADDRESS Pontweg 1, 1797 SN DEN HOORN, Texel, Netherlands.

TELEPHONE Administration: +31 (0)222 36 96 00, **Reservations:** n/a, **Fax:** +31 (0)222 36 96 59.

INTERNET Email: teso.nl@wxs.nl **Website:** http://www.teso.nl *(Dutch, English, German, French)*

ROUTES OPERATED Den Helder (Netherlands) – Texel (Dutch Frisian Islands) (20 minutes; *(1,2)*; hourly).

CONVENTIONAL FERRIES

1	MOLENGAT	6170t	80	13k	1250P	126C	19L	BA2	Heusden, NL	NL
2	SCHULPENGAT	8311t	90	13.6k	1750P	156C	25L	BA2	Heusden, NL	NL

MOLENGAT, SCHULPENGAT Built for *TESO*.

TT-LINE

THE COMPANY *TT-Line GmbH & Co* is a German private sector company.

MANAGEMENT Managing Director: Hans Heinrich Conzen & Dr Heinrich von Oertzen, **Sales Manager:** Jörg Althaus.

ADDRESS Mattenwiete 8, D-20457 HAMBURG, Germany.

TELEPHONE Administration: *Hamburg:* +49 (0)40 36 01 372, *Rostock:* +49 (0)381 67 07 911, **Reservations:** *Hamburg:* +49 (0)40 36 01 442, *Rostock:* +49 (0)381 67 07 90, **Fax:** *Hamburg:* +49 (0)40 36 01 407, *Rostock:* +49 (0)381 67 07 980.

INTERNET Email: info@TTLine.com **Website:** http://www.TTLine.de *(German)*

ROUTES OPERATED Passenger Ferries: Travemünde (Germany) – Trelleborg (Sweden) (7 hrs 30 mins; *(2,3)*; 2 per day). **Ro-pax Ferries:** Travemünde (Germany) – Trelleborg (Sweden) (7 hrs 30 mins; *(1,4)*; 2 per day), Rostock (Germany) – Trelleborg (Sweden) (6 hrs; *(5,6)*; 3 per day), **Fast Ferry:** Rostock (Germany) – Trelleborg (Sweden) (2 hrs 45 mins; *(7)*; up to 3 per day).

CONVENTIONAL FERRIES

1	NILS DACKE	26790t	95	21k	308P	-	200T	BA	Rauma, FI	BA
2	NILS HOLGERSSON	30740t	89	20k	1040P	280C	110T	BAS	Bremerhaven, GY	GY
3	PETER PAN	30740t	88	18k	1040P	280C	110T	BAS	Bremerhaven, GY	BA
4	ROBIN HOOD	26800t	95	21k	308P	-	200T	BA	Rauma, FI	GY
5	SAGA STAR	17672t	81	19k	250P	-	116T	BA	Kalmar, SW	BA
6	TT-TRAVELLER	18332t	92	18k	250P	-	150T	BA2	Fevaag, NO	SW

NILS DACKE, ROBIN HOOD Built for *TT-Line*. Primarily a freight vessel but accompanied cars – especially camper vans and cars towing caravans – are conveyed.

NILS HOLGERSSON Built as the ROBIN HOOD, a 'ro-pax' vessel. During winter 1992/93 rebuilt to transform her into a passenger/car ferry and renamed the NILS HOLGERSSON, replacing a similarly named vessel (31395t, 1987) which had been sold to *Brittany Ferries* and renamed the VAL DE LOIRE.

PETER PAN Built as the NILS DACKE, a 'ro-pax' vessel. During summer 1993 rebuilt to transform her into a passenger/car ferry and renamed the PETER PAN, replacing a similarly named vessel (31356t, 1986) which had been sold to *Tasmanian Transport Commission (TT Line)* of Australia and renamed SPIRIT OF TASMANIA.

SAGA STAR Built as the SAGA STAR for *TT-Saga-Line* and, from 1982, used on freight services between Travemünde and Trelleborg/Malmö. In 1989 sold to *Cie Meridonale* of France, renamed the GIROLATA and used on *SNCM* (later *CMR*) services in the Mediterranean. In 1993 she was chartered back to *TT-Line*, resumed her original name and was used on the Travemünde – Trelleborg service. Following delivery of the ROBIN HOOD and the NILS DACKE in 1995, she was transferred to the Rostock – Trelleborg route. In July 1997 she was purchased by *TT-Line* and in 1998 passenger facilities were completely renovated to full ro-pax format.

TT-TRAVELLER Built for *Stena Rederi*. Sister to the STENA CHALLENGER but with a lower passenger capacity. After a short period with *Stena Line* on the Hoek van Holland – Harwich service, she was chartered by *Sealink Stena Line* for their Southampton – Cherbourg route, initially for 28 weeks. At the end of the 1992 summer season she was chartered to *TT-Line* to operate between Travemünde and Trelleborg and was renamed the TT-TRAVELLER. In late 1995, she returned to *Stena Line*, resumed the name STENA TRAVELLER and inaugurated a new service between Holyhead and Dublin. In autumn 1996 she was replaced by the STENA CHALLENGER. In early 1997 she was again chartered to *TT-Line* and renamed the TT-TRAVELLER. She operates on the Rostock – Trelleborg route. During winter 1999/2000, her passenger capacity was increased to 250 and passenger facilities renovated.

FAST FERRY

7	DELPHIN	5333t	96	37.5k	600P	175C	-	A	Fremantle, AL	BA

DELPHIN Austal Ships Auto Express 82 catamaran built for *TT-Line* to operate between Rostock and Trelleborg.

Under Construction

8	PETER PAN	36000t	01	22k	744P	-	222T	BA	Bremerhaven, GY	-
9	NILS HOLGERSSON	36000t	01	22k	744P	-	222T	BA	Bremerhaven, GY	-

PETER PAN, NILS HOLGERSSON Under construction for *TT-Line* for the Travemünde -Trelleborg route. To replace the existing PETER PAN and NILS HOLGERSSON. Flagging not yet decided.

Vana Tallinn (John Hendy)

Gabriella (Mike Louagie)

UNITY LINE

THE COMPANY *Unity Line* is a Polish company, jointly owned by *Polish Steamship Company* and *Euroafrica Shipping Lines.*

MANAGEMENT Chairman of the Board: Pawel Porzycki, **Managing Director:** Ronald Stone.

ADDRESS Poland, 70-419 SZCZECIN, Plac Rodla 8.

TELEPHONE Administration: +48 (0)91 35 95 795, **Reservations:** +48 (0)91 35 95 692, (0)91 35 95 755, **Fax:** *Admin:* +48 (0)91 35 95 885, *Reservations:* +48 (0)91 35 95 693.

INTERNET Email: unity@unityline.pl **Website:** http://www.unityline.pl *(Polish, English, Swedish)*

ROUTE OPERATED Swinoujscie (Poland) – Ystad (Sweden) (6 hrs 30 mins (day), 9 hrs (night); *(1)*; 1 per day).

CONVENTIONAL FERRY

1	POLONIA	29875t	95	17.2k	920P	860C	740r	BA	Tomrefjord, NO	BA

POLONIA Train/vehicle ferry built for *Polonia Line Ltd* and chartered to *Unity Line*. Maximum trailer capacity (with no rail wagons conveyed) is approx 130.

VIKING LINE

THE COMPANY *Viking Line AB* is an Åland (Finland) company (previously *SF Line*, trading (with *Rederi AB Slite* of Sweden) as *Viking Line*). Services are marketed by subsidiary company *Viking Line Marketing AB OY* of Finland and Sweden; this dates from the time that *Viking Line* was a consortium of three operators.

MANAGEMENT Managing Director *(Viking Line AB)*: Nils-Erik Eklund, **Managing Director *(Viking Line Marketing AB OY)*:** Boris Ekman.

ADDRESS *Viking Line AB:* Norragatan 4, FIN-22100 MARIEHAMN, Åland, *Viking Line Marketing AB OY:* PO Box 35, FIN-22101 MARIEHAMN, Åland.

TELEPHONE Administration: +358 (0)18 26011, **Reservations:** +358 (0)9 12351, **Fax:** +358 (0)9 1235292.

INTERNET Email: susanne.nyholm@vikingline.fi **Websites:** http://www.vikingline.fi *(Finnish, Swedish, English)* http://www.vikingline.se *(Swedish, English)*

ROUTES OPERATED *All year:* Stockholm (Sweden) – Mariehamn (Åland) – Helsinki (Finland) (14 hrs; *(4,6)*; 1 per day), Stockholm – Mariehamn (day)/Långnäs (Åland) (night) – Turku (Finland) (9 hrs 10 mins; *(2,5)*; 2 per day), cruises from Helsinki to Tallinn (Muuga Harbour) (Estonia) (20 hrs – 21 hrs round trip; *(3)*; 1 per day) (freight vehicles are conveyed on this service but not private cars; only 1 hrs 30 minutes is spent in port). *Summer only:* Kapellskär (Sweden) – Mariehamn (Åland) (2 hrs 15 mins; *(1)*; up to 3 per day), Kapellskär (Sweden) – Mariehamn (Åland) – Turku (Finland) (8 hrs 45 mins; *(7)*; 1 per day) (peak period only). *Except summer peak period:* Cruises from Stockholm to Mariehamn (21 hrs – 24 hrs round trip (most 22 hrs 30 mins); *(7)*; 1 per day).

CONVENTIONAL FERRIES

1	ÅLANDSFÄRJAN	6172t	72	17k	1004P	200C	18T	BA	Helsingør, DK	SW
2	AMORELLA	34384t	88	21.5k	2480P	450C	53T	BA2	Split, YU	FI
3	CINDERELLA	46398t	89	21.5k	2700P	490C	60T	BA	Turku, FI	FI
4	GABRIELLA	35492t	92	21.5k	2420P	420C	65T	BA2	Split, CR	FI
5	ISABELLA	34386t	89	21.5k	2480P	364C	30T	BA2	Split, YU	FI
6	MARIELLA	37799t	85	22k	2700P	400C	60T	BA	Turku, FI	FI
7	ROSELLA	16850t	80	21.3k	1700P	340C	43T	BA2	Turku, FI	FI

ÅLANDSFÄRJAN Built as the KATTEGAT for *Jydsk Færgefart* on Denmark for the Grenaa – Hundested service. She was used on this route until 1978 when the service became a single ship operation. She was then sold to *P&O Ferries*, renamed the N F TIGER and introduced as the second vessel on the Dover – Boulogne service. Sold to *European Ferries* in 1985 and withdrawn in June 1986. In 1986 sold to *Finlandshammen AB*, Sweden, renamed the ÅLANDSFÄRJAN and used on *Viking Line* summer service between Kapellskär and Mariehamn.

AMORELLA Built for *SF Line* for the Stockholm – Mariehamn – Turku service.

CINDERELLA Built for *SF Line*. Until 1993 provided additional capacity between Stockholm and Helsinki and undertook weekend cruises from Helsinki. In 1993 she replaced the OLYMPIA (a sister vessel of the MARIELLA) as the main Stockholm – Helsinki vessel after the OLYMPIA had been chartered to *P&O European Ferries* and renamed the PRIDE OF BILBAO. In 1995 switched to operating 20 hour cruises from Helsinki to Estonia in the off peak and the Stockholm – Mariehamn – Turku service during the peak summer period (end of May to end of August). During 1997 she remained cruising throughout the year.

GABRIELLA Built as the FRANS SUELL for *Sea-Link AB* of Sweden to operate for subsidiary company *Euroway AB*, who established a service between Lübeck, Travemünde and Malmö. In 1994 this service ceased and she was chartered to *Silja Line*, renamed the SILJA SCANDINAVIA and transferred to the Stockholm – Turku service. In 1997 she was sold to *Viking Line* to operate between Stockholm and Helsinki. She was renamed the GABRIELLA.

ISABELLA Built for *SF Line*. Used on the Stockholm – Naantali service until 1992 until she was switched to operating 24 hour cruises from Helsinki and in 1995 she was transferred to the Stockholm – Helsinki route. During 1996 she additionally operated short cruises to Muuga in Estonia during the 'layover' period in Helsinki. In 1997 she was transferred to the Stockholm – Turku route.

MARIELLA Built for *SF Line*. Used on the Stockholm – Helsinki service. During 1996 additionally operated short cruises to Muuga in Estonia during the 'layover' period in Helsinki but this has now ceased.

ROSELLA Built for *SF Line*. Used mainly on the Stockholm – Turku and Kapellskär – Naantali services until 1997. She now operates 21-24 hour cruises from Stockholm to Mariehamn under the marketing name 'The Dancing Queen', except in the peak summer period when she operates between Kapellskär and Turku.

WAGENBORG PASSAGIERSDIENSTEN

THE COMPANY *Wagenborg Passagiersdiensten BV* is a Dutch public sector company.

MANAGEMENT Managing Director: G van Langen.

ADDRESS Postbus 70, 9163 ZM Nes, AMELAND, Netherlands.

TELEPHONE Administration & Reservations: +31 (0)519 54 61 11, **Fax:** +31 (0)519 54 29 05.

ROUTES OPERATED Holwerd (Netherlands) – Ameland (Frisian Islands) (45 minutes; *(2,3)*; up to 10 per day), Lauwersoog (Netherlands) – Schiermonnikoog (Frisian Islands) (45 minutes; *(4)*; up to 6 per day).

CONVENTIONAL FERRIES

1	BRAKZAND	450t	67	10.5k	1000P	20C	–	A	Hoogezand, NL	NL
2	OERD	1121t	85	12.2k	1000P	46C	9L	BA	Hoogezand, NL	NL
3	SIER	2286t	95	11.2k	1440P	72C	22L	BA	Wartena, NL	NL
4	ROTTUM	1121t	85	12.2k	1140P	46C	9L	BA	Hoogezand, NL	NL

BRAKZAND, OERD, SIER Built for *Wagenborg Passagiersdiensten BV*. The BRAKZAND is now a spare vessel.

ROTTUM Built for *Wagenborg Passagiersdiensten BV* as the SIER and used on the Holwerd – Ameland route. In 1995 renamed the ROTTUM and transferred to the Lauwersoog – Schiermonnikoog route.

Apollo (William Mayes)

Section 7 –
OTHER VESSEL

The following vessels are, at the time of going to print, not operating and are owned by companies which do not currently operate services. They are therefore available for possible re-deployment, either in the area covered by this book or elsewhere. Withdrawn vessels not yet disposed of owned by operating companies are shown under the appropriate company and marked '•'.

DIFKO Færger A/S

1	DIFKO FYN		4101t	87	12.7k	253P	170C	48T	BA	Sunderland, GB	DK

DIFKO FYN Built as the SUPERFLEX ECHO for *Vognmandsruten*. She was unused until 1995, when she was renamed the DIFKO FYN (*Vognmandsruten* having meanwhile been acquired by *DIFKO Færger A/S*) and placed on the Nyborg – Korsør service. In 1998, following the opening of the Great Belt fixed link, the service ceased and she was laid up at Helsingborg, initially in the care of *HH-Ferries* and was them to charter at short notice should one of their own vessels be unavailable. This arrangement has now ceased. In 2001 to operate between Langeland and Kiel - see late news.

Section 8 – RECENT CHANGES

CHANGES SINCE FERRIES OF THE BRITISH ISLES & NORTHERN EUROPE 1998 AND FERRIES OF THE BRITISH ISLES & NORTHERN EUROPE 1999

DISPOSALS

Because of space constraints it was not possible to include the section on disposals, name changes and company changes in *Ferries of the British Isles & Northern Europe 1999*. The following section therefore covers two years:

DISPOSALS 1998-1999

The following vessels, listed in the 1998 edition of *'Ferries of the British Isles & Northern Europe'* have been disposed of – either to other companies listed in this book or others. Company names are as used in that publication.

ANTONIO MACHADO *(Easy Line)* The purchase of this vessel did not materialise.

APOLLO *(Eckerö Line)* In 1999 chartered to *Langeland-Kiel Linien*.

BALDUIN *(Fred. Olsen Lines)* In 1999 sold to *DFDS Tor Line* and renamed the TOR NOVEGIA.

BAYARD *(Fred. Olsen Lines)* In 1998 sold to *Trasmediterranea* of Spain.

BELVAUX *(Cobelfret)* In 1998 sold to *HUAL* of Norway and renamed the CARIB STAR.

BORAC *(Fred. Olsen Lines)* In 1999 sold to *DFDS Tor Line* and renamed the TOR HUMBRIA.

BORACAY *(Fred. Olsen Lines)* In 1998 sold to *DFDS* and renamed the DANA MINERVA.

BRABANT *(Fred. Olsen Lines)* In 1998 sold to *Trasmediterranea* of Spain.

CAT-LINK I *(Cat-Link)* In 1998 sold back to *Incat*. In 1999 renamed the INCAT 035. Currently out of use.

CAT-LINK II *(Cat-Link)* In 1998 chartered to *Islena de Navigation SA (ISNASA)* of Spain and renamed the EUROFERRYS 1. In 1999 renamed the EUROFERRYS PRIMERO. She operates between Algeciras and Ceuta.

CAT-LINK III *(Cat-Link)* In 1999 sold to *Tallink* and renamed the TALLINK AUTOEXPRESS.

CAT-LINK IV *(Cat-Link)* In 1999 sold to *Mols-Linien* and renamed the MAX MOLS.

CAT-LINK V *(Cat-Link)* In 1999 charter transferred to *Mols-Linien* and renamed the MADS MOLS.

SeaFrance Cezanne (Miles Cowsill)

COLL *(Caledonian MacBrayne)* In 1998 sold to *Arranmore Island Ferries* of the Irish Republic.

COLOR VIKING *(Color Line)* In 1998 sold to *Fjord Line* and renamed the JUPITER.

CONDOR FRANCE *(Condor Ferries)* In 1998 charter terminated. Sold to *Brudy Frères* of Guadeloupe and renamed the ACACIA.

DANA HAFNIA *(DFDS)* In 1998 chartered to *Cobelfret Ferries* and in 1999 transferred to *DFDS Tor Line*.

DEUTSCHLAND (of 1972) *(DFO)* In 1998 sold to *El Salam* of Egypt and renamed the AL SALAM 97. In 1999 scrapped.

DIFKO FYN *(Vognmandsruten)* In 1998 withdrawn and transferred to new subsidiary *DIFKO Færger A/S*. Laid up at Helsingborg and available for charter to *HH-Ferries* if required.

DIFKO KORSØR *(Vognmandsruten)* In 1998 withdrawn and transferred to new subsidiary *DIFKO Færger A/S*. Laid up.

DIFKO NYBORG *(Vognmandsruten)* In 1998 withdrawn and transferred to new subsidiary *DIFKO Færger A/S*. Laid up.

DIFKO STOREBÆLT *(Vognmandsruten)* In 1998 withdrawn and transferred to new subsidiary *DIFKO Færger A/S*. Laid up. In 1999 chartered to *Easy Line*.

ESBJERG *(Scandlines (Denmark))* In 1998 sold to *Titanic Investments* of Nigeria.

EUROCRUISER *(Sally Freight)* In 1998 charter terminated. Chartered to *Stena Line (Netherlands)* and resumed the name ROSEBAY.

EUROTRAVELLER *(Sally Freight)* In 1998 withdrawn and laid up for sale. In 1990 sold to *Denval Marine* and in 2000 to operate for subsidiary *TransEuropa Shipping Lines*.

EUROVOYAGER *(Sally Freight)* In 1998 charter terminated. Immediately began operating for *TransEuropa Shipping Lines*, a company controlled by her owners

EUROWAY *(Sally Freight)* In 1998 charter terminated. Renamed the LANDI and placed on the charter market.

F.B.D. DUNBRODY *(Passage East Ferry)* In 1998 sold to *Bere Island Ferries* of the Irish Republic.

FALSTER LINK *(FL Ship Isle of Man Ltd)* In 1998 sold to *El Salam* of Egypt and renamed the TAG EL SALAM.

FENNIA *(Silja Line)* In summer 1999 to be transferred to subsidiary company *Wasa Line*.

FINNARROW *(Finnlines)* In summer 1998 transferred to subsidiary *Finnlink* to operate in freight-only mode between Kapellskär and Naantali. She did not return to *Finnlines* during winter 1998/99.

FIONA MARIA *(Comhairle Nan Eilean Siar)* In 1998 replaced by a new vessel.

GARDEN *(ArgoMann Ferry Service)* In 1999 charter terminated following delivery of the new ESTRADEN.

GRAIP *(N&T Argonaut)* In 1998 sold to the People's Republic of China and renamed the CHONG MING DAO.

HEIMDAL *(Scandlines (Denmark))* In 1998 charter terminated and returned to her owners, *Mercandia*.

INOWRACLAW *(Euroafrica Shipping Line)* In 1998 transferred to the *PolFin* service between Poland and Finland.

KING ORRY *(Sea Containers – Isle of Man Steam Packet Company)* In 1998 sold to *FION spa (Moby Lines)* of Italy and renamed the MOBY LOVE.

KJELLA *(Shetland Islands Council)* In 1998 withdrawn. Now used as a work boat.

LANGELAND III *(Langeland-Kiel Linien)* In 1998 sold to *Jadrolina* of Croatia and delivered in 1999. She has been renamed the PETAR HEKTOROVICH.

LÜBECK LINK *(Nordö Link)* No longer shown as passengers are no longer conveyed.

MALMÖ LINK *(Nordö Link)* No longer shown as passengers are no longer conveyed.

MARCELINE *(Cobelfret)* In 1998 sold to *Van Uden RoRo* of the Netherlands and renamed the BEATRIXHAVEN.

MERCANDIA I *(Litorina Line)* In 1998 sold to *Easy Line* and renamed the ANJA 11.

MERCHANT BRAVERY *(Merchant Ferries)* In 1999 transferred to *Belfast Freight Ferries.*

MERCHANT BRILLIANT *(Merchant Ferries)* In 1999 transferred to *Belfast Freight Ferries.*

MIGUEL HERNANDEZ *(Easy Line)* The purchase of this vessel did not materialise.

NAJADEN *(Scandlines (Denmark))* In 1998 sold to *E H Harms* of Germany and renamed the WILHELM KAISEN. In June 1999 to begin operating for *Elbe-Ferry* between Cuxhaven- Brunsbüttel.

NORDBY *(Scandlines (Denmark))* In 1998 sold to *Titanic Investments* of Nigeria.

NORSE LAGAN *(Norse Irish Ferries)* In summer 1998 chartered to *SeaWind Line* and operated between Stockholm and Turku. In autumn 1998 sold to *Moby Lines* of Italy for service between Italy and Sardinia and renamed the MOBY RIDER.

PATRICIA OLIVIA *(Destination Gotland)* Charter terminated at the end of the 1998 summer season; not chartered in 1999.

PEGASUS TWO *(Color Line)* Charter terminated at the end of the 1998 summer season; not chartered in 1999.

PRINCESSE CLEMENTINE *(Regie voor Maritiem Transport)* In 1998 sold to *Insel und Hallig* of Germany to start a service between Rostock and København. Renamed the ADLER BLIZZARD. This service did not start and in 1999 she was chartered to *Seajet Bahams Ltd* to operate between Palm Beach, Florida, USA and Grand Bahama Island, Bahamas. She was renamed the SEAJET KARA.

PRINCESSE MARIE-CHRISTINE *(Regie voor Maritiem Transport)* In 1998 sold to *Denval Marine Consultants* and renamed the PRIMROSE. In 1999 chartered to *TransEuropa Lines* to operate between Ramsgate and Oostende.

PRINS ALBERT *(Regie voor Maritiem Transport)* In 1998 sold to *Denval Marine Consultants,* chartered to *Sally Freight* and renamed the EUROVOYAGER. Later in 1998 chartered to *TransEuropa Lines* to continue to operate between Ramsgate and Oostende.

PRINS FILIP *(Regie voor Maritiem Transport)* In 1998 sold to *Northern Maritime* (part of the *Stena* group) and renamed the STENA ROYAL. In autumn 1998, chartered to *P&O Stena Line* for four months and used on Dover – Zeebrugge freight services. See STENA ROYAL below.

PRINSES STEPHANIE *(Regie voor Maritiem Transport)* In 1998 sold to *Insel und Hallig* of Germany to operate a service between Rostock and København. Renamed the ADLER WIZARD. This service did not start and in 1999 she was chartered to *Seajet Bahams Ltd* of USA to operate between Palm Beach, Florida, USA and Grand Bahama Island, Bahamas. She was renamed the SEAJET KRISTEN.

PRINSESSE ANNE-MARIE *(shown as sold for scrap)* In 1998 sold to *E H Harms* of Germany and renamed the JOCHEN STEFFEN in 1999.

PRINSESSE ELISABETH *(shown as sold for scrap)* In 1998 sold to *E H Harms* of Germany and in 1999 renamed the HINRICH-WILHELM KOPF .

PURBECK *(Gaelic Ferries)* In 1998 chartered to *Falcon Seafreight* to operate between Folkestone and Boulogne.

RHUM *(Caledonian MacBrayne)* In 1998 sold to *Arranmore Island Ferries* of the Irish Republic.

RIVER LUNE *(Belfast Freight Ferries)* In 1999 transferred to *Merchant Ferries.*

ROSTOCK *(DFO)* In 1999 sold to *SeaWind Line* and renamed the STAR WIND.

ROSTOCK LINK *(Scandlines (Denmark))* In 1998 transferred to subsidiary division *Amber Line* to operate in freight-only mode between Århus and Liepaja (Latvia). In 1999 chartered to *Mols-Linien* to operate freight-only between Århus and Kalundborg. In 2000 sold to *Agoudimos Lines* of Greece and renamed the PENELOPE A. To sail between Igoumenitsa (Greece) and Brindisi (Italy).

SAGA MOON *(Belfast Freight Ferries)* In 1998 transferred to *Merchant Ferries.*

SAINT KILLIAN II *(Irish Ferries)* In 1998 sold to *Marintas* of Greece and renamed the MEDINA STAR.

SAINT PATRICK II *(Irish Ferries)* In 1998 chartered to *Hellenic Mediterranean Line* of Greece (with purchase at end of five year charter period) and re-named the EGNATIA II.

SEA HAWK *(P&O European Ferries (Irish Sea))* In 1998 charter transferred to *P&O European Ferries (Portsmouth)* to operate between Portsmouth and Le Havre. Later the charter was terminated.

SOLIDOR 2 *(Emeraude Lines)* In 1998 sold to *Buquebus* of Argentina.

SOUND OF GIGHA *(Western Ferries (Argyll))* In 1998 sold to *Bilberry Shipping & Stevedoring Ltd* of Waterford, Irish Republic.

STENA ANTRIM *(Stena Line (UK))* For several months continued to operate for *P&O Stena Line.* Later in 1998 withdrawn and sold to *Lignes Maritimes de Detroit (Limadet)* of Morocco and renamed the IBN BATTOUTA. She operates between Spain and Morocco.

STENA CAMBRIA *(Stena Line (UK))* In 1998 transferred to *P&O Stena Line* and operated on the Newhaven – Dieppe service. In 1999 withdrawn and sold to *Umafisa* of Spain and renamed the ISLA DE BOTAFOC. She operates between Barcelona and Ibiza.

STENA LYNX *(Stena Line (UK))* In 1998 charter terminated and returned to owners. Subsequently renamed the AVANT.

TALLINK *(Estonian Shipping Company)* In 1998 sold to *Silver Dolphin Cruises* and renamed the EL TOR.

TOR FLANDRIA *(Tor Line)* In autumn 1998 renamed the SOUTHERN CARRIER. Charter terminated at the end of the year. In 1999 chartered to *Cobelfret Ferries*

TRANSLUBECA *(Finnlines)* In 1999 chartered to *DFDS Tor Line.*

TRIDENT 7 *(Emeraude Lines)* It is believed that in 1998 she was sold to Caribbean interests.

DISPOSALS 1999-2000

The following vessels, listed in the 1999 edition of *'Ferries of the British Isles & Northern Europe'* have been disposed of – either to other companies listed in this book or others. Company names are as used in that publication.

ALTELAND *(Transfennica)* The charter of this vessel has ended. Now operating between Finland and France.

APOLLO *(Langeland-Kiel Linien)* In July 1999 returned to *Eckerö Line* and laid up. In 2000 sold to the *Labrador Marine Inc* of Canada to operate between Blanc Sablon (Labrador) and St Barbe (Newfoundland).

ARVEPRINS KNUD *(Scandlines (Denmark & Germany))* In 2000 sold to *Tabouk Shipping* of Saudi Arabia.

BALTIC EAGLE *(Finanglia Ferries)* In 1999 chartered out. Currently in use in the Caribbean.

BERLIN EXPRESS *(Scandlines (Denmark & Germany))* In 1999 sub-chartered to *Trasmediterranea* of Spain for use in the Canary Islands and renamed the GOMERA JET. On completion of this sub-charter she was returned to her owners and did not re-enter service with *Scandlines.* In 2000 she was sold to *GA Ferries* of Greece.

European Pathfinder (John Hendy)

BOLERO *(Norfolkline)* In 2000 charter ended.

BRITTA ODEN *(DFDS Tor Line)* In 1999 charter terminated.

CONDOR 10 *(Condor Ferries)* This vessel did not return to UK in 1999 and now seems unlikely to leave the southern hemisphere at the present time.

DANMARK *(Scandlines (Denmark & Germany))* In 1999 scrapped.

DART 1 *(Dart Line)* Charter ended at the end of 1999.

DART 5 *(Dart Line)* Charter ended in early 2000 after several months out of service.

DART 6 *(Dart Line)* In 1999 charter ended. Resumed her original name, the VARBOLA. In 2000 chartered to *Merchant Ferries* for the Heysham – Dublin service.

DART 7 *(Dart Line)* In 1999 charter ended. Resumed her original name, the LIMBATU. See late news.

DEGERÖ *(Transfennica)* The charter of this vessel has ended.

DIFKO KORSØR *(DIFKO Færger A/S)* In 1999 chartered to the *Saaremaa Lævakompanii* of Estonia for service between Virtsu on the mainland and the small island of Muhu which is linked by causeway to Saaremaa. Renamed the VIIRE.

DIFKO NYBORG *(DIFKO Færger A/S)* In 2000 sold to Italian interests.

DRONNING INGRID *(Scandlines (Denmark & Germany))* In 1999 sold to Christian charity *Mercy Ships* of the USA for conversion to a hospital ship. Initially renamed the INGRID. Likely to be further renamed when she re-enters service in 2001. In 2000 renamed the AFRICA MERCY.

EVA ODEN *(DFDS Tor Line)* In 1999 charter terminated.

GABRIELLE WEHR *(P&O North Sea Ferries)* In 1999 charter terminated. In 2000 chartered to *Ferryways* to operate between Oostende and Ipswich.

GELTING SYD *(Faaborg-Gelting Linien)* In 1999 sold to *IMTC* of Spain to operate between Cadiz (Spain) and Tangiers (Morocco) and renamed the ATLAS.

HEIMDAL *(Mercandia)* In 1999 purchased by *Tele Danmark* for conversion to a cable laying and maintenance vessel.

HERALDEN *(Transfennica)* This vessel does not operate on UK routes.

ISLAND COMMODORE *(Commodore Shipping)* In 1999 purchased by *Cable & Wireless Global Marine* (part of the *Cable & Wireless Group*) for conversion to a cable laying and maintenance vessel. Renamed the WAVE SENTINAL.

JETLINER *(P&O Irish Sea)* In spring 2000 charter terminated.

JUNIPER *(TransEuropa Shipping Lines)* In 1999 returned to the Mediterranean.

KRAKA *(Scandlines (Denmark & Germany))* In 1999 purchased by *Cable & Wireless Global Marine* (part of the *Cable & Wireless Group*) for conversion to a cable laying and maintenance vessel.

LINK STAR *(Transfennica)* The charter of this vessel has ended. Now operating between Finland and Spain.

LODBROG *(Scandlines (Denmark & Germany))* In 1999 purchased by *Cable & Wireless Global Marine (*part of the Cable & Wireless Group) for conversion to cable laying and maintenance vessels. Renamed the WAVE MERCURY.

LOVISA GORTHON *(Transfennica)* The charter of this vessel has ended.

MADS MOLS *(Mols-Linien)* In 2000 charter terminated.

MAERSK ANGLIA *(Cobelfret Ferries)* In 1999 charter terminated.

MAERSK FLANDERS *(Norfolkline)* In 1999 renamed the MAERSK FRIESLAND.

MARTHA RUSS *(Transfennica)* The charter of this vessel has ended. In 1999 renamed the MED STAR. Opertaing between Sweden and Spain.

MERLE *(Belfast Freight Ferries)* In 2000 charter ended. Moved to *Dart Line* as the DART 3.

MINI STAR *(Transfennica)* The charter of this vessel has ended.

NEPTUNIA *(Estline)* In 1999 withdrawn from the Tallinn – Stockholm route. In 2000 chartered to *Falcon Seafreight.*

NORCOVE *(P&O North Sea Ferries)* In 1999 chartered ended and she returned to her owners *Bylock & Norsjöfrakt* of Sweden, resuming the name CUPRIA.

NORSE MERSEY *(P&O Ferrymasters)* In 1999 charter terminated. Chartered to *DFDS Tor Line.*

PEDER OLSEN *(BornholmsTrafikken)* In 1999 sold to *Moby Lines* of Italy and renamed the MOBY LALLY.

PEVERIL *(Isle of Man Steam Packet)* Now shown under *Sea Containers Ferries.*

PICASSO *(Falcon Seafreight)* In 1999 charter terminated. Returned to lay-up. Now shown under *Sea Containers Ferries.*

PRINS HENRIK *(Scandlines (Denmark & Germany))* In 1999 sold to *Traghetti Isole Sarde* of Italy, renamed the GIOVENTU and, in 2000, entered service between Italy and Sardinia.

RAGNA GORTHON *(Transfennica)* The charter of this vessel has ended. Now operating between Canada and the USA.

RODONA *(Cobelfret Ferries)* In 1999 chartered to *P&O North Sea Ferries.*

ROMSØ *(Scandlines (Denmark & Germany))* In 1999 sold to *Nusacom* of Indonesia. Renamed the AGOAMAS

SAPPHIRE *(Cobelfret Ferries)* In 1999 chartered to *P&O North Sea Ferries.*

SCANIA *(Scandlines (Denmark & Germany))* In 1999 sold to *Saaremaa Lævakompanii* of Estonia

SERENADEN *(Transfennica)* This vessel does not operate on UK routes.

SPROGØ *(Scandlines (Denmark & Germany))* In 2000 sold to *Tabouk Shipping* of Saudi Arabia.

STENA INVICTA (shown incorrectly under *Stena Rederi,* actually owned by *P&O Stena Line)* In 2000 chartered to *Color Line* and renamed the COLOR VIKING.

STENA PRINCE *(Stena Line)* In 1999 sold to *Traghetti Isole Sarde (TRIS)* of Italy, renamed the COMMODORE and placed on their service between Genova *(*Italy) and Palau *(*Sardinia).

STENA ROYAL *(Northern Maritime (Stena Group))* In 1999 taken on long term charter by *P&O Stena Line.* Later renamed the P&OSL AQUITAINE.

STIG GORTHON *(Transfennica)* The charter of this vessel has ended. Renamed the PUHOS.

SUPERSEACAT ONE *(SeaCat AB)* In 2000 to operate for *Hoverspeed* between Newhaven and Dieppe.

SUPERSEACAT FOUR *(Sea Containers)* In 2000 to operate for *Silja Line* (as *Silja Line SeaCat)* between Helsinki and Tallinn.

THOMAS WEHR *(P&O North Sea Ferries)* In 1999 charter terminated. In 2000 chartered to *Ferryways* to operate between Oostende and Ipswich.

TIDERO STAR *(P&O North Sea Ferries)* In 1999 charter terminated.

TRANEKÆR *Scandlines (Denmark & Germany))* In 1999 sold to *Societa di Navigazione Maregiglio* of Italy and renamed the *Isola Del Gilgio.* Used on services between Porto San Stéfano on the mainland and the islands Giglio and Giannutri.

TRANS BOTNIA *(Transfennica)* This vessel does not operate on UK routes.

TRANSGARD *(Transfennica)* This vessel does not operate on UK routes.

TRANSNORDICA *(Transfennica)* Charter now ended. Now operating for *Finncarriers* in the Baltic.

VESTFOLD *(Gøkstad AS)* In 1999 sold to *Meridiano* of Italy.

NAME CHANGES 1998-1999

The following vessels have been renamed without change of operator:

BUFFALO *(P&O Ferries (Irish Sea))* In 1998 renamed the EUROPEAN LEADER.

IONA *(Pentland Ferries)* In 1998 renamed the PENTALINA B.

LEOPARD *(P&O Ferries (Irish Sea))* In 1998 renamed the EUROPEAN NAVIGATOR.

PRIDE OF BRUGES *(P&O Stena Line)* In 1999 renamed the P&OSL PICARDY.

PRIDE OF BURGUNDY *(P&O Stena Line)* In 1998 renamed the P&OSL BURGUNDY.

PRIDE OF CALAIS *(P&O Stena Line)* In 1999 renamed the P&OSL CALAIS.

PRIDE OF DOVER *(P&O Stena Line)* In 1999 renamed the P&OSL DOVER.

PRIDE OF KENT *(P&O Stena Line)* In 1998 renamed the P&OSL KENT.

STENA EMPEREUR *(P&O Stena Line)* In 1998 renamed the P&OSL PROVENCE.

STENA FANTASIA *(P&O Stena Line)* In 1999 renamed the P&OSL CANTERBURY.

TOR BELGIA *(Tor Line)* In 1998 renamed the EVA ODEN.

TOR BRITANNIA *(Tor Line)* In 1998 renamed the TOR BELGIA.

TOR SCANDIA *(Tor Line)* In 1998 renamed the BRITTA ODEN.

NAME CHANGES 1999-2000

ESTRADEN *(ArgoMann Ferry Service)* In 1999 renamed the AMAZON.

COMPANY CHANGES 1998-1999

Color Line Service to the UK (Section 1) have been taken over by *Fjord Line*. Scandinavian services (Section 6) continue.

DFO This company has merged with *Scandlines A/S* of Denmark to form *Scandlines AG* (shown as *Scandlines, (Denmark & Germany)*).

Euroafrica Shipping Line The ro-ro service has been replaced by a container service and is thus outside the scope of this book.

Fred. Olsen Lines Services taken over by *DFDS Tor Line*.

Gaelic Ferries This operator has ceased trading.

Holyman-Hoverspeed joint venture This continues (strictly *Hoverspeed-Holyman* joint venture) but is now shown as part of *Sea Containers Ferries, Hoverspeed* as *Holyman* play no part in the operation and marketing of this service. *Holyman* involvement ceased in 1999.

Litorina Line Passenger sailings did not resume in summer 1998. The company planned a freight-only service during summer 1999 but this did not materialise.

LS-Line This operator now trades as *Ferry Serviss*.

Nordö Link This operator no longer carries passengers (ceased in December 1997).

Sally Freight The operator has ceased trading.

Scandlines (Denmark) This operator has merged with *DFO* of Germany to form *Scandlines AG*

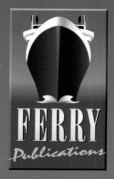

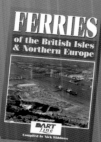

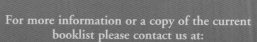

(shown as *Scandlines, (Denmark & Germany)*).

Tor Line The operator has been renamed *DFDS Tor Line*.

Truckline (passenger operations only) These are now marketed as part of *Brittany Ferries*.

Western Ferries (Argyll) This operator has ceased trading following the introduction of the EILEAN DHUIRA of *Argyll and Bute Council*. It was expected that *Stirling Shipmanagement*, who owned *Western Ferries (Argyll)*, would gain the contract to manage and operate the service but this did not happen.

COMPANY CHANGES 1999-2000

Alizés Service now joint with *Emeraude Lines*; vessel shown under this heading.

Argyll and Antrim Steam Packet Company This service will not resume in 2000.

Belfast Freight Ferries In 1999 operations merged with *Merchant Ferries*.

Delom Expected public service did not materialise. The CAP AFRIQUE continued to operate on charter to *Farmers' Ferries*, a service exclusively for livestock exports, and is now shown under this operator.

DFDS Liner Division In 1999 merged with *DFDS Tor Line*.

Faaborg-Gelting Linien In July 1999 this company ceased trading.

Ferry Serviss This service has been taken over by Russian interests. Marketed as *Baltic Express Line*.

Hoverspeed-Holyman joint venture In 1999 *Holyman's* involvement ceased.

Langeland-Kiel Linien In July 1999 this company ceased trading.

Norse Irish Ferries In 1999 taken over by *Cenargo*. Operations are being integrated with *Merchant Ferries* and they are now shown together.

P&O European Ferries (Irish Sea) In 2000 trading name changed to *P&O Irish Sea*.

SeaCat AB In 2000 the operation began to be marketed as part of *Silja Line* until the title *Silja Line SeaCat*. Now shown under *Silja Line*.

Wasa Line Trading under Finnish name, *Vaasanlaivat*. However, operated as part of the *Silja Line* network and now shown under this heading.

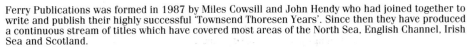

Ferry Publications was formed in 1987 by Miles Cowsill and John Hendy who had joined together to write and publish their highly successful 'Townsend Thoresen Years'. Since then they have produced a continuous stream of titles which have covered most areas of the North Sea, English Channel, Irish Sea and Scotland.

Disenchantment with writing for other magazines led the partners to launch their own quarterly journal 'European Ferry Scene' in the Summer of 1989. Now a firmly established favourite, the magazine has quickly gained praise from both the enthusiast fraternity and the ferry industry alike.

LATE NEWS

Section 1

Emeraude Lines
A Fjellstrand JumboCat 60m catamaran has been ordered for delivery in September 2000:

NEWBUILDING		2068t	00	33k	448P	51C-		A	Omastrand, NO	FR

SeaFrance
A new ship has been ordered for delivery in September 2001 (subject to confirmation). There is an option on a second vessel:

NEWBUILDING		32000t	01	25k	1900P	700C	133L	BA2	Rauma, FI	FR

Section 3

Falcon Seafreight A ship has been chartered to replace the PURBECK, which has moved to *Truckline Ferries*:

BONAVISTA	‡4078t	73	17k	36P	-	70L	BA	Capelle, NL	BA

BONAVISTA Built as the STENA SHIPPER for *Stena AB* of Sweden. On completion, demise chartered to *Union Steamship Co* of New Zealand and renamed the UNION WELLINGTON. In 1977 chartered to *Aghiris Navigation* of Greece and renamed the ALPHA EXPRESS. Later that year, renamed the STENA SHIPPER and used on a variety of services. In 1980 chartered to *Sealink UK*; rail tracks were fitted and she was operated on the Harwich - Zeebrugge train ferry service, being renamed the SPEEDLINK VANGUARD. In 1987 the charter was terminated, and, after a brief period as the CARIBE EXPRESS, she was renamed the STENA SHIPPER. In 1988 she was chartered to *Kirk Line* of the Cayman Islands for service in the Caribbean and renamed the KIRK SHIPPER. In 1989 she was chartered to *Truckline Ferries*, renamed the NORMANDIE SHIPPER and inaugurated a Caen - Portsmouth freight service. In 1996 she was laid up. In 1999 she was sold to *Adecon Shipping Management* of Canada and renamed the BONAVISTA. In 2000 chartered to *Falcon Seafreight*.

P&O Irish Sea A fourth ship has been chartered for the Liverpool - Dublin service. She is to be named the CELTIC SUN:

CELTIC SUN		7800t	98	17k	12P	-	88T	A	Huelva, SP	ES

CELTIC SUN Built as the LEMBITU for *Estonian Shipping Company*. On completion chartered to *P&O European Ferries (Irish Sea)* and placed on their Liverpool Dublin route whilst the BUFFALO was being lengthened (renamed the EUROPEAN LEADER on re-entry to service). In Autumn 1998 she was chartered to *Dart Line* and placed on the Dartford - Vlissingen route. In 1999 she was renamed the DART 7. In Autumn 1999 the charter was ended and she was chartered to *Cetma* of France, resumed the name LEMBITU and used on services between Marseilles and Tunis. In 2000 she was chartered to *P&O European Ferries (Irish Sea)* and later renamed the CELTIC SUN.

Truckline Ferries The PURBECK has been chartered to *Truckline Ferries* to operate between Caen and Portsmouth (6 hrs; 1 per day).

Section 4

Difko Færger A/S reopened the Langeland - Kiel route on 1st May 2000 using the DIFKO FYN (shown in Section 7). Two sailings per day, crossing time 2 hrs 45 mins.

INDEX

ABEL MAGWITCH	163
ADMIRAL OF SCANDINAVIA	66
ALANDIA	175
ÅLANDSFÄRJAN	204
ALLASDALE LASS	106
AMANDINE	126
AMAZON	124
AMORELLA	204
ANJA 11	174
ÁRAINN MHÍR	98
ARAN EXPRESS	162
ARAN FLYER	162
ARAN SEABIRD	162
ASK	190
ATLANTIC II	84
AURORA AF HELSINGBORG	192
BALMORAL	163
BALTIC EIDER	139
BALTIC JET	186
BALTIC KRISTINA	178
BALTIC STAR	166
BARFLEUR	60
BASTØ I	168
BASTØ II	168
BELNAHUA	98
BEN-MY-CHREE	84
BERGEN	180
BIGGA	116
BIRKA PRINCESS	168
BOHUS	169
BONAVISTA	219
BRAKZAND	205
BRAMBLE BUSH BAY	160
BRAVE MERCHANT	73
BRETAGNE	60
BRUERNISH	101
CAEDMON	121
CAILIN AN AISEAG	108
CALEDONIAN ISLES	101
CANNA	101
CAP AFRIQUE	138
CAROLINE RUSS	159
CARRIGALOE	107
CCTL HAMBURG	124

CELANDINE	126
CELTIC STAR	146
CELTIC SUN	209
CENRED	121
CENWULF	121
CHRISTIAN IV	169
CINDERELLA	204
CLANSMAN	101
CLAYMORE	89
CLEMENTINE	126
COLL	98
COLOR FESTIVAL	169
COLOR VIKING	169
COMETA	143
COMMODORE CLIPPER	62
COMMODORE GOODWILL	128
CONDOR 9	64
CONDOR EXPRESS	64
CONDOR VITESSE	64
CONTENDER	144
COTE DES ISLES	69
COURIER	162
COUTANCES	159
CROMARTY ROSE	116
CROWN OF SCANDINAVIA	173
CYMBELINE	126
DANA ANGLIA	66
DANA CIMBRIA	133
DANA CORONA	133
DANA FUTURA	133
DANA HAFNIA	133
DANA MAXIMA	133
DANA MINERVA	133
DANIEL QUILP	163
DART 2	128
DART 3	128
DART 4	128
DART 8	128
DART 9	128
DART 10	130
DAWN MERCHANT	73
DELPHIN	202
DEUTSCHLAND	190
DIAMANT	84
DIFKO FYN	208
DONEMARK	162
DOUBLE O SEVEN	162

DRAÍOCHT NA FARRAIGE	162
DRONNING MARGRETHE II	190
DUC DE NORMANDIE	60
EARL SIGURD	109
EARL THORFINN	109
EBENEZER SCROOGE	163
EDGCUMBE BELLE	162
EDMUND D	113
EGLANTINE	126
EIGG	101
EILEAN BHEARNARAIGH	106
EILEAN DHIURA	98
EILEAN NA H-OIGE	106
ELK	150
ERNEST BEVIN	121
EUROPEAN AMBASSADOR	74
EUROPEAN CAUSEWAY	74
EUROPEAN ENDEAVOUR	146
EUROPEAN ENVOY	146
EUROPEAN FREEWAY	150
EUROPEAN HIGHLANDER	146
EUROPEAN HIGHWAY	152
EUROPEAN LEADER	146
EUROPEAN NAVIGATOR	146
EUROPEAN PATHFINDER	146
EUROPEAN PATHWAY	152
EUROPEAN PIONEER	146
EUROPEAN SEAFARER	146
EUROPEAN SEAWAY	152
EUROPEAN TIDEWAY	150
EUROPEAN TRADER	146
EUROVOYAGER	157
EYNHALLOW	109
F.B.D. DUNBRODY	99
FANTAASIA	199
FELIX	193
FENCER	162
FENJA	190
FENNIA	194
FILLA	116
FINNARROW	179
FINNBIRCH	139
FINNCLIPPER	179
FINNEAGLE	179
FINNFELLOW	179
FINNFOREST	139
FINNHANSA	179

FINNJET	194	HOTSPUR IV	163	LOCH RANZA	101
FINNPARTNER	179	HOVERSPEED GREAT		LOCH RIDDON	101
FINNRIVER	139	BRITAIN	84	LOCH STRIVEN	101
FINNROSE	139	HOY HEAD	109	LOCH TARBERT	101
FINNTRADER	179	IDUN VIKING	162	LOCHMOR	101
FIVLA	116	ISABELLA	204	LOCHNEVIS	101
FREEDOM 90	162	ISLE OF ARRAN	101	LOFOTEN	182
FREJA VIKING	162	ISLE OF CUMBRAE	101	LORD OF THE ISLES	101
FRIESLAND	173	ISLE OF INISHMORE	70	LOVERVAL	126
FRIGG SYDFYEN	190	ISLE OF INNISFREE	70	LYNHER	161
FRISIA I	184	ISLE OF LEWIS	101	LYONESSE LADY	108
FRISIA II	184	ISLE OF MULL	101	LYRA	126
FRISIA V	184	JAMES NEWMAN	121	MAERSK EXPORTER	144
FRISIA VI	184	JENACK	118	MAERSK FLANDERS	144
FRISIA VIII	184	JENS KOFOED	169	MAERSK FRIESLAND	144
FRISIA IX	184	JOCHEN STEFFEN	176	MAERSK IMPORTER	144
FYLGA	116	JOHN BURNS	121	MAI MOLS	184
GABRIELE WEHR	138	JONATHAN SWIFT	73	MAID OF GLENCOUL	108
GABRIELLA	204	JUNO	101	MALLARD	160
GALWAY BAY	162	JUPITER	101	MAREN MOLS	184
GEIRA	117	JUPITER	69	MARIELLA	204
GEORG OTS	199	KAHLEBERG	190	MARTIN CHUZZLEWIT	163
GITTE 3	174	KARL CARSTENS	190	MAX MOLS	184
GLENACHULISH	107	KAUNAS	183	MECKLENBURG-	
GLENBROOK	107	KENILWORTH	162	VORPOMMERN	190
GOD MET ONS III	118	KING HARRY FERRY	160	MELOODIA	199
GOLDEN MARIANA	109	KING OF SCANDINAVIA	66	MELUSINE	126
GOOD SHEPHERD IV	117	KINGSWEAR BELLE	162	MENJA	190
GOSPORT QUEEN	162	KLAÌPEDA	183	MERCANDIA IV	180
GÖTALAND	192	KOADA	117	MERCANDIA VIII	180
GOTLAND	172	KONG HARALD	182	MERCHANT BRAVERY	142
GRAEMSAY	109	KONINGIN BEATRIX	187	MERCHANT BRILLIANT	142
GREAT EXPECTATIONS	163	KONINGIN BEATRIX	92	MERCHANT VENTURE	142
GREIFSWALD	190	KRONPRINS FREDERIK	190	MERSEY VIKING	73
GRIMA	117	KRONPRINS HARALD	169	METTE MOLS	184
GRY MARITHA	108	LADY OF MANN	84	MIDNATSOL	182
GYLEN LADY	109	LAGAN VIKING	73	MIDNIGHT MERCHANT	74
HAMLET	190	LARKSPUR	157	MIDSLAND	173
HAPPY HOOKER	162	LEIRNA	117	MIE MOLS	184
HARALD JARL	182	LITTLE ISLAND FERRY	161	MIKHAIL SHOLOKHOV	166
HAVELET	64	LIV VIKING	162	MISNEACH	99
HEBRIDEAN ISLES	101	LOCH ALAINN	101	MOLENGAT	201
HEBRIDES	106	LOCH BHRUSDA	101	MOONDANCE	155
HENDRA	117	LOCH BUIE	101	MORVERN	98
HIGHER FERRY	160	LOCH DUNVEGAN	101	MOUNTWOOD	163
HINRICH-WILHELM KOPF	176	LOCH FYNE	101	MÜNSTERLAND	176
HOLGER DANSKE	190	LOCH LINNHE	101	NARVIK	182

NEPTUNIA	136	P&OSL PICARDY	80	QUIBERON	60
NEW ADVANCE	117	P&OSL PROVENCE	80	RAASAY	102
NIEBOROW	186	PALANGA	183	RAPIDE	84
NILS DACKE	202	PASEWALK	124	RED EAGLE	114
NILS HOLGERSSON	202	PAULINE RUSS	159	RED FALCON	114
NO 4	118	PENTALINA B	113	RED JET 1	114
NO 5	160	PETER PAN	202	RED JET 2	114
NORBANK	150	PETER WESSEL	169	RED JET 3	114
NORBAY	150	PETERSBURG	190	RED OSPREY	114
NORCAPE	150	PEVERIL	153	REEDHAM FERRY	161
NORDHAV	143	PHILIP PIRRIP	163	REGINA BALTICA	178
NORDIC JET	186	PICASSO	153	RENFREW ROSE	163
NORDKAPP	182	PIONEER	101	RHUM	98
NORDLANDIA	175	PLYM	161	RICHARD WITH	182
NORDLYS	182	POLARLYS	182	RIVER LUNE	142
NORDNORGE	182	POLONIA	204	RIVERDANCE	155
NORKING	150	POMERANIA	186	ROBIN HOOD	202
NORLAND	76	POOLE SCENE	162	RODONA	150
NORMANDIE	60	PORTA FERRY	118	ROGALIN	186
NORMANDY EXPRESS	69	PORTSMOUTH EXPRESS	80	ROSE OF ARAN	162
NORMANDY	70	PORTSMOUTH QUEEN	162	ROSEANNE	158
NORQUEEN	150	POVL ANKER	169	ROSEBAY	156
NORRÖNA	91	PRIDE OF BILBAO	78	ROSEHAUGH	108
NORSE MERSEY	133	PRIDE OF CHERBOURG	78	ROSELLA	204
NORSEA	76	PRIDE OF FLANDERS	150	ROSLAGEN	175
NORSKY	150	PRIDE OF HAMPSHIRE	78	ROTTUM	205
NORSTAR	76	PRIDE OF HULL	76	ROVER	162
NORSTREAM	150	PRIDE OF LE HAVRE	78	ROYAL DAFODIL	163
NORSUN	76	PRIDE OF PORTSMOUTH	78	RÜGEN	190
NORTHERN MERCHANT	144	PRIDE OF RATHLIN	74	RUSS	166
OBBOLA	153	PRIDE OF ROTTERDAM	76	SAGA MOON	142
ODIN SYDFYEN	190	PRIDE OF SUFFOLK	150	SAGA STAR	202
OERD	205	PRIDE OF THE TYNE	163	SANDEFJORD	169
OILEAN ARANN	162	PRIMROSE	158	SAPPHIRE	150
OLDENBURG	163	PRINCE OF SCANDINAVIA	66	SASSNITZ	190
OOST-VLIELAND	173	PRINCESS OF SCANDINAVIA	66	SATURN	102
ORTVIKEN	153	PRINS JOACHIM	190	SCHIEBORG	126
OSTFRIESLAND	176	PRINS JOHAN FRISO	187	SCHLESWIG-HOLSTEIN	190
ÖSTRAND	153	PRINS RICHARD	190	SCHULPENGAT	201
OUR LADY PAMELA	121	PRINS WILLEM -		SCILLONIAN III	108
OUR LADY PATRICIA	121	ALEXANDER	187	SEA SPRINTER	162
P&OSL AQUITAINE	80	PRINSES CHRISTINA	187	SEA WIND	193
P&OSL BURGUNDY	80	PRINSES JULIANA	187	SEACAT DANMARK	196
P&OSL CALAIS	80	PRINSESSE BENEDIKTE	190	SEACAT ISLE OF MAN	84
P&OSL CANTERBURY	80	PRINSESSE RAGNHILD	169	SEACAT SCOTLAND	84
P&OSL DOVER	80	PURBECK	136	SEAFRANCE CEZANNE	90
P&OSL KENT	80	QUEEN OF SCANDINAVIA	173	SEAFRANCE MANET	90

SEAFRANCE MONET	90	STENA DISCOVERY	94	TOR HOLLANDIA	133
SEAFRANCE NORD PAS-DE-CALAIS	155	STENA EUROPE	197	TOR HUMBRIA	133
		STENA EXPLORER	94	TOR NORVEGIA	133
SEAFRANCE RENOIR	90	STENA GALLOWAY	92	TOR SCANDIA	133
SEAGARD	159	STENA GERMANICA	197	TOR SELANDIA	133
SHANNON DOLPHIN	116	STENA GOTHICA	133	TOR SUECIA	133
SHANNON WILLOW	116	STENA HOLLANDICA	94	TRANQUILITY	162
SHAPINSAY	109	STENA JUTLANDICA	197	TRANS FENNIA	159
SHEARWATER 5	114	STENA LYNX III	94	TRANSBALTICA	139
SHEARWATER 6	114	STENA NAUTICA	197	TRANSEUROPA	179
SHIELDSMAN	163	STENA SAGA	197	TRANSLUBECA	179
SIER	205	STENA SCANDINAVICA	197	TRELLEBORG	192
SILESIA	186	STENA SEARIDER	156	TRIDENT 5	69
SILJA EUROPA	194	STENA SEATRADER	156	TT-TRAVELLER	202
SILJA FESTIVAL	194	STENA SHIPPER	126	TUNGENES	143
SILJA SERENADE	194	STENA VOYAGER	94	TYCHO BRAHE	190
SILJA SYMPHONY	194	STRANGFORD FERRY	118	ULYSSES	73
SILVIA ANA L	172	SUPERFAST VII	199	UNDINE	126
SKAGEN	169	SUPERFAST VIII	199	UNITED CARRIER	159
SKÅNE	192	SUPERFAST IX	199	UNITED EXPRESS	159
SLINGEBORG	127	SUPERFAST X	199	UNITED TRADER	159
SOLENT ENTERPRISE	162	SUPERFERRY	95	URD	190
SOLIDOR 3	68	SUPERSEACAT ONE	84	URIAH HEEP	163
SOLIDOR 4	68	SUPERSEACAT TWO	84	VAL DE LOIRE	60
SOUND OF SANDA	120	SUPERSEACAT THREE	84	VALENTINE	126
SOUND OF SCALPAY	120	SUPERSEACAT FOUR	196	VANA TALLINN	199
SOUND OF SCARBA	120	SUPERSTAR EXPRESS	74	VARAGEN	109
SOUND OF SHUNA	120	SYMPHORINE	126	VARANGERFJORD	162
SOUND OF SLEAT	120	TALLINK AUTOEXPRESS	201	VARBOLA	142
SOUTHERN CARRIER	126	TAMAR	161	VESTERÅLEN	182
SPAARNEBORG	126	THE PRINCESS ANNE	84	VICTORINE	126
SPHEROID	142	THE PRINCESS MARGARET	84	VIKINGLAND	189
SPODSBJERG	190	THE SECOND SNARK	162	VILLUM CLAUSEN	169
ST CATHERINE	121	THE TOM AVIS	161	VILNIUS	183
ST CECILIA	121	THE TOM CASEY	161	VISBY	172
ST CLAIR	111	THJELVAR	172	WASA QUEEN	194
ST FAITH	121	THOMAS WEHR	138	WAVERLEY	163
ST HELEN	121	THOR SYDFYEN	190	WESTERLAND	189
ST OLA	111	THORA	117	WESTFALEN	176
ST ROGNVALD	152	THORSVOE	109	WILHELM KAISEN	176
ST SUNNIVA	111	TOR ANGLIA	133	WILKINS MICAWBER	163
STAR WIND	193	TOR BELGIA	133	WOODCHURCH	163
STENA BRITANNICA	94	TOR BRITANNIA	136	YOKER SWAN	163
STENA CALEDONIA	92	TOR CALEDONIA	133		
STENA CARISMA	198	TOR DANIA	133		
STENA CHALLENGER	92	TOR FLANDRIA	133		
STENA DANICA	197	TOR GOTHIA	133		

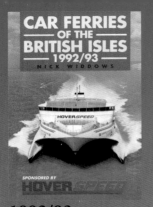

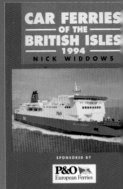

STILL AVAILABLE

BACK ISSUES OF

FERRIES OF THE BRITISH ISLES AND NORTHERN EUROPE

from

**Ferry Publications
PO Box 9, Narberth,
Pembrokeshire, SA68 0YT
Tel: 01834 891460 Fax: 01834 891463**

1992/93

Sponsored by Hoverspeed. Detailed review and
information on the Ferry Industry in the UK. Price £5.50.
(European and Overseas orders add £1.00 p&p)

19

Sponsored by P&O European Ferries. Detailed review
information on the Ferry Industry in the UK. Price £
(European and Overseas orders add £1.00

1999

Sponsored by Dart Line.
Features include History of Dart Line Europe.
Review of the Ferry Industry 1998.
Fast Ferry Review. The Rise of the Ro-Pax.
Price £10.35.
(European and Overseas orders add £1.00 p&p)

1995

Sponsored by Stena Sealink.
Round Britain Review.
Price £8.50.
(European and Overseas orders add £1.00
p&p)

19

Sponsored by Sally
History of Sally Ferries at Ram
Round Britai
Northern Europe R
HSS Review. Price £
(European and Overseas orders add £1.00

1997

Sponsored by
Commodore. Features
include History of
Commodore Shipping
Company, Development
of the Fast Ferry Industry.
Round Britain and
Northern European Ferry
Reviews. Price £9.35.
(European and Overseas orders
add £1.00 p&p)

1998

Sponsored by Ramsgate
Port. Features include
Round Britain Review,
Fast Ferry Industry
and Scandinavian
Ferry Review.
184 pages. Price £10.35.
(European and Overseas
orders add £1.00 p&p)